B"H

Happy Purim

2022 - 5782

◆━━━━━━━━◆

Thank you for the support and
kindness you have shown.

May Hashem bless you with
long life, good health, prosperity,
much nachas and joy.

*Rabbi Yonah & Leah Fradkin
and all of us at Chabad*

my *lives changed*
story 2

Editor-in-Chief: *Rabbi Elkanah Shmotkin*
Managing Editor: *Rabbi Yechiel Cagen*
Line Editor: *Mrs. Uriela Sagiv*
Production Manager: *Rabbi Yecheskel Posner*
Layout: *Levi Weingarten*
Design: *Shimon Gorkin*

718-774-6000
jem@jemedia.org

Comments and Permissions
For comments, corrections, or new information; inquiries with regard to republishing text, images, or documents from this book; or for educational discounts for groups or organizations, please write to us at mystory@jemedia.org.

ISBN: 978-1-93-234911-5
Library of Congress Control Number: 2017934411

Printed in China

ב"ה

my *story*
lives ↳ changed

2

thirty-three individuals share their
personal encounters with the Rebbe

Based on testimonies recorded
by the **MY ENCOUNTER WITH THE REBBE**
oral history project by
JEWISH EDUCATIONAL MEDIA

Preface

What makes a leader?

Our world is preoccupied with leadership—perhaps more accurately, with its absence. Think tanks analyze what critical attributes a leader must possess. Universities offer courses to educate young leaders, while foundations provide fellowships to ensure that prospective leaders can hone their skills. Yet, as valuable as all these efforts might be, they fail to capture the essence of what leadership—certainly Jewish leadership—is about.

THE MIDRASH TELLS US that several of our nation's earliest leaders began as shepherds. Indeed, G-d did not choose them for their focused adherence to His mission—though they certainly fulfilled His will dutifully—nor for their vision, their genius, or even their ability to influence others. They were deemed worthy of the responsibility because of how they tended to their sheep.[1]

Once, as he cared for his flock, Moses saw a young lamb wander away. As it ran through a thicket to a small watering hole, Moses gave chase, and then waited as the lamb drank. After it had quenched its thirst, he gently lifted the sheep onto his shoulder and carried it back to the flock. Said G-d, "Since you tended to the sheep with such love — by your life, I swear you shall be the shepherd of My flock, Israel."

Later, Moses would confront Pharaoh, split the sea, and speak to G-d "like a man speaks to his fellow."[2] Yet the Book of Zohar refers to Moses simply as, *"Ra'aya Mehemna*—the Faithful Shepherd."[3]

His defining moment would come in the wake of the people's travesty and betrayal—the making of the Golden Calf, when G-d was prepared to destroy them and make a new nation of Moses and his offspring. Moses rejected the proposition and shattered the tablets of the Ten Commandments, deciding that it would be better to destroy the work of G-d's hand than to sacrifice His people.[4]

Ever since, this has been the template for Jewish leaders: shepherds who do not lose sight of the people, their shortcomings, and their needs.

MUCH HAS BEEN WRITTEN about the impact of the Rebbe's leadership. He thought broadly and boldly, and dared to transform the face of world Jewry. Not content with retrenchment of a people decimated by the scourges of Nazism and Communism, he sought to influence the Jewish world. In fact, his stated goal was to affect the *entire* world in ways unprecedented, and to bring about its ultimate redemption.

Yet, ever the faithful shepherd, the Rebbe related to each person as an individual first, concerned with *their* world, *their* needs, and *their* realities.

ONE OF THE MOST BELOVED JEM projects is *Here's My Story*, the weekly publication culled from the *My Encounter with the Rebbe* oral history project, which collects testimonies of people's interactions with the Rebbe. While some individuals relate the Rebbe's advice on matters of global import, most tell of his attention to the seemingly mundane areas of their lives.

In this book, we present a selection of thirty-three stories. Many are published here for the first time, while others are more complete versions of the most beloved weekly stories, alongside a selection of photos and documents. Each account reveals a glimpse of the Rebbe's far-reaching wisdom, as it was applied with sensitivity and care.

More than any course or program possibly could, they provide every reader with a road map to true Jewish leadership.

Jewish Educational Media

---

1. *Shemot Rabbah* 2:2.
2. Deuteronomy 34:10.
3. Zohar, vol. 2 (p. 21a).
See also *Tanya*, ch. 42 (p. 117).

4. *Midrash Tanchuma Parshat Ki Tisa*:30, quoted by Rashi on Exodus 34:1. See the Rebbe's exposition on this event: *Likkutei Sichot*, vol. 34, p. 217.

Contents

SECTION TWO
NO PERSON TOO SMALL, NO PROBLEM TOO BIG

SECTION THREE
THINK BIGGER

SECTION FIVE
THE POWER OF A *MITZVAH*

Introduction

My Story 2: Lives Changed

On a Shabbat afternoon in the spring of 1986,[1] the Rebbe spoke to thousands who had gathered at a *farbrengen*. His talk concerned the story of Ezekiel, whom G-d had instructed: "Son of man, prophesy over the valley: 'Dry bones, hear the word of G-d!'"[2] Ezekiel was charged with informing the bones of G-d's message of hope: "I will endow you with the spirit of life; you will come alive."

In his signature style, the Rebbe declared that this charge was given not to Ezekiel alone, but to every Jew. "If you know the *Alef-Bet* of Judaism you must share it with someone else. If you are a 'son of man'—a human being with a compassionate heart—share the life of *Yiddishkeit* with someone who knows less than you. Call out to the dry bones, 'Hear the word of Hashem!'"

FROM THE DAY IT WAS PUBLISHED in 2017, *My Story* became an instant classic. It has since been reprinted several times and translated into Hebrew and Russian, with additional languages in the works. The first-person testimonies have stirred something in readers well beyond what we could have imagined. The stories resonate; they grab people and engage them.

Much like the revival of the Jewish people anticipated in Ezekiel's vision, it is not only the Rebbe's wisdom and loving guidance that lies at the heart of every story; it is also each person's living, distinct voice and unique circumstances—the "flesh, sinews and bones"—that enable the story to come to life and to breathe life into others.

THE REBBE PATIENTLY LED a generation that believed, "Our bones have dried up, our hope is lost, we have been cut off," helping this generation find confidence in a living, optimistic future. The first-person narratives in *My Story 2: Lives Changed* are each a thread in a tapestry that spreads across the globe, retelling the Rebbe's role in the revival of these individuals, while influencing the revival of Jewry as a whole—not unlike the sight described by Ezekiel: "The spirit came into them, and they lived and stood on their feet: a very great army—exceedingly so."

THE *MY ENCOUNTER WITH THE REBBE* ORAL HISTORY PROJECT, from which these stories are culled, has become a vibrant, international, collaborative project. To those who sent in leads for interviews; to the families who lent their living rooms to be invaded by cinematographers, sound recorders, interviewers and interviewees; and especially to the interviewees, who share their most personal experiences with the rest of us: Thank you for taking part in this global initiative. No doubt, these stories will continue to play a role in amplifying the Rebbe's teaching, inspiration and vision for a world perfected and redeemed.

And to those who haven't yet shared your experiences, we implore you, from the bottom of our hearts, to please do so. To those who know someone who should be interviewed, please email us at interviews@jemedia.org. The Rebbe was talking to *you* that Shabbat afternoon. We each have a role to play in endowing others with life and spirit.

May we merit speedily in our days the time when the sadness of exile transforms into the joy of redemption, when "I will open your graves and cause you to come out, My people, and bring you home to the Land of Israel."

Rabbi Elkanah Shmotkin

Executive Director, JEM

Rabbi Yechiel Cagen

Director, My Encounter with the Rebbe

---

1. *Torat Menachem*, 5746, pp. 200 – 202.   2. Ezekiel 37:1–14.

EDITOR'S NOTE

The stories in this book are first-person recollections of events and conversations with the Rebbe. While we have worked to authenticate each story and believe them to be accurate, the obvious should be noted: In some cases, the statements attributed to the Rebbe appearing in quotation marks are likely not his exact statements. Rather, they reflect the person's own recollection and/or interpretation of the Rebbe's words.

NURTURING MIND, BODY AND SOUL

DR. JAN JACOBSON SOKOLOVSKY

The Smile from Ear to Ear

A story about a few good listeners

Dr. Jan Jacobson Sokolovsky is an attorney who presently lives in Jerusalem.
She was interviewed in her home in October of 2018.

I would like to tell you the story of my son Danny and of the Rebbe's influence on the trajectory of his life.

In 1966, I had given birth to Danny, the youngest of my three sons. As he grew, he did not speak anywhere near as early as his brothers. When I asked the pediatrician, "Why is Danny not speaking yet?" I was told that he might have a hearing problem. After some testing, the pediatrician confirmed that, indeed, Danny had a severe hearing problem.

At eighteen months of age, he was fitted with a hearing aid. In those days, that meant wearing a harness that carried battery-operated equipment which was connected by wires to the buttons in his ears. It was not a very pleasant setup, to say the least. Danny was an active toddler, and it was a constant battle to prevent him from pulling out this contraption and throwing it on the ground. Eventually, though, he understood that this bulky contraption helped him communicate with his friends.

To be clear, by no means were we strangers to the problems faced by hearing-impaired children. Our oldest son, Barry, had begun to lose his hearing when he was four years old, and it continued to deteriorate until he was seven. But Barry had already learned to speak quite well before his hearing loss. Danny would have to learn to speak after he had lost his hearing—an overwhelming challenge for a young child.

In the summer of 1967, we moved to the Jewish community in Skokie, Illinois, so that Barry, our oldest, could start first grade in a Jewish day school there, and Danny would be able to enroll in a special education

Rabbi Shlomo Zalman
Hecht with Myron
Jacobson at Barry's Bar
Mitzvah. 1974.

*Courtesy of Jan
Jacobson Sokolovsky*

program at Northwestern University that had a big center for young children with hearing problems.

Back then, there was a huge disagreement among educators as to whether hearing-impaired children should learn to communicate with sign language, or they should be taught how to talk. Northwestern University was on the side of trying to teach them to talk, so this is the kind of therapy Danny received until he was three, when he was enrolled in a special education nursery program in our local school district.

IT WAS SHORTLY AFTER WE MOVED TO SKOKIE that we were introduced to Rabbi Shlomo Zalman Hecht, the Rebbe's emissary to Chicago. Although he was not the rabbi of our synagogue, my husband—Dr. Myron Jacobson—and I eventually developed a very close relationship with him.

When it was almost time for Danny to enter first grade, we told Rabbi Hecht that we planned to keep him in the public school system, which had an excellent program for the hearing impaired. We believed that Danny could not succeed in a Jewish day school where he would

also have to learn Hebrew; we feared that a bilingual program would be too much for him.

Rabbi Hecht was not sure we were making the right decision. "This is too serious an issue for you to decide by yourself," he told us. "You have to ask the Rebbe."

We had never met the Rebbe, but Rabbi Hecht arranged an audience, which took place late in the spring of 1972.

We were given an appointment for 3:00 AM, so we arranged to fly in for just that one night. We met with the Rebbe who, thanks to Rabbi Hecht, was well-versed in all the details of our situation. We felt that he was totally concentrating on the issue that was critical to us: the life of our son.

WE EXPLAINED OUR INTENTIONS FOR DANNY — we wanted to keep him in a special education program in the public school and hire a private tutor so he could learn Hebrew at his own pace — and we asked the Rebbe what he thought of the plan.

The Rebbe converses with a couple during a meeting of the Machne Israel Special Development Fund. 4 Tishrei, 5750-1989.

Sam Shlagbaum, The Living Archive

"I don't believe that public school will be good for Danny," he responded. "You can't know what will happen to him there. A Jewish boy needs to be educated in a Jewish environment."

"What would the Rebbe suggest?" I asked.

And this is where the Rebbe surprised us by making a completely out-of-the-box suggestion.

"Tell me," he said. "Who is Danny's teacher in public school? Is she Jewish?"

We confirmed that his teacher was a Jewish woman, who was a marvelous educator.

"How about," the Rebbe proposed, "if instead of sending him to public school with a tutor in Hebrew, you sent him to the Jewish day school where his brothers go, and ask this teacher to tutor him in English?"

He painted a vivid picture for us: "Consider how Danny will feel on the first day of school when he sees his brothers getting on the school bus on their way to the Jewish day school, while he heads out to someplace entirely different. How will that make him feel?"

We got the point and we agreed. We thought it was brilliant—indeed, we were literally overwhelmed by the ingenuity of his advice.

The Rebbe understood that if Danny went to public school, he might get a good education, but he would constantly be reminded of how different he was from his brothers. And in addition, the Rebbe explained to us, he wouldn't be in the atmosphere of a Jewish day school.

The Rebbe understood Danny better than anyone else, which is why he suggested turning our plan upside down—instead of public school with a Hebrew tutor, let's do Hebrew school with an English tutor.

We had underestimated Danny's abilities, but the Rebbe had no doubt about his potential. It was as if the Rebbe put himself in Danny's head and knew that a bilingual program would not be overwhelming to such an intelligent child.

We were pleased with the idea and eager to give it a try. As we were leaving, the Rebbe added, "If, in the future, the possibility arises of an operation on the ear, Danny should undergo it," and he blessed us that it should succeed.

Apparently, the Rebbe was aware that an operation for Danny's condition was available, but at that time and for many years thereafter, it was very risky. This surgery involved a cochlear implant, which meant

Danny follows his brothers Barry and Michael onto the bus for his first day of Jewish day school. 1972.

Courtesy of Jan Jacobson Sokolovsky

drilling a hole in the head and then into the ear. It didn't always work and, when it didn't, it made things even worse, so it was not something to be undertaken lightly. But when it was successful, it gave the severely hearing-impaired individual a chance to truly hear. So we kept this possibility in the back of our minds, knowing that, when the time was right, we had the Rebbe's blessing to go ahead.

WHEN WE RETURNED HOME, we went to speak with the teacher, who immediately agreed to the Rebbe's plan, even though she had never before done any private tutoring (nor has she since). And we sent him to the Jewish day school as the Rebbe recommended.

I have a picture of Danny getting on the bus together with his brothers on the first day of school. He has his lunch box, and he's looking at me with a smile that goes from ear to ear. I think it's the best picture of Danny that I ever took.

We would never have thought of this idea on our own. And certainly the teacher would never have thought of it. Nobody would have. But there it was, right in front of us.

Jan with her son Danny.

*Courtesy of Jan
Jacobson Sokolovsky*

The teacher turned out to be a godsend. She came over to our house several times a week after school and tutored Danny in English and whatever else he needed.

Danny succeeded in his studies and he certainly benefitted from the Jewish atmosphere of the school, as the Rebbe had predicted. He went on to graduate from Yeshiva University and then immigrated to Israel.

EVENTUALLY WE WERE ADVISED THAT THE OPERATION, which was initially highly experimental, had become standard and carried much less risk.

So, in 2005, Danny received a cochlear implant, which was a great success. As we drove home from Hadassah Hospital after the operation, Danny remarked that he could hear the music from the car radio, and he asked me if the ticking sound he heard was a drum. It was just the turn signal. He had never even known that there was such a sound.

I was often brought to tears watching Danny discover a totally new world of sound. He later said that the first week after the operation was one of the happiest of his life. He heard the door open when somebody walked in—he didn't have to be surprised to see people suddenly appearing in front of him. He heard coins dropping. Birds were singing for the first time and dogs were barking.

"I never could have heard any of this without the operation," he told me. "But I always knew that one day I would be able to hear. I had the Rebbe's blessing waiting in my pocket." ■

Amazing Is Not Enough

When you truly want to change the world,
it's best to start with yourself

Mr. Gordon Zacks was an American businessman, philanthropist, and expert on Middle East policy, who served as an advisor to President George H. W. Bush. He was interviewed in his home in Kennebunkport, Maine, in August of 2007.

While serving as the chairman of United Jewish Appeal's Young Leadership Cabinet, I gave the keynote address at an assembly of three thousand delegates from around the United States and Canada who made up the Council of Jewish Relations and Welfare Funds. Apparently the Rebbe heard about my speech, and he invited me to come in for a private audience.

Before I describe that memorable meeting—which I will never forget if I live to be a hundred—I need to explain how I came to give that speech that attracted the Rebbe's attention.

I was born in 1933 in South Bend, Indiana, to parents who married in the middle of the Great Depression, but who nevertheless went on to live the American Dream. My mother, Florence, invented the foam rubber slipper, and together with my father, Aaron, founded the RG Barry Corporation, which eventually became the world's largest supplier of comfort footwear.

I was twelve years old when World War II ended and, therefore, old enough to learn what the Nazis had done to the Jews. I felt very powerless, very angry and very confused as to why such a horrible thing could be allowed to happen in the modern world. I was also deeply affected by the founding of the State of Israel in 1948, and I resolved to be a part of the rebirth of my people.

The first thing I did was organize a fundraising campaign in my high school for the United Jewish Appeal's efforts to resettle Holocaust survivors. With time, I rose through UJA's ranks, and in the thirty years

Gordon making a phone call as a member of the student council at Bexley High School in Ohio. 1950.

Courtesy of Kim Zacks

I was with the agency, I traveled to over seventy countries to study the condition of Jewish life all over the world. At the same time, I made over fifty trips to Israel, developing a deep understanding of the challenges facing the Jewish people and the Jewish state.

Because of this, I was invited to give the keynote address about which the Rebbe had heard. The topic of my speech—echoing the theme of the conference—was "Youth Looks at the Future." I spoke about what had been accomplished in the twenty-plus years since the founding of the State of Israel, during which time Jews in the free world had collaborated to rescue and resettle close to three million Jews from hostile lands and bring them to freedom. "But what will the next twenty years bring?" I asked. If we don't repair Jewish education and make it relevant, exciting and appealing to young Jews growing up in the free world—where they have so many options, and where anti-Semitism is no longer the defining factor of Jewish reality—we could lose more Jews through assimilation than we've saved through affirmation.

And so I suggested that we create what I called an "Institute for Jewish Life"—endowed with $100 million of State of Israel bonds—to generate innovative, experimental ideas in the field of Jewish education to try to find relevant and exciting ways to keep young Jewish people Jewish.

Gordon delivering a speech at a UJA event. Late 1960s.
Courtesy of Kim Zacks

I REMEMBER ARRIVING AT CHABAD HEADQUARTERS in January of 1970 at about eleven o'clock at night. As I walked in, the Rebbe stood up to greet me, and I was confronted by his crystal clear eyes penetrating mine, peering into my soul. His presence was so intense — there was such energy emanating from him — yet I felt a sense of serenity and peace. This was a very strange combination and that made it all the more impressive. I think this is why my memory of this meeting remains so vivid.

He began to speak. He didn't say, "Welcome," he didn't say, "Hello," and he didn't say any words of greeting. He opened with: "Mr. Zacks, I have read your speech, and it is clear to me that you have taken good care of your mind. I look at you, and it's clear to me that you have taken good care of your body. What are you doing for your soul, Mr. Zacks?"

That was the opening of a conversation which lasted an hour and a half.

His response to my appeal for the founding of an "Institute for Jewish Life" that would experiment with new ways of attracting Jewish youth was: "The house is on fire, and we have no time to experiment. We need proven firefighters to put out the flame." He went on to explain that there were outreach programs worldwide that were successfully combating the problems I was concerned about and proposed that I support those organizations, as they could certainly put that hundred million dollars to good use.

I was not convinced. "Rebbe, there are millions of Jewish souls whose houses are on fire and who need salvation, but who have lost your number," I said. "They're not going to call you because they are not prepared to pay the price in lifestyle change that is required to be religious."

"With the help of G-d," he responded, "they'll find the number."

"But even if so," I countered, "they will come and see that they don't want to be here. It's too much of a change for them; they can't make that kind of commitment. They need to find some meaning in the lives they are leading now, so that they are not focused on material things only. That's why we have to search for a new way of making Jewish education appealing to them."

He looked at me thoughtfully. "Do you believe in revelation?" he asked.

"I believe in G-d, but I'm not sure I believe He reveals Himself to human beings. I believe that the Bible was inspired by G-d, but I haven't yet accepted the fact that it's written by G-d word for word."

I doubt that the Rebbe thought he could convince me to change my mind on the spot with what he said next, but he certainly gave me food for thought.

"When I was studying in Paris, I learned about how incredibly organized the universe is — how there are laws that govern the movement of all the stars and planets and constellations in the universe. And how extraordinarily complex the human body is, with billions of cells which are constantly reproducing and sustaining it. So, do you think it is conceivable that there is a rule that governs everything in life, but not humans? Do you think that G-d placed us here to fend for ourselves without a rule book, without a road map, without guidance? Why would He do that? And how can you expect to discover on your own the mysteries of the universe without help from G-d?"

It was clear to me that the Rebbe knew what he was talking about. He wasn't a casual observer of the universe; he was a deep student of it; and it only reinforced his conviction about G-d as the creator of the universe and as the author of the ultimate guidebook to its workings — the Torah.

"MR. ZACKS," HE SAID TO ME, "your problem is that you are trying to find the road map through your head — you're trying to think yourself to G-d. But you can't think yourself to G-d. First, you have to experience the why and the how of being Jewish. By living the Jewish lifestyle, you will discover G-d, for He is within you. The mistake you are making is trying to connect to Him through your head, when you have to connect to Him through your heart, through Jewish experience."

He followed that up with an offer to send a *chasid* to live with me for a year to teach me. "If at the end of the year you will have found G-d in your heart, you will have received the greatest gift a person can receive in life. But if I'm wrong, and you will not have discovered G-d, what will you have lost? Weigh a year against eternity. What difference does a year make against an eternity of connection to G-d?"

"Did you ever read *Zorba the Greek*?" he asked.

After I recovered from my shock, I said that I did.

The Rebbe gives *lekach* to an individual at the door of his *sukkah*. Hoshana Rabbah, 5738-1977.

Levi Freidin,
The Living Archive

"Do you remember where the student and Zorba are on the beach discussing the meaning of life? And Zorba says to the student, 'A man's head is like a grocer; it keeps accounts.... It never risks all it has; always keeps something in reserve. It never breaks the string.' Mr. Zacks, you haven't been able to break the string, but you must. You must release yourself from your mental approach to G-d and come with me on the journey of the heart."

That's what the Rebbe said, if you can believe it. He was quoting *Zorba the Greek* to me.

His point was that my effort to find G-d intellectually was flawed, and until I was willing to open myself to an experience that would move my heart and soul, I was unlikely to succeed in discovering G-d as a force that informs my choices.

It was a lot to take in, and I answered that I would really have to think about it.

"Good," he said, "I want you to think about it, and I want you to think about what needs to be done to save the Jewish people from the fires of assimilation."

Gordon Zacks in front of RG Barry, a company established by his parents, which he directed. Circa 2012.

Courtesy of Kim Zacks

He also said something else that was very profound and very real: "Remember, if you want to change the world, you have to change yourself. When you change, it's like dropping a pebble in a lake—the ripples that go out from the point of contact will influence all those around you. If you become connected to G-d in your soul and, as a consequence, behave in a manner that G-d would require of you, it will impact the people around you. And the power of that change is the first and most important step towards making the world a better place."

That, in a nutshell, was our conversation.

ALTHOUGH I NEVER SPECIFICALLY DID what he wanted me to do, meeting him had a profound impact on the life choices that I made from that day forward.

Following that meeting, I began to contemplate how I would go on to serve Israel and the Jewish people. I actually gave consideration to becoming a rabbi, but once I found out what a rabbi actually does, I knew it was not for me. I gave consideration to running for office, becoming a US senator, but I learned that politicians spend too much time trying to get reelected rather than serving their constituents. And I gave consideration to immigrating to Israel, but what Israel needed then were farmers and, since I had no idea how to plant a flower, it was clear that this was not where I belonged. So I rejected each of those options and decided that the most effective role that I could play was as a volunteer—a role I was already playing in some respects.

To do it right, I sought out successful volunteers and asked them how to succeed at volunteering in the Jewish world. And they said, in so many words, "First, you have to have passion; second, you have to have knowledge; third, you have to have time — and it helps if you have money."

That is when I decided that the best course for me was to go into business and build a large organization that would give me both time and money to do what I really wanted to do for the rest of my life. So I went into the family business which was then still a small emerging concern, and I went forward from there, building it into the company it has become. Over time, I connected with Max Fisher, the Detroit-based philanthropist and diplomat, and he became my mentor as I climbed up the levels of leadership, locally, nationally and internationally.

Artillery is offloaded in Israel as part of the US airlift during the Yom Kippur War.

Harry Heist, US Air Mobility Command Museum

IN 1973, WHEN ISRAEL CAME CLOSE to losing the Yom Kippur War—indeed it came within twenty-four hours of being destroyed and was only saved by President Richard Nixon's order to launch the biggest airlift of armaments since World War II—I shifted my priorities to political action, becoming involved with AIPAC (the American Israel Public Affairs Committee) and with Jewish advocacy.

In 1978, I was asked to support the presidential campaign of George H. W. Bush. But although I greatly admired the man, I declined because I saw that he was totally ignorant about the Middle East and might cause, with all good intentions, irreparable harm to Israel. However, he was willing to be educated, to travel to Israel and learn all that he needed to know, and after I worked with him to develop a detailed policy for the Middle East, I took on a senior role in his campaign. He lost the nomination to Ronald Reagan but joined the Republican ticket as vice-president, and I served as his advisor on the Middle East for the eight years he held that office and another four after he was elected president. He was not reelected in 1992 however and, at that point, I decided that I had two new roles to play—one was in the field of Jewish education, and the other in developing leadership for the American Jewish community.

Why specifically Jewish education?

Well, the Rebbe had something to do with that.

OVER THE YEARS, the Rebbe wrote me five letters, in which he repeatedly returned to the subject of our original discussion — Jewish education.

"In the present emergency, there is no time for indulging in research," he wrote in a letter dated September 23, 1976, "inasmuch as ignorance of Judaism is now so prevalent that we have to speak in terms of making sure that the children should receive the very basics of our Jewish heritage."

He mentioned that he had seen my name listed in the press among top Jewish leaders, and he wanted to refresh my memory about our discussion some six years prior and to urge me to use my influence to sound an alarm:

> The urgency of this matter has increased even further since our meeting in view of the unfortunate deterioration of the general moral atmosphere, not to mention the religious

Leaders of the National Republican Jewish Coalition meet President Reagan and Vice President George H.W. Bush in the Oval Office. Gordon Zacks and Max Fisher are seated closest to the president. Early 1980s.

Courtesy of Kim Zacks

atmosphere, in the United States.... Unless a major effort is undertaken to strengthen the Torah education of our young generation, it is easy to visualize the consequences. Much more could and should be said on the subject, but from the impression I gained of our meeting and discussion, I believe that no further elaboration is needed.

His other letters were in a similar vein, stressing the dire need for Torah education, and also encouraging me to open up my own head and heart to learning how to be Jewish. But I did not have a chance to discuss any of this with him in person for eighteen years after our original meeting.

In 1988, I came to see the Rebbe with my youngest daughter Kim. She had become Torah observant, and she wanted to go to Crown Heights one Sunday when the Rebbe was giving out dollars.

Beginning two years prior, when he was eighty-four, the Rebbe started passing out dollars which the recipients were to give to charity. His reasoning: When two people meet, something good should result for a third.

Kim asked me to go with her. I didn't call anybody to get any special consideration; I simply took a cab with my daughter to Crown Heights and waited in line outside the Rebbe's home with everybody else. The line went on forever; we must have stood there for an hour and a half.

To my surprise, he recognized me immediately. "It's been many years since I've seen you," he said with a smile. "And I will be very happy when you add to your activities in spreading Judaism."

That was my cue to introduce my daughter, who was dressed in the style of an observant woman. "This is only the beginning," he said. "She must influence her father and her mother and all the members of the family.... This will not affect her respect for you. While honoring her father and

Kim Zacks in Columbus, Ohio. 1991.
Courtesy of Kim Zacks

RABBI MENACHEM M. SCHNEERSON
Lubavitch
770 Eastern Parkway
Brooklyn 13, N. Y.
_____
HYacinth 3-9250

מנחם מענדל שניאורסאהן
ליובאוויטש
_____
770 איסטערן פּאַרקוויי
ברוקלין, נ. י.

By the Grace of G-d
20th of Elul, 5732
Brooklyn, N. Y.

Mr. G. Zacks
140 N. Parkview Ave.
Columbus, Ohio 43209

Greeting and Blessing:

I duly received your letter of July 31st with enclosure,
and regret the delay in my reply, all the more regrettable
since there was also a delay in your writing, while time is
truly of the essence.

I trust you will not take amiss my candid remarks on how
I feel about the matter, since my approach is based on the
principle of our Sages of blessed memory, namely that the
essential thing is the deed.

Having read your letter very carefully, the first question
that occurred to me was what will the Jewish children gain
from our exchange of correspondence? What have they gained,
and what will they gain today or tomorrow? Since you are a
successful businessman, I trust it is not necessary to elabo-
rate on this approach.

With regard to the enclosed prospectus for "The Institute
for Jewish Life" - far be it from me, of course, to minimize
the esteem and honest intentions of the individuals who are
involved in this project. However, as mentioned above, looking at it from the practical viewpoint, one thing seems to me
quite certain, that for the next three years this project will
not contribute anything tangible to all those children who
need Jewish education now, while the hundreds and thousands of
dollars which this project will cost could have immediately
been used to pay the salaries of hundreds of teachers and
scholarships to scores of Jewish children for their Jewish
education, even on an elementary level.

Needless to say, I can see that just as it is necessary
to plan for the present and for the immediate future, it is
also necessary to plan for the distant future. However, this
is the normal approach under normal circumstances. By way of
example, treating a patient, it is necessary both to alleviate
his condition immediately as well as to have a plan for long-
term treatment and cure, but when the condition of the patient
is so serious that he may not be around in the distant future,
a long-term plan will not help him much. Such is also the
situation of many of our Jewish children and youth, a large
proportion of whom may unfortunately not be around to benefit
from any long-range investigations, research, and the like

A letter from the Rebbe to Gordon Zacks.
Courtesy of Kim Zacks

The Rebbe converses
with an individual
during a meeting of
the Machne Israel
Special Development
Fund. 7 Tishrei,
5751-1990.

*Sam Shlagbaum,
The Living Archive*

mother, she can influence you in very gentle form."

Then the Rebbe wished me to have good news to share, adding, "Don't wait as long as since I last spoke with you. At the time, we talked about about good news in spreading Judaism, especially in the realm of Jewish education."

He remembered precisely what we spoke about eighteen years before, as if our earlier conversation had not been interrupted by time!

I thought, "How many people does the Rebbe meet in the course of a year?" The night I met him there were three hundred people waiting—just that one night! I couldn't even comprehend how many people he must have seen and spoken to over the course of the eighteen years that had passed. What an incredible mind he had, with an instant recall that is extraordinarily rare on this planet.

"You're amazing!" I exclaimed.

Without a pause, he replied, "What is the benefit to the community that I am amazing? But I'll try to cash that in, and you will help me."

He then gave us several dollar bills. Turning to Kim, he said, "This should be the beginning of the fulfillment of the prophecy that in the end of days children will influence their parents—in a gentle manner, but in an effective manner." As we were leaving, the Rebbe called out after me, "No hard feelings for my preaching."

I didn't understand, and he repeated what he said.

"I have only deep feelings in my heart—and in my head," I said. "And I am trying to do what you asked of me."

"As soon as possible," he urged.

I chuckled at his insistence, and he said, "I am not satisfied—that is my character; I cannot help it." ■

PROFESSOR MORDECHAI SHANI

House of Healing

Human doctors, spirited patients, and other
building blocks of proper healthcare

Professor Mordechai Shani served as the director of the Chaim Sheba Medical Center at Tel HaShomer for thirty-three years, founded the School of Public Health at Tel Aviv University and served two terms as the director of Israel's Ministry of Health. He was interviewed in his office in March of 2013.

After the death of the famed Israeli doctor, Professor Chaim Sheba, with whom I worked for a number of years, I became the director of the Chaim Sheba Medical Center at Tel HaShomer, the largest hospital in Israel with an annual budget of $600 million a year. In my capacity as director I came to the United States periodically for fundraising purposes, and on one such occasion in 1976, Yossi Ciechanover, the Israeli Defense Ministry representative in New York, invited me to join a group of Israeli officials who were going to meet the Lubavitcher Rebbe.

As an amateur historian, the Rebbe had always intrigued me because he was an extraordinary phenomenon in the ultra-Orthodox world. He had studied mathematics, physics and philosophy at the University of Berlin; he then went on to Paris to continue his studies in mathematics and electrical engineering at an elite school and, later, at the Sorbonne. Although he exposed himself to exact sciences, they didn't harm his faith or religious observance — just the opposite; he seemed to have synthesized the world of religion with the world of technology. This made him a truly unique person in my eyes.

Indeed, observing him for the first time proved quite an experience.

It was Simchat Torah and several thousand *chasidim* were in attendance; the atmosphere was very joyous and lively, but when the Rebbe walked in, everyone stood still — you could hear a pin drop. The awe and reverence with which those present held the Rebbe was palpable.

At some point during the night, I was introduced to him, and in that brief exchange, the Rebbe asked me why, in Israel, we call a hospital a

beit cholim, meaning "house of the sick." He expressed the opinion that it should be called *beit refuah*, "house of healing," explaining that it was not just a matter of nomenclature but a true statement of a hospital's purpose—to bring about complete healing which, in itself, would encourage the patients. He then invited me for a discussion after the holiday celebrations, saying with a smile, "Perhaps we should meet and continue this conversation when it's more calm and quiet."

THAT MEETING TOOK PLACE A YEAR LATER in the Rebbe's modest office, which, in my opinion, matched his personality. During this friendly conversation lasting about half an hour, we did not discuss personal issues, nor did we engage in a formal dialogue. Rather, it was a give-and-take between two people coming from different worlds and holding sometimes similar, sometimes contrasting points of view. The conversation was conducted in a mixture of languages—in Yiddish, which I spoke a little thanks to my grandmother, and in English, but mostly in Hebrew. For the most part, we spoke about the practice of medicine.

First of all—and this was so characteristic of the Rebbe—he saw the patient's soul as the source of his or her strength. He said that the stronger our connection is to our souls, the better we can cope with life. "The health of the soul and the health of the body are intertwined," he explained.

As well, he spoke about the *mitzvah* of visiting sick people, emphasizing how important it is for the patient's recovery that he or she not feel alone. (And I might add that this is one of the beautiful things about Israel's ultra-Orthodox community, which makes such a point of assisting the sick and strengthening their spirit.)

The Rebbe also voiced his opinion that people must be taught that they are responsible for their own health. Yes, doctors can guide and help patients, but the primary responsibility lies with the individuals themselves. Those who do not take care of themselves—who do not eat well, sleep enough or exercise enough—will impair their health no matter what the doctors do.

Today, there is a push in medicine toward "patient empowerment," where we try to impress upon people that they have an obligation to look after their own health and not rely on the doctors. But the Rebbe was speaking to me about this forty years ago—before anyone was even

Professor Shani giving a speech in front of the Sheba Medical Center. Beside him are Professor Baruch Padeh and Prime Minister David Ben-Gurion.

Sheba Medical Center

Professor Shani (C.) guiding Senator Ted Kennedy on a visit to the Sheba Medical Center. 1971.

Sheba Medical Center

thinking about it! Only recently has it become popular to emphasize that preventive medicine requires the individual to take responsibility.

Another issue that we discussed was the place of technology in medicine. Back in the 1970s, before the age of the personal computer, technology was not yet a central nor dominant tool of the medical world. The problems related to technology in medicine would not become apparent for years to come. But here, too, the Rebbe was ahead of his time. He said something tremendously forward-thinking: "It is up to you, the doctor, to determine whether technology will be used for the benefit of humanity."

He worried that technology might create distance between the doctor and the patient: "At the end of the day," he said, "the attention of the doctor, the human being, is most important; and while technology can be a helpful tool, it cannot become a replacement for listening and caring."

He was so very right. If a doctor works strictly according to protocol, he will often administer many unnecessary tests or, worse, misdiagnose. The most important starting point is to listen to the patient and try to understand what his or her needs are. But, unfortunately, for many doctors today, technology has become the central means of practicing medicine instead of a helping tool, sometimes to the detriment of the patient. So the Rebbe had every reason to be concerned.

He also expressed concern about the state of medical services in Israel, a country that did not have socialized medicine back then. At the time of my meeting with the Rebbe, medical insurance providers in Israel were allowed to reject applicants, and people ended up without any coverage. It became clear, as he spoke, that the Rebbe was familiar with the health-care systems in Germany and France, both of which had begun providing medical insurance for their entire populations. They did not leave any person to contend alone with the high cost of healthcare, and the Rebbe wanted Israeli politicians to understand that they must do the same. In effect he was saying: "It cannot be that a Jew in the Land of Israel does not have access to health insurance. A Jewish society cannot abandon its sick and poor."

Incidentally, some eight or nine years later, I served on the Netanyahu Commission, which dealt with this very issue. As a result of the commission's report, a law — the National Health Insurance Law — was passed, compelling the government to provide funding so that everyone had access to health services. And I felt this was done in the spirit of the Rebbe's vision.

Professor Shani shaking hands with Prime Minister Benjamin Netanyahu.

Sheba Medical Center

AS OUR CONVERSATION WAS WRAPPING UP, the Rebbe returned to the point he made at our first meeting and offered this advice to me as a doctor and director of a hospital: "Don't focus on illness, focus on wellness. Make the hospital a place that seeks to improve people's health, not a place that emphasizes how sick they are."

I walked out of that meeting with the Rebbe extraordinarily impressed. As someone who interacts regularly with people in the religious world, I can testify that it is a rare phenomenon to meet a Torah scholar who can also converse about science and medicine. But the Rebbe did more than converse; he wasn't merely knowledgeable—he had vision. He foresaw how rapidly the world was progressing, and he anticipated the forthcoming problems that medical professionals had barely begun to think about.

Most people cannot see the forest for the trees, but the Rebbe was able to see the forest from above—to understand the world of medicine from a global perspective, to understand what is important and what is less important. This ability made him unique and, in this respect, the Rebbe cannot be compared to anyone I know.

In hindsight, I believe that my meeting with him has had no small influence on my own approach to these issues and my own vision of the role of medicine in society.

Certainly, the Rebbe helped me solidify my outlook on healthcare— that it is a path of service to others. I never went into private practice; I stayed in public health my entire life.

WHEN HE AND I SPOKE ABOUT the role of the hospital, I mentioned to him the problems facing a psychiatric hospital in Bnei Brak. The Rebbe asked me why I wasn't involved. I told him I had tried to get involved, but sadly, it didn't work out. To which the Rebbe replied, "You'll go back there."

He was right. I have now been in Bnei Brak, at the Mayanei Hayeshua Medical Center, for the last fifteen years, serving as its governor. As such, I have a large role in influencing the hospital's path, and I've done so in accordance with the Rebbe's guidance.

During our meeting, as we were speaking about the doctor-patient

Professor Shani holding his award for the Israel Prize of 2009.

relationship, and the interplay between academia and patient care, he cautioned me, "Be careful not to academicize the hospital too much. Too much emphasis on academia could harm the relationship between doctor and patient." So, when the subject was broached recently at Mayanei Hayeshua, I said, "Gentlemen, I was advised by the Lubavitcher Rebbe not to promote academia too much, because the Rebbe emphasized that doctors should be people first, not academics."

And when I needed to deal with the government concerning the problems with Israel's mental health services, I did so in the Rebbe's spirit, maintaining that you can't separate one's health from their soul. When I convinced the deputy minister of health to support mental health reform, I did so quoting the Rebbe.

In 2009 I received the Israel Prize for Lifetime Achievement and Contribution to Society and Country. And I believe that this serves as testimony to how the Rebbe's guidance has impacted my life. ■

MR. YOSEF LAUTENBERG

The Exceptional Name Change

Wheelchairs, crutches and a synagogue full of heroes

Mr. Yosef Lautenberg is the cofounder of the IDF Disabled Veterans' Organization and the founder of the Beit Halochem centers, a network of rehabilitation and sports facilities for wounded Israeli soldiers. He was interviewed in his office in Tel Aviv in August of 2009.

I was injured during Israel's War of Independence in the Battle for Jerusalem. This battle began immediately after the UN passed the partition plan on November 29, 1947, which divided the remaining lands of the British Mandate for Palestine between the Jews and the Arabs. Already at the time, the local Arabs were engaging in acts of terrorism that steadily grew worse. Their main focus was Sha'ar HaGai, the mountain pass connecting Jerusalem to Tel Aviv, through which all the supplies reached the Jews of the city. I was a member of the units that escorted the supply convoys to protect them from the constant attacks, and I well remember coming in with the food trucks to Jerusalem, where the residents of the besieged and battered city would be anxiously awaiting our arrival.

By spring of 1948, with the date for the end of the British Mandate rapidly approaching, Sha'ar HaGai was under complete control of the neighboring Arab villagers. Jerusalem was under total siege. Some 100,000 Jews were trapped in the city, their lives depending on us on the outside. We knew that if we didn't subdue the Arab villagers along the way, Jerusalem would fall. And if Jerusalem fell, it would be doubtful if the State of Israel would ever be established. That was what everybody felt.

On the 8th of May, my unit—the Harel Brigade—got an order to assist in conquering Bayt Mahsir, the largest Arab village, located nine kilometers west of Jerusalem. During this battle, a Jordanian Legion fighter managed to come within a few meters of my position. Just then,

Yosef (R.) during Israel's War of Independence.

Courtesy of Yosef Lautenberg

my machine gun, a German Spandau, jammed and, as a result, he suc-ceeded in firing a string of bullets directly at me, wounding me severely.

Next to me was a machine-gunner who was shot in the head. At first, I thought he was dead, but then I heard him say: "Yoske, don't leave me here...." I pulled him out to safety, dragging him behind me, and after two hours, the medics reached us. When we came to the hospital I was put in a cast because my pelvis was broken and I underwent a series of surgeries. All in all, I was hospitalized for over two years.

During the time I was at Tel HaShomer Hospital, I cofounded an organization for those who were disabled in the War of Independence. Our goal was to assist, in a practical way, all those who had been injured in the war and to represent their interests to government institutions, in order to effectuate better rehabilitation services. Back then such services virtually did not exist, but the need was dire. Six thousand Israelis — or one percent of the entire Jewish population — had died in the War of Independence, and an equal number were left permanently handicapped from their injuries.

Yosef (front, center)
with some of his fellow
soldiers in the hospital.

*Courtesy of
Yosef Lautenberg*

Our efforts succeeded, and through the intervention of Prime Minister
David Ben-Gurion, we received a donation to build Beit Kay in Naha-
riya — a place for injured veterans to recover and readjust to civilian
life — which opened in 1958.

MEANWHILE, I GOT ON WITH MY LIFE. I married, raised a family, and went
to work for the Ministry of Defense. But then I got another idea to help
disabled veterans.

By way of background, I need to mention that Israel had been participating in sports competitions for the handicapped since the idea
first surfaced on the world scene in 1952. And we have excelled, despite
the scant resources available to us. I wanted to encourage this initiative
and, in 1970, I came up with the idea of building a network of sports
facilities where disabled veterans would feel at home, where they could
socialize and take part in a range of rehabilitation services.

I raised the funds and started building the first Beit Halochem

("Warriors' House") in Tel Aviv, planning to open it in late 1973. But the Yom Kippur War intervened and the opening had to be postponed.

Yom Kippur was a very difficult war, with almost 2,700 IDF soldiers killed—including my son Eitan, to my great sorrow—and many others left permanently scarred by their injuries and experiences.

In March of 1974, the Tel Aviv Beit Halochem finally opened its doors, becoming the biggest sports center in the world for the disabled. And I must mention that the people of Chabad immediately offered to collaborate with us, and the veterans were invited to be guests of honor for the Jewish holidays in Kfar Chabad.

Chabad *chasidim* had always supported us—visiting the wounded in the hospital during all the wars—and now they supported us in this effort as well. I will never forget the *chasidim* dancing on Simchat Torah with wheelchair-bound veterans who were missing both legs. Yet everyone danced and danced with tremendous joy. It was a remarkable scene.

AND THAT BRINGS ME TO MY ENCOUNTER WITH THE REBBE. In 1976, I led the Israeli delegation—including many veterans who had suffered serious injuries in the Yom Kippur War—to the Paralympics in Toronto,

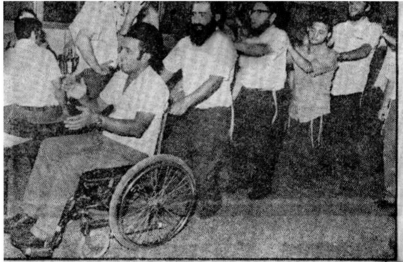

Chabad *chasidim* celebrating with the group of "exceptional" soldiers upon their return to Israel.

מצאנו צה״ל״ — זהו אות חדש, שהוומצא על־ידי הרבי מליובאביץ׳ ושניתן לחברי משלחת נכים לאולימפיאדה בטורונטו. הספורטאים שבו ארצה דרך ניו־יורק, ושם זכו לקבל מי הרבי את האות החדש. בתמונה: צעירי חב״ד בארץ אוהמול בכפרם את המשלחת

The Israel paralympic team. Yosef is second in line.

Courtesy of Yosef Lautenberg

where we won third place out of the forty countries participating. Since we were not so far from New York, I had the idea of bringing the group to meet the Rebbe after the games. When I called Chabad Headquarters in New York to arrange the visit, I received an immediate and enthusiastic response.

On the appointed date, we all arrived—two busloads of us—and we were given a tour of the place, then ushered into the main synagogue. The *chasidim* welcomed us warmly, but they were not allowed into the synagogue with us. There were strict orders that only we should be present for our special audience with the Rebbe.

As we awaited the Rebbe, a holy atmosphere permeated the place; I, for one, was filled with tremendous emotion.

When the Rebbe came in, he addressed us in Hebrew, even though generally his public speeches were in Yiddish. What he said was recorded on tape:

> Just as all Jewish people from different parts of the globe are able to unite together, rising above the bounds of space, so too are they able to transcend the limitations of time. This explains the power of the Jewish nation, an Eternal People.

Although we are called "the smallest amongst the nations," we are fewest only in one particular place or time. But in truth, all Jews — from Mount Sinai until the end of generations — are responsible for one another, making up one entity, one nation, so we are numerous and powerful even in quantity compared to the other nations. The Jewish people's ability to transcend the bounds of space and time stems from their ability to harness the spiritual to overcome the physical, and to prioritize quality over quantity....

He was saying this to people who were missing limbs, who had been severely injured, and his words truly touched our hearts. Some of us were religious, others were secular, but we all responded to the Rebbe's words.

He went on to say that even if a person has a physical shortcoming, it is no reason to be downcast. Quite the contrary, because he is lacking something physical — especially if he suffered the injury while protecting the Jewish people in the Holy Land — this is proof positive that the Creator has endowed him with great spiritual power. Such a person is not merely "equal" to those around him, for his superior spirit enables him to overcome any physical shortcoming. In other words, he is able

The Rebbe greets members of the delegation and hands them dollar bills to be given to charity. 23 Av, 5736-1976.

Courtesy of Ofer Tzur

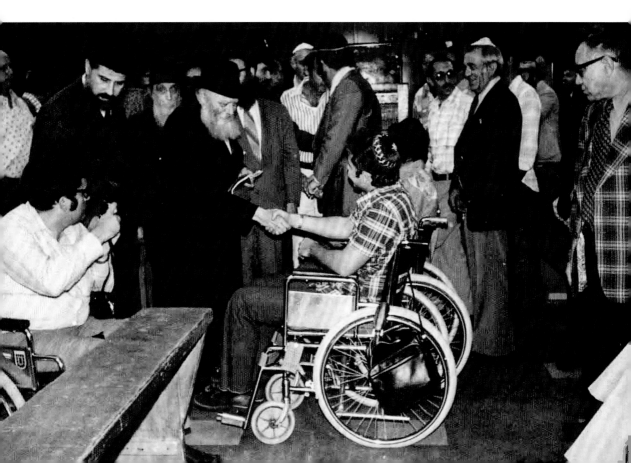

The Rebbe greets
members of the
delegation and hands
them dollar bills to be
given to charity.
23 Av, 5736-1976.

*Yossi Melamed,
The Living Archive*

to find a way to succeed above and beyond an ordinary person.

And then the Rebbe stunned us all:

> I do not approve of the term "handicapped," which suggests
> some kind of inferiority. To the contrary, we must empha-
> size that this person has been endowed by the Creator with
> abilities above and beyond those of ordinary people. This
> person is special and exceptional, and was given strength to
> overcome hardships and obstacles which an ordinary human
> being cannot. Therefore ... I would like to suggest that the
> name be changed from "*nechei*—handicapped" to "*metzuya-
> nei*—exceptional"—whether exceptional by an act of war, or
> otherwise. And this change in name is not merely semantics;
> rather, it describes the situation most accurately.

I sat there transfixed, listening to him. Having spent my entire life in this
field, I've met people who were severely wounded—who were blinded,
who were paralyzed, and more—and yet, with whatever function they
had left, they achieved more than anyone could have possibly imagined.
Someone who doesn't know this field would never believe it. But the
Rebbe understood this completely.

The Rebbe addressing the delegation
of "exceptional" soldiers.
23 Av, 5736-1976.

Yossi Melamed, The Living Archive

At the end of his talk, he said:

> When Jews meet, they extend their hands to one another in order to express the fact that they are one. This is alluded to in our Torah, which was given through Ten Commandments — five commandments engraved on one tablet and five on the other. When two Jews shake hands, the five fingers of one person meet the five fingers of the other, and together they reflect the Ten Commandments, and the Ten Divine Utterances with which G-d created the world, and G-d's Divine Providence over every single individual, wherever he may be. Therefore, before we conclude, I would be honored if I could shake each of your hands and greet each one of you individually with [the traditional Jewish blessing] "*Aleichem Shalom*—Peace be upon you." ... And I would also be honored to present each one of you with a dollar, which I thank you in advance for donating to charity upon your return to the Holy Land.

When the Rebbe came down from the stage, he shook the hand of each member of our delegation—something which we were told was unprecedented. It was a sight to behold!

The Rebbe greets members of the delegation and hands them dollar bills to be given to charity.
23 Av, 5736-1976.

Yossi Melamed,
The Living Archive

This took at least an hour, maybe more, but the Rebbe made sure to greet and converse with each and every one of us.

This encounter with the Rebbe was very emotional for us all. We felt that this man truly loved us—that he loved those who had sacrificed their bodies for the preservation of the Land of Israel—and that he even worried about us. He told us to intensify our security by making sure our *mezuzot* were in order. And he even offered to send his emissaries in Israel to our homes to help us with this.

But, most of all, he truly understood us.

The Rebbe understood—and this bears repeating—that we must always look at what *is*, not at what *isn't*. As he said, if we only connect with the special spiritual energy gifted to us by the Creator, we can touch the stars. And we all need to remember this. ■

DR. REUVEN FEUERSTEIN

Minding the Mind

*The adventures of a modern-day
mental health hero*

Dr. Reuven Feuerstein was a developmental cognitive psychologist and founder of the International Center for the Enhancement of Learning Potential, based in Jerusalem. His applied systems of structural cognitive modifiability have been implemented in over eighty countries across the globe. He was interviewed in his office in June of 2011.

As a psychologist practicing in Israel during the 1940s, I worked with Holocaust survivors, many of them children who were absolutely traumatized by what they had endured. For example, I saw a seventeen-year-old boy who weighed only seventy-five pounds, and who would look at every scrap of food as if he was starving; he would steal and hoard food every chance he got.

Of course, people were asking, "Is there hope for children like this? Will they ever be able to build a future? Will they ever be able to forget what they've been through?" Many were of the opinion that there was nothing we could do to help these children because they had seen too much of the world's evil.

But I thought, "We cannot afford to lose even *one* child."

Subsequently, I went to study at the University of Geneva under Jean Piaget and Carl Jung and others, and in 1954, I founded the International Center for the Enhancement of Learning Potential (ICELP) in Jerusalem, dedicated to a theory I developed, which I called the theory of malleability of intelligence.

Basically, I said, "Yes, we can help these children and *all* children, no matter their developmental problems. We can help them change because they are human beings who have a divine spirit in them."

At the time I advanced this theory—that human beings are modifiable, that they are not necessarily limited by their genetics—it was considered heresy. People simply did not believe that the brain could change, although now it is an accepted fact that there is no part of the body as flexible and changeable as the brain.

Dr. Feuerstein
delivering a class.

Courtesy of the
Feuerstein family

THE REBBE KNEW ABOUT MY WORK and supported it completely. We
had initially met in 1964 when I first visited the US and, on each of my
subsequent trips—as a visiting professor at Yale University—I made
it my business to come meet the Rebbe. He frequently sent children to
me—some with developmental problems, some with Down syndrome,
and some who were epileptic. Wherever I went, people were coming
up to me, saying, "The Rebbe wants you to see our child." As well, I received many letters from the Rebbe about particular children whom
he wanted me to see.

Each time that he sent me a referral, it was accompanied by his
blessing, "*Zayt matzliach*—May you be successful." With that blessing,
I got a feeling of empowerment—that, no matter how very difficult the
case, I could help this particular child. It became clear to me that he
believed that even people with genetic or chromosomal disorders could
be turned into functioning individuals and could even study Torah.

Indeed, it was from the Rebbe that I got the idea that such a thing could happen, and I have proof with my very own grandson who has Down syndrome, yet he has learned in *yeshivah* and graduated high school, passing the final examinations.

But, back then, it was considered daring to suggest such things, because people didn't believe such dramatic change was possible. I was often challenged: "How do you dare tell people that this child will ever be able to speak? How dare you hold out hope that this child will be able to read ... to finish school ... to go to *yeshivah*?"

I dared to say these things because of my interactions with the Rebbe. And, by 1980, nobody was asking me such questions anymore because my ideas had caught on everywhere—in America, in Africa, even in the Amazon rainforest. I had three books published and was frequently invited to lecture in universities. And I do not believe that I could have managed any of this were it not for the great inspiration and assurance that the Rebbe gave me.

ON ONE OCCASION, I came to ask for advice regarding my work with Native Americans.

At that time, Native Americans had a problem, in that the US government did not consider their languages acceptable for teaching in schools. And I was invited—as a specialist in the field of cultural differences, who could speak to the need for transmission of culture and tradition—to appear before the US Congress on behalf of the Navajo people and explain that these people need to use their native language, which should be taught in their schools.

Apparently, I convinced Congress and, afterwards, several Navajos came to study with me, going on to start a whole program of my teachings in their community. They also invited me and my entire family to come stay with them on the reservation and teach their people how to preserve the transmission of their culture.

But I was not sure that, according to Jewish law, I could accept their invitation. I did not know whether Torah considered their beliefs and the symbols that they used to be idolatry. But if it did, how could I—a Jew whose entire religion stood against idolatry—tell these people to continue their traditions?

Not knowing what to do, I came to New York and asked the Rebbe's secretary, Rabbi Leibel Groner, to convey my question to the Rebbe: "Can I tell the Navajo people to transmit their culture to the next generation, or would I be encouraging them in idolatry?"

The Rebbe's answer came during a *farbrengen*, when he spoke about the *Sheva Mitzvot Bnei Noach*—the seven universal laws dating back to the time of Noah—which prohibit idolatry, blasphemy, murder, theft, sexual immorality, and animal cruelty, and which prescribe the establishment of courts of law. "It is our duty as Jewish people," the Rebbe said, "to assist the various cultures in their task of fulfilling the Seven Laws of Noah. They are who they are, but it is our duty to influence them to keep G-d's law."

Afterwards, he called me up for a *l'chaim*, and he shook my hand.

I walked away knowing what I had to do. I taught the Navajos the concepts of Mediated Learning Experience (MLE)—a pedagogical belief system through which I was able to teach the word of G-d—and I believe they use this system to this day.

AFTER I WAS APPOINTED VISITING PROFESSOR AT YALE IN 1980, I continued to develop new training modalities demonstrating that you can create new synapses within the brain, new connections that didn't exist before, and in this way help children with the most devastating conditions.

I'd like to give just two examples:

There was a boy with a brain condition which made it very difficult for him to focus and, therefore, to hear what people were saying to him—his ability to listen was extremely limited. But the Rebbe gave me his special blessing for this boy. And despite his brain condition, the boy started to learn and became much more focused in his behavior, even becoming a part of the religious world.

Another case—the most difficult one of my entire career—also came to me through the Rebbe. I cannot reveal all the details because of patient privacy issues, but I can say that this boy was diagnosed as mentally defective in the country of his birth and was placed in a

The Rebbe hands a
dollar to a young
boy for him to give
to charity. 11 Tishrei,
5750-1989.

Levi Freidin,
The Living Archive

school for deficient children. There he lived among troubled youth and
was influenced by their bad behavior. Consequently, he became a real
problem, and nobody believed he would ever be able to function as a
normal, independent human being.

At some point, his father went to see the Rebbe, and the Rebbe told
him to bring his son to me, which he did.

The son came here to Israel and was placed with a Chabad family.
He learned to read. And he would often sit by my door reading from the
Book of Psalms because it is a Chabad custom to read the entire book
over the course of each month. The boy did this for the three years that
he was with us.

Thank G-d, all went very well, and I felt that we had done what the
Rebbe asked us, and empowered us, to do. We had been successful. But,
after this boy left us, he ended up in the gravest danger. He went to a
place from which few people return. He was involved with promiscuous
people — people who were taking drugs and doing much more than

Dr. Feuerstein in
conversation.

*Courtesy of the
Feuerstein family*

that. I would say that there was no sin in the world that these people
didn't commit.

When I heard what had happened, I contacted the Rebbe, who said,
"Don't give up on him. Send somebody to find him, bring him back and
continue."

I did not believe that a rescue effort would succeed, but the Rebbe
had instructed me to try, so I did. I sent somebody to take this young
man away from these terrible people, and we successfully coached him
back to a healthy and moral lifestyle. He had been lost, yet he came
back, and today he is the father of four children, two of them learning
in *yeshivah*.

I want to say that, as a psychologist, I could never have believed that
such a turnaround was possible. Usually, in such cases, we just give up.
But the Rebbe did not give up.

Clearly, psychology is very limited in its understanding of the other.
It's very much affected by, and related to, our understanding of ourselves. But the way the Rebbe understood the condition of the individual was altogether different. And this is why he thought that everyone
could be helped. His was a very different way of seeing the human
being—not as a reflection of the self but as a divine spirit that, at the
core, can never be corrupted.

RABBI YAAKOV YITZCHAK BIDERMAN

Ignore the Ridicule

A remarkable turning point in
man's search for meaning

Rabbi Yaakov Yitzchak Biderman has served as the Rebbe's emissary in Vienna, Austria, since 1980. He presently directs the Chabad institutions throughout the country and also serves as the spiritual leader of the Heichel Menachem Synagogue. He was interviewed in Brooklyn, New York, in January of 2012.

As an emissary of the Rebbe, I have encountered many difficulties and challenges, but in the hardest of times, I always tried to remember that it was the Rebbe who sent me here, it was the Rebbe who prepared me for this role, and it is the Rebbe who will ensure the success of my mission because the Rebbe is always with me in spirit.

I learned that he was looking out for my well-being and guiding me from a distance in the summer of 1970 when I was just a twelve-year-old boy. I had come from Israel to Chabad's Camp Gan Israel in Montreal, Canada, where I found myself feeling very lonely and longing to return home. All the campers spoke a language that I did not speak and shared inside jokes and school references that were foreign to me. I felt like an outsider, and although the counselors tried to make me feel included, they were responsible for hundreds of kids and could hardly give a single child undivided attention.

At some point during the summer, the director of Torah studies at the camp, a young man named Michoel Slavin, went to visit the Rebbe in New York on the occasion of his birthday. During that visit, the Rebbe said to him, "There is an Israeli boy in your camp by the name of Biderman who doesn't speak English, and who might be lonely and isolated. Try to see if you can make him feel more included."

Michoel took the Rebbe's words to heart, and he started studying with me, helping me prepare for my Bar Mitzvah. And then things began to change for me. The other kids noticed that although I could not communicate in English, my Hebrew was better than theirs, which helped me excel in Torah studies. They noticed that I was good at soccer, and that impressed them. As a result, I began to feel more accepted and began to like camp. Indeed, the experience proved so positive for me that I ended up staying on at the Chabad *yeshivah* in Montreal.

Attending a Canadian camp might have seemed like an unusual choice for a twelve-year-old Israeli boy, but it happened as a result of a suggestion from my mother's father, Rabbi Avraham Parshan. Originally a Sochotchover *chasid*, when he immigrated to Toronto in the 1950s he became very connected to the Lubavitcher Rebbe. And he was more than happy when I decided to stay in Canada to learn in a Chabad *yeshivah* there (after receiving the Rebbe's approval, of course).

On my father's side, there was also a bit of a Lubavitch connection. Although my paternal grandfather, Rabbi Moshe Mordechai Biderman, was the Lelover Rebbe, he had sent his sons, my father and my uncles, to Chabad schools in Tel Aviv when they were kids. I remember that he would speak with great admiration of the Lubavitcher Rebbe, and once he said: "The Lubavitcher Rebbe works wonders. He is a miracle worker because, as Rabbi Aaron of Karlin used to say, the greatest miracle is to bring G-dliness into Jewish hearts!"

Camp Gan Israel, Montreal. Summer, 1981.

Courtesy of Rabbi Pesach Sperlin

Rabbi Yaakov
Biderman (C.) listens
to a conversation
between his uncle,
Rabbi Avraham
Biderman (R.) and the
Rebbe. 28 Cheshvan,
5752-1992.

*Chaim B. Halberstam,
The Living Archive*

FAST FORWARD TO 1981 WHEN, after graduating *yeshivah*, becoming an ordained rabbi and getting married, my wife Edla and I were appointed as the Rebbe's emissaries to Austria.

Shortly after we arrived in Vienna, I received a letter from the Rebbe encouraging our efforts. He wrote, "Wishing you success in your holy work, and especially with the preschool."

This was puzzling as we hadn't established a preschool yet. But then — literally a few days later — a group of parents came to us and asked if Chabad could open a preschool for their children.

I was astonished and could not help but feel that, as I experienced before, the Rebbe was looking after every individual Jewish child from a distance.

All this was made clearer to me a few years later, when my uncles, Rabbi Shimon and Rabbi Alter Biderman, visited the Rebbe. At the end of that audience, which lasted quite some time, the Rebbe mentioned that their nephew was "doing great and wonderful things in Vienna." My uncles reported this to my father, who in turn mentioned it to his father, the Lelover Rebbe, adding that he didn't understand what the

The Lelover Rebbe, Rabbi Moshe Mordechai
Biderman
Courtesy of Rabbi Yaakov Biderman

Lubavitcher Rebbe could have meant. "Yaakov Yitzchak is having a very difficult time there. He hasn't seen much success yet."

(This was before everything developed in Vienna. The Chabad community center didn't yet exist, the institutions with hundreds of students were not yet established, even the Chabad House was not yet founded. We were working out of our home, inviting guests for Shabbat and giving a few Torah classes. There were no "great and wonderful things" to speak of.)

After hearing what my father reported, the Lelover Rebbe thought for a good while and then said, "You should know that *tzaddikim* see past, present and future at one glance. If the Lubavitcher Rebbe said it, that's how it is. And if you don't see it now, then you will see it in the future."

ONE OF THE MOST STARTLING EXAMPLES of the Rebbe's vision was brought to my attention during my service in Vienna. It involved the famed psychiatrist, Dr. Viktor Frankl, the Holocaust survivor who became the founder of logotherapy and author of the classic, *Man's Search for Meaning*.

Every year since we had arrived in Vienna, before Rosh Hashanah, we would send a Hebrew calendar to all the Jewish families in the city. And every year, Dr. Frankl would send us a humble donation in return. It was a mystery to me why he chose to donate specifically to Chabad, a religious organization dedicated to spreading *Yiddishkeit*, when he himself was not active in any Jewish community. I did not inquire, however, and the mystery was not solved until many years later.

In 1994, I received a visit from an elderly woman who identified herself as Marguerite Chajes, who greeted me with, "I have a surprise for you. You might think that you are the Rebbe's first emissary in Austria, but you are not. I was the first."

I was indeed surprised to hear that, but then she explained what she meant.

In 1958, during an audience with the Rebbe, she had mentioned that she wanted to visit Austria, a country where she had been raised but from where she had fled before the start of the war. Hearing this, the Rebbe asked her to contact his office before her trip, as he had a particular mission for her.

A few months later when she was ready to go, she did this. The Rebbe's secretary told her that she was to contact a Dr. Viktor Frankl in Vienna and relay a message to him in the Rebbe's name: "Don't despair. Don't take any of the ridicule you are facing to heart. Continue to disseminate your teachings. Be strong." And the Rebbe sent his blessings for success.

Now I need to explain that, at that time, Dr. Frankl was not yet the famous professor he would later become. He had studied with Sigmund Freud before the war, but after his experiences in the concentration camps, where his whole family was murdered, he departed from the Freudian view. He concluded that man's deepest drive is not towards pleasure but towards meaning. Indeed, man is searching for meaning in life all the time — even in the most dehumanizing situations — and mental health is very much related to faith and values. This conclusion served as a basis for his form of existential analysis which he called logotherapy.

But this flew in the face of the accepted notions of the day. And although he was appointed to head the prestigious Vienna Polyclinic of Neurology after the war, his ideas were subjected to tremendous ridicule by proponents of Freudian psychoanalysis,

Marguerite Chajes

Dr. Frankl delivering
a lecture at the
Polyclinic in Vienna.
1966.

Viktor Frankl Archive/
Imagno/
picturedesk.com

which was mainstream. People would even heckle him in the middle of his lectures. He was so hurt by this reaction that when Marguerite came to search for him at the clinic, she was told that he hadn't come to the office in a while. So she went to his home.

She told me that, when she arrived, she was surprised that the woman who opened the door and identified herself as Dr. Frankl's wife did not appear to be Jewish at all, and that there was a crucifix hanging on the wall. She thought it was very odd that the Rebbe would send her to encourage someone like that. (Only later did she learn that, after the Holocaust, Dr. Frankl had married a devout Catholic woman, and that the crucifix obviously belonged to her.)

Nonetheless, Marguerite was determined to fulfill her mission and, when Dr. Frankl appeared, she told him that she had a message for him from the Lubavitcher Rebbe. He invited her to sit down, and she said, "Rabbi Schneerson asked me to convey to you that you should not give up. Be strong. Don't be embarrassed by those who ridicule you. Continue on your path. You will prevail."

His response to those words shocked her. She said that she had never before seen an adult—never mind a personality of Dr. Frankl's stature—break down in such bitter tears. It took him some time to compose himself, and then he showed her the papers that were lying on the table—they were immigration documents for Australia. He was so crushed by the treatment he had suffered that he had decided to leave Vienna. But after absorbing this message from the Rebbe, he felt encouraged. He told her, upon parting, "I will find strength to return to my work. I will continue."

Shortly thereafter, he published the English version of his book, *A Psychologist Experiences the Concentration Camp*, under the title *Man's Search for Meaning*. It became a huge bestseller, which has sold over sixteen million copies and has been translated into two dozen languages.

This was such a remarkable story—that the famed Viktor Frankl might not have had the impact he'd had on the world were it not for the Lubavitcher Rebbe!—that I needed to confirm it. I decided to meet Dr. Frankl myself. He was very old by then, nearly 90; still, I took a chance and called him. He answered the telephone himself but said he was very weak and could not meet with me. He sounded a bit impatient, and it was clear that he was not well. Nonetheless, I asked him, "Does the name Lubavitcher Rebbe or Rabbi Schneerson mean anything to you?"

The moment that he heard the Rebbe's name, his tone changed completely. "Certainly, certainly, the name Rabbi Schneerson means a lot to me. I owe him a great deal," he said to me in German. "I respect the Rebbe very much. He helped me at an extremely critical moment. I owe him a great deal."

And, indeed, so do many others.

Millions of people benefitted from the Rebbe's message to Dr. Frankl. I cannot imagine what would have occurred if not for the

Rabbi Yaakov Biderman speaking at the annual International Conference of Chabad Emissaries. 5748-1987.
Courtesy of the Chabad Library

Viktor Frankl with a patient. 1952.
Viktor Frankl Archiv/Imagno/picturedesk.com

Rebbe's perfectly-timed words of encouragement.

But I have also wondered what led the Rebbe to take an interest in Viktor Frankl in the first place. As far as I know, Dr. Frankl had never communicated with the Rebbe, yet the Rebbe took pains to offer him encouragement and to support his work. It would seem that the Rebbe did this not only out of personal concern for Dr. Frankl's welfare, but also in order to advance a philosophy which he felt ultimately fosters belief in G-d, a spiritual perspective and good values. The fact that this constitutes the real cure to a suffering soul is something the Rebbe himself taught repeatedly.

I just can't help but marvel at the Rebbe's sensitivity, wide reach and vision that have impacted my life to a remarkable degree, as well as the lives of so many millions of others. ■

NO PERSON TOO SMALL, NO PROBLEM TOO BIG

MRS. ESTHER MENTZ

Shopper's Assistance

A Brooklyn girl finds a loving father after all

Mrs. Esther Mentz has worked as a social worker and directed an organization that helped the elderly receive proper care. After retiring, she continues to work with the needy on a volunteer basis. She was interviewed in her home in Brooklyn in November of 2010.

I never knew what it is to have a loving parent, and the Rebbe gave me the closest thing to that. He made me feel that he understood me completely, and, when I was in his presence, I felt like I was the only person who mattered. So, of course, I was drawn to him—he was like a father to me.

I came to know of Chabad in 1954 when I first moved from Rhode Island to New York after high school. I had been raised in a nonreligious family and had had very little in the way of Jewish education, but after my mother passed away when I was sixteen, I started to educate myself. Eventually, one of my teachers helped me move to East Flatbush, in Brooklyn, so that I could further my Jewish learning. There lived the Rebbe's distant cousin, Reb Zalman Schneerson, and he became my tutor in Chasidic literature. Because of this association, I was brought into the Chabad community, and I would catch glimpses of the Rebbe at the *farbrengens* and other special occasions. Even though he was a larger-than-life figure for me, I did not have any personal, face-to-face encounters with him for many years.

In 1955, I went on a date with a Chabad *chasid*, Binyamin Mentz, and we eventually decided to get married. But it took some time to get the Rebbe's approval.

Not knowing me or my family, presumably the Rebbe wanted to do some research before he would give his approval. Once the Rebbe was

satisfied, he went out of his way to make sure my wedding was very special, since I had no mother, and my father was very opposed to my religious lifestyle.

The Rebbe officiated at our wedding and, not only that, he made sure that the wedding hall was filled to the brim. It seemed to me at the time as if every young *yeshivah* student and every seminary girl in Brooklyn had come to dance with us. I did not know—in fact, I did not learn for many years—that this was the Rebbe's doing. He made sure that my wedding was a most joyous occasion.

WHEN WE FIRST GOT MARRIED, my husband wasn't yet earning much of a living. Times were tough, to say the least. As Passover was approaching, I had no idea how we were going to manage. I had to buy all the special food, plus I could not use the regular dishes that had come in contact with leavened products (*chametz*). But how was I supposed to get new dishes?!

So, as any good *chasid* would, I wrote to the Rebbe about my problem. Immediately, I got a response from the Rebbe's secretary, Rabbi

Hodakov, who informed me, "The Rebbe said to buy whatever you need — whatever it costs — and put it on his bill." And he directed me to a housewares store on Kingston Avenue and Montgomery Street in Crown Heights.

I was mindful of the fact that I was spending the Rebbe's money, so I bought the minimum that I needed. I mean, how could I in good conscience spend a penny more than I had to? I bought two or three of everything, no more: a couple of forks, knives, spoons, and the cheap glass dishes that were popular at the time — two or three white ones for dairy and two or three green ones for meat, plus a couple of pots.

I submitted the bill to the Rebbe's office, carefully listing all my purchases because I felt he should see where his money went. Before long, I got a call from Rabbi Hodakov. "The Rebbe wants to know — where are your dishes?" So I told him, "I got the little glass dishes. You know, the green and the white!"

"But what about the ones you are going to use for the *seder*?"

"I am going to use the same ones for the *seder*."

This did not satisfy the Rebbe. Rabbi Hodakov called me again to say that the Rebbe wanted me to go back to the store and buy a proper set of Passover dishes and silverware as well as other appropriate utensils.

"It seemed to me at the time as if ... every seminary girl in Brooklyn had come to dance with us." 2 Adar, 5716-1956.

Courtesy of the Mentz family

I didn't do it. I couldn't bring myself to spend other people's money. The next thing I know, the Rebbe ordered it all and had it delivered to my house! The plates and soup bowls had daffodils in the middle, and there was a matching sprig of daffodils on the silverware.

I was in shock!

I could not get over the fact that the Rebbe did not want me to feel that I was missing something. He would not have me feel less than anyone else, if he could help it.

In general, men don't care about these things. Men care about the *seder*, not whether the dishes match. But a woman likes to set a nice table. The Rebbe understood this, and he wanted me to have the same things as every other family.

That's how much he cared. I still get shivers when I think of it.

Every year after that, he remembered us. He'd send us fifty dollars for Passover, with a note that we should use it for food.

Eventually, the time came when we could afford to buy the food, and so I returned the check. In response, a message came back, "You don't have to use it just for food. This is for Passover, when there are many other expenses."

The following year, he increased it to a hundred dollars. That was the Rebbe—he understood that I would not abuse his generosity, so

The silverware that the Rebbe sponsored.

Courtesy of the Mentz family

he increased it to make sure I spent it on other things that he knew I really needed.

The Rebbe's caring and sensitivity were unmatched, even when it came to a woman he barely knew and with whom he had never spoken.

THE FIRST TIME THAT I ACTUALLY SPOKE with the Rebbe was when I was pregnant with my daughter. Back then, it was the custom for every woman in the community to get a blessing from the Rebbe during her pregnancy.

I went to see him, frightened to death. Even though he had been so kind to me, he was still *the* Rebbe, whom everyone held in awe. But he put me at ease immediately with his smile, and he graciously offered me a seat, though I had been told beforehand that a *chasid* does not sit in front of the Rebbe.

From that point on, I related to him as a father and went to him with my problems.

There came a time when the one wig with which I covered my hair — since a married woman's hair is meant to be covered — wore out completely. So I started wearing hats and scarves. My father passed away in January of 1961, and, when I flew down to Florida for the funeral wearing my winter hat, people looked at me strangely as sweat poured down my face in the terrible heat. I had been so upset about the passing of my father, I had not taken into consideration that Florida's weather wasn't like New York's, but once I was at the cemetery, what could I do?

I was so terribly embarrassed by my appearance that, on my return, I went to the Rebbe and told him about the incident. "What happened to your *sheitel*?" he asked. "It wore out," I replied, "and I don't have the money to buy another one."

The Rebbe became visibly upset and said, "A woman should never be placed in a position where she has to make a choice between feeling like you felt, or taking off her hair covering. That should never be."

Not long after that, I got a call from Rabbi Hodakov who said that he had orders from the Rebbe to tell me to go to the best place for wigs, order a *sheitel* for myself, and send him the bill. He stressed that it should be the *best* place and the *finest* wig.

So I did just that. I went to a place that made theatrical wigs, and they made me a beautiful *sheitel*. I recall that it cost more than $500, and I felt great wearing it.

The Rebbe had such tremendous sensitivity to everyone's feelings that he understood a woman's sense of self. He understood that I didn't feel good about myself. He wanted me to feel like a woman should feel and not be embarrassed because I didn't have the money to look decent.

This trait of his—the ability to understand and empathize; his great compassion—was so rare and so beautiful.

HE SHOWED THE SAME KIND of sensitivity to children. I remember our family coming for an audience in 1959 on the occasion of my husband's birthday. Hendy, my precocious two-year-old daughter, was running around the Rebbe's office. To her mind this was a wonderful playground with all kinds of drawers to open, full of fun things to pull out.

I was so embarrassed, as was my husband, and he was trying to get her under control. But she wasn't paying any attention to him—she had a mind of her own.

After a while the Rebbe took matters into his own hands. He called her over and said, "Let me show you something." He took out a pencil and a piece of paper and began drawing. He drew a house made out of the letters of the Hebrew alphabet, so that the *chet* was the house, the *hei* was the door, the *yud* was the door handle, the *lamed* was smoke coming out of the chimney, and so forth. Hendy was fascinated. Then the Rebbe asked, "Would you like to have it?" but she said, "No." My heart fell. I wanted to frame it for posterity—but she didn't take it.

On our way out, the Rebbe gave her a silver dollar and she was happy with that. How I would have loved for her to take that picture home with her! But, I still have the special memory of the Rebbe interacting with a little girl.

Hendy and Chaim Mentz. 1961.
Courtesy of the Mentz family.

The Rebbe hands a dollar to a young girl. 11 Tishrei, 5752-1991.
Levi Freidin, The Living Archive

Binyamin with his
children, Hendy and
Chaim, near their
Crown Heights home.
1962.

*Courtesy of
the Mentz family*

He didn't have his own children, but he had an incredible appreciation for everyone else's. You could see him beaming when he was with little kids. He was able to bring himself down to the level of a two-year-old and draw her a picture. It was truly something sweet to see.

ANOTHER TIME I CAME TO HIM to confide that I was finding it hard to make friends among the Lubavitch women. In those days, they were mostly immigrants from Europe, Yiddish speakers, while I was an American who did not know their language. Furthermore, my background was different from theirs and that made me an outsider. This was hurtful to me, and so I went to discuss it with the Rebbe.

He heard me out and asked me what I thought the underlying problem was. "Did you have a problem making friends with other religious girls when you were in the Bais Yaakov seminary?"

"No. I had lots of friends," I said. Thus, we identified that the problem was primarily a language barrier.

"So why not make friends outside of Lubavitch?" he suggested.

It was a brilliant idea. There were plenty of religious women in the neighborhood with whom I had more in common — why I had thought that I could only associate with Lubavitch women, I don't know. But I immediately saw how right the Rebbe was — there was more than one way to slice it, and we are all Jews, after all.

AS I GREW MORE CONFIDENT in my role as a religious wife and mother, and as the Lubavitch community became more Americanized, I made inroads among the women and even came to play a significant role. Indeed, in 1974, I became copresident—together with Malka Sarah Kuperman—of N'shei Chabad, the Chabad Women's organization.

When I did, I decided I wanted to do something memorable other than hold meetings. It occurred to me that Crown Heights really needed a Bikur Cholim Society, a group of women volunteers to visit the sick. By then the population had greatly increased, with young people who had newly returned to their Jewish roots settling in the neighborhood. Many of these young *baalei teshuvah* did not have a family support system. Life was difficult for them, money was short, and some of their families were not pleased that their children had become observant. When they got sick or the women gave birth, they didn't get many visitors at the hospital.

Lefferts General Hospital happened to be around the corner from where I lived, and that seemed as good a reason as any for me to help them out. So this is what I did: I visited these young newly-religious women in the hospital, and I found they needed to pour out their hearts to

A N'shei Chabad gathering in 1957. The Rebbe's mother, Rebbetzin Chana, stands fourth from the right.

Courtesy of Malka Sarah Kuperman

Nostrand Avenue in
Crown Heights. 1970.

Brian Merlis
Collection

someone. They needed to tell someone about the difficulties they were handling at home, how upsetting this or that child was, that they didn't know how to take care of the baby, that they had no one to help them.

As I listened and learned about the problems of these young newcomers, I found that there was an urgent need for a free supply of special baby formula. One of my children had needed it, and it cost close to fifty dollars a week which I didn't have, so I could empathize with mothers in the same situation.

I ended up doing these two things — visiting sick women in the hospital, and raising money for babies who needed special formula. And I also did a third thing — something that I called a *"Mesibat Shabbat on Sunday."* This "Sunday Shabbat party" was a gathering for children who were not well — handicapped in some way. In keeping with society's approach to such problems back then, these children were often hidden from the general population and didn't receive the care they would nowadays.

Beth Rivkah Elementary School allowed us to use their building and the seminary girls got involved, so there was a one-on-one ratio — one child to one adult — because these children were all differently affected and needed special attention. Various women volunteered to pick up the children, Lipskier's grocery store supplied snacks, Rimler's supplied prizes and games, and a retired teacher came on board to organize the program. We did lots of nice things — like going to the zoo, for example — and I pulled it all together.

AFTER A TIME, HOWEVER, I said I can't do this anymore. I was tired; it just took too much out of me, and it took me away from my children. They were home on Sunday, but I wasn't. So I decided it was time to quit.

The next time I saw the Rebbe, I informed him, "This is the last year, and then I'm letting it go."

"Why?" he asked. "You're doing a great job!"

"I'm tired," I said. "I'm doing it singlehandedly. I don't want to do it anymore."

He looked at me. "You're tired? You don't want to do it anymore?" Then he said something that pierced my heart: "What should the Rebbe say: 'The Rebbe is tired, he doesn't want to do it anymore'? But the Rebbe continues doing it. He needs to keep doing it, even when he gets little cooperation."

"I'm not the Rebbe," I countered.

"And you're not doing the job of a Rebbe — you're doing the job that you can do." He was so cajoling with that smile of his. "Can you continue for another year?" he asked.

If the Rebbe asks you like that, you cannot say no.

I just would like to emphasize that the Rebbe never asked anyone to do more than he did. He always did more than anyone else.

So I agreed and I continued for another two years.

IN 1979, Binyamin and I divorced. I recall coming to see the Rebbe and telling him that I would soon be moving out of Crown Heights. The conversation was brief, as my thirteen-year-old son was there, having come to receive the Rebbe's blessing on the occasion of his Bar Mitzvah.

The Rebbe greets
Esther and her son
Chaim on the "Sunday
Dollars" receiving line.
3 Av, 5751-1991.

Chaim B. Halberstam,
The Living Archive

The Rebbe looked at me. "You're leaving Crown Heights?"

"Yes," I confirmed.

"Will you continue to be my friend?"

I was so stunned by his question that you could have knocked me over with a feather. But I managed to say, "I will always feel about you as I do now."

"Will you come back and visit?"

I promised I would.

But it was about ten years before I returned. When I walked in, the Rebbe's face lit up with a big smile and he declared, "My friend has returned!"

It gave me such goosebumps that he remembered the words he had spoken to me so many years before. He was such a busy man, a world-class leader; so many people had passed through his door, yet he remembered our last conversation. Like only a father could. ■

RABBI NOCHUM STILERMAN

A Delivery Boy's Life

A wealth of wisdom from a most unlikely source

Rabbi Nochum Stilerman, a financial consultant and fundraiser, has raised over $400 million for various Jewish causes over the past fifty years. He is also known for his seminars, in which he teaches the tools of his trade. He presently lives in Har Nof, Jerusalem, where he was interviewed in March of 2016.

Whenmyfamilyimmigrated to the United States from Soviet Russia in February of 1951, we were relocated by the American Jewish Joint Distribution Committee to Crown Heights, Brooklyn, where my father established the first grocery store that was closed on Shabbat.

My father was an observant Jew, and all his friends told him that he would not survive in this business being closed two days out of the week—on Shabbat and Sunday—as, in those days, the so-called "blue laws" forbade being open on Sunday. But my father could never do business on Shabbat, and he wondered if he should give up on this venture. Not knowing what to do, he decided to seek advice from Rabbi Menachem Mendel Schneerson, the new Lubavitcher Rebbe. Although my father was not a *chasid*, it seems that back in Russia he'd had some contact with Chabad, so he felt this was the right address for his question.

The Rebbe advised him to trust in G-d and go ahead, and my father opened a store at 333 Albany Avenue, between Union Street and Eastern Parkway.

At that time I was about nine years old, and I became a delivery boy for my father, a job which I did for the next ten years. Using a three-wheeled pushcart, I would make deliveries to his customers—and he had some famous customers. Among them were the Rebbe and his wife (Rebbetzin Chaya Mushka), the Rebbe's mother (Rebbetzin Chana), and the Rebbe's mother-in-law, the widow of the Previous Rebbe (Rebbetzin Nechama Dina).

Reb Yankel Lipskier
Levi Freidin, The Living Archive

Our other famous customers included the Kozhnitzer Rebbe, the Bobover Rebbe, the Kozlover Rebbe, the Kerestirer Rebbe and the Novominsker Rebbe. The business never made a fortune, but we worked very hard and managed to make ends meet. I myself had to get up at five in the morning to start preparing the deliveries, and my father, who woke up even earlier than me, stayed in the store until eleven at night.

Then, one day—it was in 1953 or 1954, as I recall—a Lubavitcher named Yankel Lipskier came to my father and said he wanted to open another grocery store in the neighborhood, just one block away from ours. My father said to him, "There isn't enough business for one family, how can there be for two? Besides, the wholesale kosher distributors won't deliver to you since they are already delivering to me." (There were only three distributors of kosher products at the time—Balsam, Kehal and Mehadrin.)

But Lipskier pleaded that he needed to make a living, and so my father proposed, "Let's go to the Rebbe—whatever he says, I will do."

After hearing both sides, the Rebbe stated, "Under ordinary circumstances, Mr. Stilerman would be correct—the two of you can't make it. But I assure you that G-d will provide a livelihood for both of you."

Because he had full faith in the Rebbe as a man of G-d, my father agreed. Not only did he allow Lipskier to open a competing grocery store, but he gave him a loan to start the business! He lent Lipskier three thousand dollars, which would be more than thirty thousand dollars today. Imagine a competitor opening a business a block away from you, and you giving him thirty thousand dollars to help him succeed and possibly put you out of business!

But my father did it, because he trusted the advice of a *tzaddik*. In his mind, there was no question—if the Rebbe said they would both

make a living, then that's what would surely happen. So why shouldn't he give a loan to a fellow Jew?

And then he helped him in other ways. At first Balsam, the kosher milk distributor, would not deliver to Lipskier. So my father ordered extra and had me haul the milk crates on my pushcart to his competitor. If Lipskier ran out of a product, my father would send it over from his own inventory. I remember it well, as I was the one who would have to deliver it all. It seemed to me that this was a ridiculous arrangement, and yet it worked. Somehow, they both made a living, as the Rebbe had promised they would.

I VIVIDLY RECALL making deliveries to the Rebbe's mother, Rebbetzin Chana. An outgoing and joyful woman, she always had a nice thing to say and a smile on her face. Whenever I came, she treated me kindly, offering me a glass of milk — hot in the winter, cold in the summer — accompanied by sponge cake.

Lipskier's grocery store, after it was bought by new owners.

Levi Freidin, The Living Archive

Rebbetzin Chana, the Rebbe's mother.
16 Adar II, 5719-1959.
Courtesy of Sima Paltiel

She would urge me to sit down, and I didn't realize until later that I was sitting in the Rebbe's chair. But the Rebbetzin told me to sit there—how was I to know?

I grew very fond of Rebbetzin Chana. She gave me the feeling that she was like my bubby, that she really cared about me—the little kid schlepping her groceries. She would always ask about my family, and sometimes, when I couldn't bring her groceries and another delivery boy did, she would call my father to ask if I was okay.

While I was drinking the milk, Rebbetzin Chana would ask me to tell her stories. So I would relate bits out of *Talks and Tales*, the children's monthly magazine, a subscription that had been a present from Rebbetzin Chaya Mushka, who always encouraged me to read so I would improve my English.

One day, I said to Rebbetzin Chana, "I read a funny story and I was wondering if it is true." She asked, "What is the story?" So, I told her what I read—that when the Previous Rebbe was a little boy, he asked his father whether the angels can count.

His father responded that the Angel Michael counts the psalms each person recites and, with them, he creates a chandelier that lights up in Heaven above and on earth below for that person. "Is this true?" I asked her.

"Not only is the story true," she answered me, "But that is what really happens."

"In that case, I will recite a psalm," I declared. "I won't say the whole Book of Psalms, but I will say one or two chapters, because I would also like a chandelier."

At that she smiled and said, "In order to have a chandelier, you have to build a house. A house stands on a foundation of Torah and *mitzvot*. Once you have the foundation, you can have a house, and then you can start thinking about a chandelier."

I looked at her and said "I understand," but I didn't really. What I did understand was that this chandelier would never be mine, because the way to get it seemed like a very complicated program.

She must have intuited my reaction and mentioned something to the Rebbe, because the next time I made a delivery to her and the Rebbe was there, he asked me, "What's going on with the palace that you are building?"

Puzzled, I looked at him, "What palace?"

"I hear you want to have a chandelier, so you must be building a palace!"

MEANWHILE, I CONTINUED to deliver to Rebbetzin Chana, and one time I was moved to ask her, "What is the Rebbe's favorite prayer?"

At that time, it was very hard for me to pray because, usually, by the time the *minyan* gathered for morning prayers, I had been running around with my pushcart for a good two hours and was too exhausted to concentrate. So I wanted to identify the most important prayer in order that I could recite at least this one prayer with total concentration.

She answered, "All the prayers are important, but yes, there might be one that is more important than the rest. I don't know what that is for the Rebbe, but the next time I see him, I will ask him on your behalf."

Of course, I expected that the answer would be the *Amidah*, which is the cornerstone of Jewish prayer. But I hoped it would be something shorter.

The following week, when I delivered the groceries, she said, "I have an answer to your question." She paused, as I waited with great anticipation.

Then she said, "You know, I am so happy you asked because I wouldn't have known that he had a favorite prayer."

I was holding on to my seat.

"It's a very short prayer," she continued. "The very first prayer that we say in the morning, *Modeh Ani*: 'I give thanks before You, living and everlasting King, that You restored my soul to me with compassion; great is Your faithfulness.'"

"That's it?" I asked.

"Yes," she said. "That's his favorite."

I was surprised but also very happy to hear it. And I adopted this prayer as my own personal favorite as well.

Sometime later, I heard the Rebbe give a talk on the subject of *Modeh Ani*. He explained that the message of this prayer is that G-d has a lot of faith in us, so let's not disappoint Him. How do we know that He has so much faith in us? Because He gave us another day of life, even though He doesn't owe it to us.

It became my life's goal not to disappoint G-d in what I accomplished during each day. I learned that from the Rebbe, by way of the good offices of Rebbetzin Chana.

ON OCCASION, WHEN I DELIVERED to Rebbetzin Chana, the Rebbe was there, since he visited his mother every day. And I would later joke that, as far as I know, I'm the only one in Chabad for whom the Rebbe opened the door. I would ring the bell and, instead of Rebbetzin Chana, he'd be the one to let me in and help me carry the packages inside.

The first time it happened, Rebbetzin Chana introduced me to him as "my friend Nochum," and the Rebbe responded, "If you are a friend of my mother, you are my friend too."

And indeed, I felt that I was. From the time of my Bar Mitzvah, I was always able to get an audience with the Rebbe whenever I had something on my mind. All I had to do was ask his secretary, Rabbi Hodakov, and I was in. When I saw the Rebbe, he always made a point of asking about my parents. He was interested in how my father was doing in the business, how my mother's asthma was coming along, and so forth.

On one occasion he gave me a blessing which I cherish to this day. He said, "Your father and mother should be very proud of you, and G-d should be proud of you, but the main thing is that you should be proud of yourself."

This blessing became my motto, and it has followed me all the days

of my life. I have often asked myself, "Am I proud of what I'm doing? Will I be glad tomorrow that I did this or that today? Am I actualizing my potential?" And I have passed this insight on to my children.

The Rebbe gives *lekach* to a boy at the door of his *sukkah*. Hoshana Rabbah, 5729-1968.

Chaim B. Halberstam, The Living Archive

WHEN I REACHED MARRIAGEABLE AGE, I was still working for my father, delivering groceries by pushcart. After I started dating, I vividly recall my humiliation one morning, when the young lady I met the night before passed me on the street while I was wheeling my pushcart.

This pushcart had iron wheels, and it made a lot of noise. I didn't need a horn to honk—everybody knew I was coming down the street. When she saw me, I was so very embarrassed. To cover up how I felt, I joked, "Do you want a ride?" But truly, I just wanted the earth to swallow me up.

It bothered me so much that I brought it up to the Rebbe the next time I saw him. He said, "I understand how you feel, but remember

The Stilermans
at their wedding.
March 13, 1966.

*Courtesy of
Rabbi Stilerman*

that, by helping out in the store, you are honoring your father and your mother. This is to your merit, and you don't need to be embarrassed."

His words entered my heart; I believed him totally, and my attitude changed completely. Now, as I wheeled my pushcart around Crown Heights, I smiled. Not long after, I married an amazing, G-d fearing, young woman who lived a short distance from the store. And here I stand today, the father of seven children, and grandfather of many grandchildren and great-grandchildren. ■

MRS. DIANE ABRAMS

Grandma Rachel's Legacy

*Reflections on the courageous Jewish woman
of yesterday, today and tomorrow*

Mrs. Diane Abrams practiced law in Manhattan, New York, and created and taught the nation's first "Women and the Law" course at NYU Law School. Presently, she works as a real estate broker. She was interviewed in her home and her office in January of 2002 and August of 2013.

The first time I met the Rebbe was just after I had become engaged to my husband, Robert Abrams — Bob — who was then the borough president of the Bronx. This was in 1974, a time when I was a matrimonial lawyer. Previous to that, I taught the *Women and the Law* course — which I originated in 1969 — at the University of Pennsylvania and New York University law schools.

Rabbi Israel Mowshowitz of the Hillcrest Jewish Center, with whom Bob worked, suggested that we visit the Rebbe to receive a blessing for our marriage. Although neither of us had a connection to Lubavitch, the Rebbe graciously gave us his blessing, for which we were grateful.

After our marriage, we were invited to a *farbrengen* at 770 Eastern Parkway, and then we began seeing the Rebbe several times a year on public and private occasions.

During one of our meetings, I mentioned to the Rebbe that I had written an article about my grandmother — my father's mother, Rachel — published in the summer of 1974 in *Jewish Life* under the title "Grandma Lives." The Rebbe expressed interest in reading it, so I sent him a copy.

I had decided to write this article after becoming involved in the women's movement in the late 1960s, a time when Judaism was being criticized for its approach to women. Many critics, who were not necessarily knowledgeable about Jewish life, claimed that Judaism looked down upon women or denigrated women or considered them irrelevant in the public arena. Yet my grandmother — who was a very traditional, Torah-observant woman — held a highly respected place in both her

Diane's grandmother, Rachel Schulder.
Courtesy of Diane Abrams

family and her community.

Therefore, I felt strongly that there did not have to be a conflict between feminism and Judaism. Jewish women could take the Torah seriously, have a significant role within Judaism, and have an equal role in society. Writing my grandmother's story was my answer to those who did not understand how a woman could be loyal to Jewish tradition and also play an important role in the larger world.

After the Rebbe read my article, he told me that I should expand on it and write a book about my grandmother, perhaps foreseeing some of the conflicts that would arise around women's roles. I tried to do what he suggested, but I never completed the manuscript.

DURING OUR MEETINGS, as the Rebbe talked with Bob about issues of mutual concern, frequently, he would turn to me in the middle of the conversation to ask, "What do you think about this issue? What is your opinion? These are the days of women's liberation!" Knowing that I was a feminist lawyer who had opinions on the issues of the day, he wanted to hear what I had to say. Each time Bob and I visited him—even after Bob became the attorney general for the State of New York and there were pressing matters to discuss—he always made a point of inviting my input as well.

We were privileged to visit with the Rebbe many times and also to attend his *farbrengens*. I would feel very uplifted by those events and so I always looked forward to attending.

I recall one *farbrengen* in 1975, when Bob and I, along with a number of dignitaries, came to join the twenty-fifth anniversary celebration of

GRAND

Broom. This was a three story building, and on the ground floor there was a store, with a sign in the window, "A. SCHULDER AND SONS." "A. Schulder" represented my grandfather, Abraham Schulder, and "sons" were my father William and his brother Michael.

My grandfather lived on the first floor, one flight up, and we resided on the top floor. We had no bathtub, and when we had to take a bath, we would go to my grandfather's apartment, since he had a bathtub off the hall. Our toilet was also located in the hall, but it did not have a door, only a curtain that could be drawn across the opening.

In the top floor apartment, the center room was the kitchen, which had a large coal stove. The bedrooms were on the periphery, and alongside the kitchen was the dining room.

I know that you want to know more about my mother, and the mere mention of her name brings back many loving memories. She was beautiful to look at, and a delightful person with which to speak. She had a dulcet soft sweet voice, and did not know the meaning of malice. I think that she acquired this trait from her father, who was also a soft spoken man. My mother lived an unhurried life, being an individual who you would say had the trait of quiet efficiency.

I remember Peasch time, which was when we all got new clothing. My mother took me to a store, and she would always get me a suit that was one size larger, saying, "You'll grown into

all set up for Shabbos dinner.

Q. On Friday night, was there anyone at the table other than the family?

A. Yes, we always had an *Orech* (guest)—that is, a poor boy or man whom my father would bring home from shul to have the Friday night dinner with us. Sometimes there were three or four such guests.

Q. How did grandma know how much to cook?

A. She really didn't, but she always cooked extra, and there was enough for everybody. In those days, we were considered to be fairly well-to-do family.

When we moved to Williamsburg, the number of Shabbos guests increased. I'll never forget my grandfather's admonition to my father that we were all going to become *goyim* when we moved from the East Side to Williamsburg—even though everybody knows how religious the Williamsburg community is.

When we lived in Williamsburg, we used to *doven* at Yeshiva Torah VoDaath. There were always out of town students who did not have any place in which to eat their Shabbos meals, and my father would usually bring home three or four for dinner. The other members of the congregation would do likewise, so nobody was ever left without a Shabbos meal.

Q. Do you remember any other incidents from when you were a child?

A. My mother liked it very much when her father, Moshe Shochet, would visit us in Williamsburg. He al-

would see an immaculate white table-cloth on top of the dining room table, with the candelabra, candles and plates

Diane Schulder is a highly successful attorney, specializing in matrimonial law. A graduate of Columbia Law School, she conceived and taught the first course on "Women and the Law" at the University of Pennsylvania and New York University. She is currently engaged to Bronx Borough President, Robert Abrams.

ways had a little satchel and would bring us goodies from the slaughterhouse, such as Kishkes and other interesting types of food. Even though he was a very poor man, he would always bring us children a few packs of gum.

My maternal grandfather was a Shochet, and he would spend many hours immersed in study. He had many Gemorahs, and when we looked at him after his death, we saw that the pages that refer to the temple were filled with teardrops.

THE MOTHER'S ROLE

Q. Now I'd like to come to the main focus, which is the kind of person that grandma was. Naturally, every person is different, and just because she was a wonderful person does not necessarily mean that it was all due to the kind of culture and community in which she lived. Still, I believe that there was a certain relationship between the kind of community in which she lived and the kind of person that she was. I wonder if you could just describe here what she did every day, what was her work, and how she was regarded by the other members of the family.

A. Basically, my mother was very much like most Jewish mothers. She took care of the children, saw that we were clothed, fed and that we went to school. In those days there were not many Yeshivahs, and I used to go to *Cheder* after public school. My mother would see to that, and when we were

Excerpts from Diane's article published in *Jewish Life*.

Courtesy of Diane Abrams

the Rebbe's assumption of Chabad leadership. Bob went to the men's section to present the Rebbe with a congratulatory proclamation, while I went upstairs with the women.

Bob made his presentation and the Rebbe thanked him, humbly noting that he was receiving the proclamation on behalf of the Chabad movement rather than as a distinction for himself, personally. He then asked, "Is Mrs. Abrams also here?" Bob confirmed that I was there and pointed up to the women's section. "I'm very happy!" the Rebbe responded.

TEN YEARS LATER, IN 1985, we had a fateful meeting with the Rebbe on Hoshana Rabbah, the seventh day of Sukkot.

I was almost forty-eight years old and the mother of one child—our daughter Rachel, named after my grandmother—but I very much wanted another. When I consulted a doctor, however, I was told that, due to my age, I had less than a five percent chance of becoming pregnant. I sought the opinion of a second doctor who was a bit more encouraging.

Meanwhile, Bob and I didn't breathe a word about our hopes to anyone. We didn't even tell our parents or close friends; we were just praying for another child.

It was at this time that we came to see the Rebbe, as we did annually on Hoshana Rabbah when he was distributing honey cake at the door of his *sukkah*. To our great surprise, totally out of the blue, the Rebbe looked at me and said with a smile, "I give you a blessing for an addition to your family within the next year."

I was stunned! How could he have known that this was exactly what we were praying for? We hadn't told a soul!

Seven weeks later — I remember it was on Thanksgiving — I took a home pregnancy test, but I couldn't believe my eyes. I awakened my daughter Rachel and asked her, "Tell me what color is this, white or blue?"

"It's blue," she replied.

I still couldn't believe it. "Are you sure it's not white?"

"Mom, I'm sure. It's blue."

Immediately, I went to take another test at my doctor's office. After the results came back, the doctor called and said, "The test is positive for pregnancy, but there must be an error. We'd better test again."

"I give you a blessing for an addition to your family within the next year."
The Rebbe blesses Diane at the door of his *sukkah*. Hoshana Rabbah, 5746-1985.

Levi Freidin,
The Living Archive

With Becky in hand, Diane and Bob return to the Rebbe. Hoshana Rabbah, 5747-1986.

Levi Freidin, The Living Archive

The third test confirmed beyond a shadow of a doubt — I was pregnant. And I was very, very happy.

On July 31, 1986, just a few months before my forty-ninth birthday, I gave birth to Becky — Benyamina — a healthy girl who has brought us great joy and who has been called by some "the Rebbe's baby."

Subsequently, I learned that just about the time I was giving birth, Rabbi Yehuda Krinsky, the Rebbe's secretary, phoned our house. When Rachel picked up the phone, he asked her, "How is your mother?" The Rebbe had instructed him to call and inquire after my well-being at the very moment I was delivering Becky. Hearing this later really touched me.

The following year on Hoshana Rabbah, we went to visit the Rebbe. "I see you brought the addition to your family," the Rebbe remarked, repeating the exact words he had used in his original blessing to us.

Bob said, "Rebbe, we want to thank you."

"Don't thank me," the Rebbe replied, and he pointed to the sky.

I have often wondered: Did the Rebbe have special powers so that his blessings could cause a woman to give birth? Or was it that he created a positive, calm influence that was conducive to good things taking root? Or was it his extraordinary sensitivity to other people that created a new reality? How was he able to know what we were hoping and praying for although we never mentioned it? How was he able to give a blessing that came true?!

I have no answers to these questions; I can only testify to the facts and that the Rebbe was always seeking to understand the person before him and how he could help each person live up to his or her highest potential.

AS FOR HIS ADVICE TO ME TO WRITE A BOOK about my grandmother, I hadn't realized how much it mattered to him — not until the summer of 1991.

Bob and I had come to see him a few days after the Crown Heights riots, when Bob was meeting with community leaders. I was startled when the Rebbe turned to me and said, "You promised me some time ago that you were going to write a memoir about your grandmother. What happened to the book?"

This was totally unexpected. I felt so embarrassed that I turned beet red. "Well ... I'm doing something in that direction," I stammered. "I'll inform you as it comes along."

Diane and Bob walk Becky down the aisle.

Courtesy of the Abrams family

"It's taking you too long," he chastised me with a fatherly smile. "You have much more to do after you finish it."

He lit a fire under me, and from that day forward for all of the next year, I worked hard on that project. I conducted a great deal of research, even traveling to Eastern Europe to the place where my grandmother was born, and I wrote a draft of the book, but it was never published.

Nonetheless, my efforts back then opened the way to other fascinating and productive avenues. For one thing, together with my friend Adele Tauber, I wrote a book about my family based on oral histories, which was privately printed for my parents' sixtieth wedding anniversary. From there I began to delve into genealogy and went on to learn more about my family, as I tried to fulfill the task that the Rebbe set before me. And I am now, finally, completing a new version of the manuscript he wanted me to write, entitled *My Grandmother's Candlesticks: Feminism and Judaism*, which I hope to see published soon.

The Rebbe always made me, as well as others, feel that he wanted us to do good and important things. A great leader always brings out the best in his followers, and the Rebbe certainly did that throughout his long and productive life.

RABBI HERBERT WEINER

The Tenth Mystic

*The relentlessly searching mind meets
the endlessly caring heart*

Rabbi Herbert Weiner was one the founders of Temple Israel in South Orange, New Jersey, which he led for nearly thirty-five years before immigrating to Israel. He is best known for his book, Nine and a Half Mystics, *an introduction to Kabbalah originally published in 1969. He was interviewed in his home in Jerusalem in May of 2007.*

I was not raised in a religious home, nor was I given a Jewish education. The extent of my childhood exposure to Judaism was a single trip to a synagogue, arranged by a well-meaning uncle, on the occasion of my Bar Mitzvah. In college, I was active in Hillel, the Jewish organization on campus, and I spent a week at Avuka, a Zionist camp in the Catskills. This was the era of Hitler—World War II was about to begin—and I was keenly aware of my Jewish identity.

Eventually, I ended up at the Jewish Institute of Religion (since merged with Hebrew Union College), which was a very unusual place, as it had students from all streams of Judaism—Reform, Conservative and Orthodox, and even total nonbelievers. This is where I was ordained as a Reform rabbi in 1948.

During my rabbinic studies, I became interested in Jewish mysticism and came to learn with a Kabbalist by the name of S. Z. Setzer, in a basement on East Broadway. I ended up writing an article about him for *Commentary* magazine, the leading postwar journal of Jewish affairs. This article, which appeared in the November 1952 issue, garnered a lot of attention and led to other assignments for me.

In 1954, *Commentary* asked me to write an article about Chabad-Lubavitch. The editor who gave me the assignment seemed to think that this Chasidic sect was making waves all over the world and was worth looking into; he told me to go down to the Chabad headquarters at 770 Eastern Parkway and see what was happening over there.

At that point, the Rebbe had been leading Chabad for about three

The Rebbe speaks at
a children's parade in
front of 770.
Lag B'omer, 5717-1957.

The Living Archive

years and was already becoming famous, but frankly, I myself had not heard much about him or the Chabad movement. Nonetheless, I made an appointment to see him and was told I would have to wait for a month. The Rebbe's calendar was fully booked because so many people were seeking his counsel.

Meanwhile, there was going to be a *farbrengen*, a festive gathering of *chasidim*, which the Rebbe would lead, so I decided to attend that. As I recall, the Rebbe began with a complex Torah issue and then continued to delve deeper, from outer levels to inner levels to the innermost levels, and into the hidden teachings — the mystery of it all. Of this I understood absolutely nothing. But after an interval of singing and toasting *l'chaim*, the Rebbe spoke again. This time — although it was in essence a reiteration of his first talk — the Rebbe brought the lofty ideas down to earth. He spoke in simple Yiddish, expressing his ideas clearly.

I left the *farbrengen* feeling that it had been an interesting — yet frustrating — evening. There was no question about the sincerity of the faith demonstrated by the Lubavitch *chasidim*, but it was a faith completely beyond my understanding and, I suspected, beyond the comprehension of most modern people.

Still, I did not give up and returned for my private audience with the Rebbe. During that audience and the one that followed a year later, he spoke to me in Yiddish and I spoke to him in English. In this way we understood each other perfectly, yet were each able to express ourselves best in our native languages.

Rabbi Weiner
Courtesy of the Weiner family

I had prepared a series of questions to ask him, but it was he who started off by interviewing me. He asked me what kind of work I did and what I had studied. My reporter's notebook remained closed, while I found myself chatting freely about matters I had not expected to discuss. I think an hour passed before I got to my prepared questions.

Today, I do not recall everything that I asked him in that interview or the subsequent one, each of which lasted more than two hours. But some exchanges stand out clearly in my memory — and indeed, are recorded in the *Commentary* articles I subsequently wrote.

ONE EXCHANGE HAD TO DO WITH the nature of evil and Chabad's special interpretation of the oneness of G-d. The Rebbe explained that inasmuch as Judaism believes that there is nothing other than G-d, evil has no real existence. But for man to have true freedom of choice, it must *appear* to have a real existence. He used a metaphor to explain the idea: For a man to cut another with a knife seems to us an evil thing. Yet, there are occasions — surgery, for example — when a good purpose is being served by such action. So, too, what appears evil in our sight is really good in the light of a higher wisdom. To believe otherwise, to believe that evil has an independent existence, is to be driven in the end to the conviction that there are two divine powers rather than one. The oneness of G-d implies that, ultimately, everything can be explained and justified. "To divide things into separate compartments," the Rebbe concluded, "and to say that this belongs to G-d and this doesn't, is idolatry."

In a later exchange, I expressed my frustration at not being able to understand Chabad. I had spent more than a year interviewing members of the movement, but I could not quite grasp the reasons for the loyalty of Chabad *chasidim*, the continued vitality of the organization, and its resistance to the degeneration common to religious dynasties. The obvious explanations did not really satisfy me. After all, other religious groups were driven by the same feeling of historic mission and the same sense of community, yet they did not thrive or even survive. So what made Chabad different? What made Chabad so successful?

In an effort to solve the enigma of Chabad, I resolved to ask even the most provocative questions of the Rebbe. I dove in: "Does Chabad's success stem from its utter dependence on the Rebbe? And if so, is that not a sign of weakness?"

The Rebbe answered without hesitation, as if he had dealt with the question before. "A weak person is usually overcome by the environment in which he finds himself. But our *chasidim* can be sent into any environment, no matter how strange or hostile, and they maintain themselves within it. So how can we say that it is weakness which characterizes a *chasid*?"

I pressed from another angle, telling him that I sensed a desire in Chabad to oversimplify—to strip ideas of their complexity, merely for the sake of a superficial clarity. As a matter of fact, his *chasidim* seem to have one thing in common: a sort of naive look in their eyes that a sympathetic observer might call spiritual purity (*tmimut*), but that might less kindly be interpreted as simplemindedness, the absence of inner struggle.

Although the words I spoke were harsh, the Rebbe showed no

resentment. "What you see in their eyes is the absence of a *kera!*" he answered.

"A what?" I asked, not understanding.

"Yes, a *kera*—a split," he repeated, hesitating for a moment before continuing: "I hope you will not take offense, but something tells me you don't sleep well at night, and this is not good for your longevity. Perhaps if you had been raised wholly in one world or in another, it might be different. But this split within you comes from trying to live in two worlds."

The Rebbe's answer gave me an opening, and I pivoted to the personal: "But you, too, have lived in two worlds. Your *chasidim* are rather proud of the fact that you once attended the Sorbonne. Why then do you discourage them from studying in the 'other world'?"

"Precisely because I have done it, I know the value of that study,"

The Rebbe shares a moment with Rabbi Weiner while distributing *lekach* at the door of his *sukkah*. Hoshana Rabbah, 5748-1987.

Levi Freidin, The Living Archive

the Rebbe replied. "I do recognize its usefulness.... We need engineers and chemists, but engineering and chemistry are not the most important things. Besides, to attend college does not mean only to learn facts. It means exposure to certain circles and activities which conflict with a believer's values and faith. It's like taking a person from a warm environment and throwing him into a cold-water shock treatment several times a day. How long can he stand it? In addition, college studies take place usually before the age of thirty, when one's character is not yet crystallized. Too much exposure at that stage is dangerous."

THIS LED ME TO ANOTHER QUESTION: How did the Rebbe know better? How could he assume responsibility for giving advice not only on religious matters, but on medical problems or business affairs, especially when he knew that in the eyes of those he was advising, his advice was binding?

The Rebbe did not seem offended by this question either. "To begin with," he replied, "it is always easier to run away from responsibility. But what if your running might destroy the community? And what if they put the key into your pocket and walk away? What can you do then?"

The Rebbe seemed to be hinting, I thought, at the fact that he had to be persuaded to take on the role of Rebbe and that he had reluctantly accepted the leadership of Chabad. Yet, he had taken it on, and he was guiding the movement with a strong hand.

I asked how he reconciled his practice of giving advice in material matters with the fact that the Alter Rebbe, the 18th-century founder of Chabad, had expressly told his *chasidim* that they must not ask him for help in nonspiritual matters. I had the *Tanya,* the Alter Rebbe's *magnum opus,* with me and I began flipping through it to find the proof, but the Rebbe interrupted my search.

"You are referring to his letter number twenty-two," he said, smiling. "Despite that letter, the Alter Rebbe did give advice in material matters."

Sensing after a moment that his explanation did not satisfy me, the Rebbe added: "When a person comes with a problem, there are only

A *Time* magazine article published in March, 1957, based on the reporting of Rabbi Weiner.

RELIGION

The Lubavitchers

A rundown, three-story building at 770 Eastern Parkway, Brooklyn is the hub and powerhouse of one of the most intense religious brotherhoods in the modern world: the Lubavitcher movement. In Communist Russia and North Africa, Australia and all over the U.S., an estimated 10,000 followers of this Hasidic sect look to Brooklyn for light and guidance, for it is the home of their Rebbe,* Menachem Mendel Schneerson. He is the seventh leader of the Lubavitchers, a man whose wisdom is believed by his followers to be something more than human.

Few outsiders have made the effort to try to understand this paradoxical sect of highly organized, missionary-minded mystics, strongest remnant of the great age of Hasidism, that inspired Eastern European Jewry during the 18th and 19th centuries. In the March and April issues of *Commentary*, Reform Rabbi Herbert Weiner of Temple Israel in South Orange, N.J. presents the results of a year-long study of the Brooklyn Lubavitchers.

Joyous Mysticism. The Lubavitcher movement, deriving its name from a small town in northern Russia, was founded by Shneur Zalman (1747-1812), a brilliant young Talmudist in White Russia who became a disciple of Hasidism. This was a movement of holy men (*zaddiks*) and their followers who reacted against the arid, hairsplitting Talmud-boring of 17th century Judaism with a kind of joyous mysticism; they have often been compared to the followers of St. Francis of Assisi. Shneur Zalman burned with Hasidism's *hitlahavut* (spiritual enthusiasm), but he recognized the need for organization and teaching as well, and he steered a middle course between mystical rapture and the traditional emphasis on study. He gave his followers and their descendants a highly organized religious school system, a missionary tradition and a lively concern for health and material welfare that kept the movement alive (often underground) through persecution, war and revolution.

In 1940 the sixth Rebbe, Joseph Isaac, arrived in New York City, an ill and exhausted refugee from Communist imprisonment and the German bombardment of Warsaw. But in the decade before he died, he planted the Lubavitcher movement deep in the U.S. He organized "Torah Missions," and set up Lubavitcher Bible classes, founded a publishing house to turn out textbooks in English and Hebrew, dispatched missionaries all over the world. After his death in 1949, he was succeeded by his son-in-law, Menachem Mendel, who, like all Rebbes, added Schneerson to his name in honor of Founder Shneur Zalman.

Long Discourse. Author Weiner describes his visit to a *farbrengung*, an annual festivity in celebration of Joseph Isaac's release from Communist prison. The courtyard adjoining the Brooklyn headquarters was jammed with Lubavitcher men at benches and tables, many of them in long black coats or full jackets and large-brimmed black hats. Some wore the *gartel*, a black silk cord bound around the waist to symbolize the distinction between the "higher" and "lower" parts of man. As soon as blue-eyed, black-bearded Menachem Mendel arrived, he was handed a bottle of whisky, which he passed to outstretched hands below him, and almost

RABBI MENACHEM MENDEL SCHNEERSON
A little Moses in Brooklyn.

immediately bottles of whisky and paper cups appeared on all the tables.

Then there was singing, followed by toasts ("*L'chayim!*"—to life), followed by more singing, and the first of many talks by the Rebbe, during which everyone remained standing. The Rebbe spoke on the four levels on which, according to the Hasidim, the Bible is written: *p'shat* or literal meaning, *d'rush* or simple allegory relating to moral teachings, *remez* or "the hint" of the mystical relation between man and God, and *sod*, the secret, dealing with esoteric cosmological matters accessible only to students of the cabala.*

Every Lubavitcher who possibly can comes to consult the Rebbe on any aspect of his life—financial, moral or medical. It is in the medical field that Rabbi Mendel has performed many feats that Luba-

vitchers do not hesitate to call miraculous. The Rebbe himself—he studied science at the Sorbonne—merely says: "Sometimes all that is necessary to know what a man's troubles are is to spend a half hour observing how he looks. and how he moves his hands, and then to try identifying with him."

The Danger of Compromise. Russian-born Rabbi Mendel, like all Lubavitcher Rebbes, looks upon himself as spiritual "shepherd" of all Jews everywhere— Hasidic or not. He lives modestly with his wife in their $75-a-month flat, devotes his whole time to the Torah, to his flock and to directing missionary work among Jews who have fallen away from the Orthodox faith. As he sees it, the most important injunction for Jews is not to compromise in matters of faith and observance. "Compromise is dangerous because it sickens both the body and the soul . . . One must do everything, but at the same time we welcome the doing of even a part. If all we can do is to save one limb, we save that. Then we worry about saving another. A man may say, 'I would like to be whole, but I can't. My evil impulse prevents me, or I have to make a living, or I don't have the time' . . . The great fault of Conservative and Reform Judaism is not that they compromise but that they sanctify the compromise [and] still the conscience."

His followers are sure that he is right, and every year some 100 young Lubavitcher missionaries travel all over the U.S. to spread his word to other Jews. Often they find little or no understanding. But, says one of his disciples of the Rebbe: "He is to us what Moses was to Israel in his time. Not that the Rebbe is to be compared to Moses, 'like whom there has been none other since.' But the Rebbe is like a little Moses."

---

* A Hasidic term for leader, stemming from the Hebrew rabbi, meaning teacher.

* An esoteric system of speculation on metaphysics which went in for much symbolical manipulation of words and names. The cabala originated in Palestine but came under strong Babylonian influence between 500 and 900 A.D. Its best-known work, the *Zohar*, compiled in the 13th century, had a profound influence on Hasidism.

Rabbi Weiner in
Kibbutz Hulda in
Israel. 1946.

*Courtesy of
the Weiner family*

two alternatives—either send them away, or try to help them. Each person knows their own problem best, so one must try to unite oneself with them and help them dissociate from their own ego. Then, one can try to understand the role of Divine Providence in this particular case."

He delved into this issue further when I asked him to explain the power of his blessing.

"It is possible for a Rebbe to awaken powers slumbering within a person," he said. "It is also possible to bring a person into contact with a higher level of powers outside their own soul. A person lives on one floor of a building and needs help from the floor above; if they can't walk up themself, someone else must help them."

"Does that mean that the Rebbe can help one go up to a higher spiritual plane?"

"That's the hardest way," answered the Rebbe. "The easier way is to bring these powers down upon them."

A DISCUSSION OF FAITH FOLLOWED, with me suggesting that many people would like to believe but find it hard. The Rebbe disagreed. "It's not so hard for people to believe. Even atheists, when pressed into a corner, come up with belief."

When I protested that in most cases doubt seems to overwhelm faith, the Rebbe nodded in agreement. "There can be doubts. To question G-d, however, is the first indication that one believes in something. You have to know something about G-d to even question Him. But we must try to overcome doubts by constantly feeding the spirit. Just as a body that has been kept healthy can overcome a medical crisis, so a soul can defeat its crises and its doubts if it is constantly kept healthy."

"But why are there so many without faith?" I continued to press.

The Rebbe looked directly at me. "They are afraid of the consequences of faith.... They are afraid that they might have to abandon some of their comforts or give up cherished ideas. They are afraid of changing their lives."

"The great fault of Conservative and Reform Judaism," the Rebbe continued, "is not that they compromise, but that they *sanctify* the compromise, still the conscience, and thereby leave no possibility for return."

The Rebbe was clearly against compromise in matters of faith. He brought up the story of the Prophet Elijah who, in his day, confronted Jews worshipping both G-d and the idol Baal. Elijah demanded that they take a stand: "How long will you keep wavering between two opinions? If the L-rd is G-d, follow Him. If Baal is, follow him!"

"Compromise is dangerous," the Rebbe said, "because the one who compromises tries to mediate between religion and the demands of his secular environment, and is therefore unable to distinguish the truth."

Chabad differs ent on, in that the movement encourages

every Jew not to compromise—to observe as many of the commandments as he or she can, even if only a few. "It's important to know
that one must do everything, but at the same time we welcome the
doing of even a part. If all we can accomplish is to save one limb, we
save that. Then we worry about saving another." This is the only way,
he concluded, because, otherwise, a Jew who wanted to return would
not know what there is to return to.

In response to my question about the unethical behavior of some
so-called religious people, the Rebbe insisted that even those who
are religious and not ethical—while some secular people are highly
ethical—would be much worse off if they were not religious at all,
as they would have no incentive to improve.

When it came time for me to leave, the Rebbe stopped me. "Wait—I would like to ask you a question: How is it that you are not Orthodox?" Surprised, I mumbled something about not being able to believe that the whole of the Torah was given by G-d, and I left it at that.

The Rebbe never forgot our exchange. And subsequently, he returned to this one part—that I needed to be a Torah-observant Jew—over and over again.

That message was repeated when my mother died in 1969, and the Rebbe sent me an unusual condolence letter. "I was saddened to hear of the passing of your mother," he wrote. "May you not know any sorrow in the future...."

It was a brief but warm expression of sympathy, followed by a one-page postscript, in which he tried to appeal to my heart to be an example within the Reform movement of a Jew who fully observes the Torah. He closed with a half-page explanation of why he wrote his appeal this way:

> This entire piece has been written as a PS and on a separate sheet, not because it is of lesser importance [to what is] preceding it. On the contrary! However, our Sages wisely reminded us that allowances should be made for a person in distress. The thought might just occur that here comes a man who ... wishes to take advantage of a profound and unhappy experience in order to advance his ideals. But in truth ... these ideals are not only mine but also yours.

INDEED, THEY WERE. And I did what he asked of me. In fact, sometimes I felt like I was the Rebbe's emissary to the Reform movement. Whenever there was a meeting or convention, I would stand up and say: "I've been asked by the Rebbe to raise the issue of greater observance..."

Truth be told, the Reform movement did become more and more observant; it also became more respectful of *chasidim* and more respectful of the Rebbe. I am not saying that this happened because of my prodding, but I do believe that the Rebbe foresaw this turn of events.

The last time I spoke with him was in March of 1991. I stood in line with hundreds of others as the Rebbe gave out dollars for charity. When my turn came, I mentioned my book *Nine and a Half Mystics*, which featured chapters describing nine mystics, the Rebbe among them, and an essay by me—the "half," the incomplete believer.

I explained that a revised edition of the book would be published soon and that I wrote even more about the Rebbe in the last chapter. He responded that there was "much good" in my book, but then returned to his theme:

"I believe that now you can openly confess that you are an Orthodox Jew. You must make it public that you are an Orthodox Jew, and certainly were an Orthodox Jew during the times and years when you were making speeches in your temple."

He asked me not to be offended by his remarks—and, of course, I was not; in fact, I told him I would take his words to heart.

Indeed, when I retired from Temple Israel, where I had served as rabbi for nearly thirty-five years, there was a goodbye dinner, and I used that occasion to make the announcement he asked of me. "I have

Rabbi Weiner addressing his congregation.

Courtesy of the Weiner family

something I must tell you," I said. "After I wrote *Nine and a Half Mystics*, the Lubavitcher Rebbe told me that I should make it *Ten Mystics*. I shouldn't remain a *half*. And I do want to become *ten*. I have always been an Orthodox Jew, even if I have not been observing the Torah to the letter. But now I really want to be an Orthodox Jew in every sense of the word."

Upon hearing my announcement, the president of the congregation, Herb Iris, picked up a glass of wine and declared, "*L'chaim* to your Rebbe! And about being Orthodox—we always knew you were an Orthodox Jew!" ■

RABBI SHMARYA KATZEN

To Reach the Littlest Sparks

Reflections of a beloved kindergarten teacher

For forty-seven years, Rabbi Shmarya Katzen taught young children at the United Lubavitcher Yeshiva in Brooklyn. He was interviewed in the My Encounter Studio in July of 2018.

My story begins at the University of Maryland, where I was studying engineering and where I was first introduced to Chabad. Although my parents weren't religious, I had grown up in a traditional Jewish atmosphere, and I had gravitated to other Jews at the university, occasionally participating in Hillel House programs. It was there, in 1964, that two graduate students named Larry Levine and Joel Sinsky suggested that I explore Chabad.

I had no idea what Chabad was, what Lubavitch was, but I felt very empty inside—something within me was yearning to be satisfied—and I followed their suggestion to go to New York for Shavuot, when we celebrate receiving the Torah at Mount Sinai. Arriving at the Chabad Headquarters at 770 Eastern Parkway, I sensed the excitement in the air, as though it was only ten minutes ago that G-d gave the Torah to the Children of Israel.

I was warmly welcomed in the home of Rabbi Yossel Goldstein, where I spent the holiday. I found it to be an amazing experience. I remember sitting at the holiday table while Rabbi Goldstein spoke words of Torah and feeling that something very mystical was going on. He said that every soul comes down into this world with a mission to fulfill, and wherever you find yourself is not an accident, but an act of Divine Providence—you are supposed to be right there.

After this experience, I returned for a summer program at Chabad to learn more about Judaism, and then went back to the university for the fall term. But something strange was happening to me—I found that I couldn't study—try as I might to open the books, I couldn't do it. I was drawn to return to New York.

I ended up writing to the Rebbe, telling him that I wanted to leave the university, that I had lost interest and it wasn't for me any longer, but I wasn't sure what to do next.

I didn't get an answer right away, so I just packed up and arrived at 770, where I found a letter from the Rebbe waiting for me. He wrote:

The *Baltimore Sun* reports on Rabbi Katzen in a chess tournament at age 16. December 30, 1959.

> The attainment of good is unfortunately not always very easy. And usually, the more the thing is desirable, the more difficult it is to obtain. Therefore, when one finds extraordinary difficulties or obstacles, this in itself is often a sign that the thing desired is very worthwhile. As for a practical solution to your problems, you should discuss them with your local friends who are *yirei shamayim* [G-d-fearing] to whom you could explain all the pertinent details, or who may already know them from experience.

Now, I had already made my decision to leave the university, but I did consult with a friend, nonetheless, who recommended that I tell the Rebbe more about my background and my dissatisfaction with secular learning, and that I ask for a blessing for my *yeshivah* studies.

I wrote again, and this time the Rebbe responded right away. Among other things, the Rebbe explained to me why I was never satisfied up to this point: "It's impossible for a Jew to feel satisfied unless he first satisfies his soul."

I knew that my instincts had been right—I had to sit and learn Torah in order to give my soul what it needed.

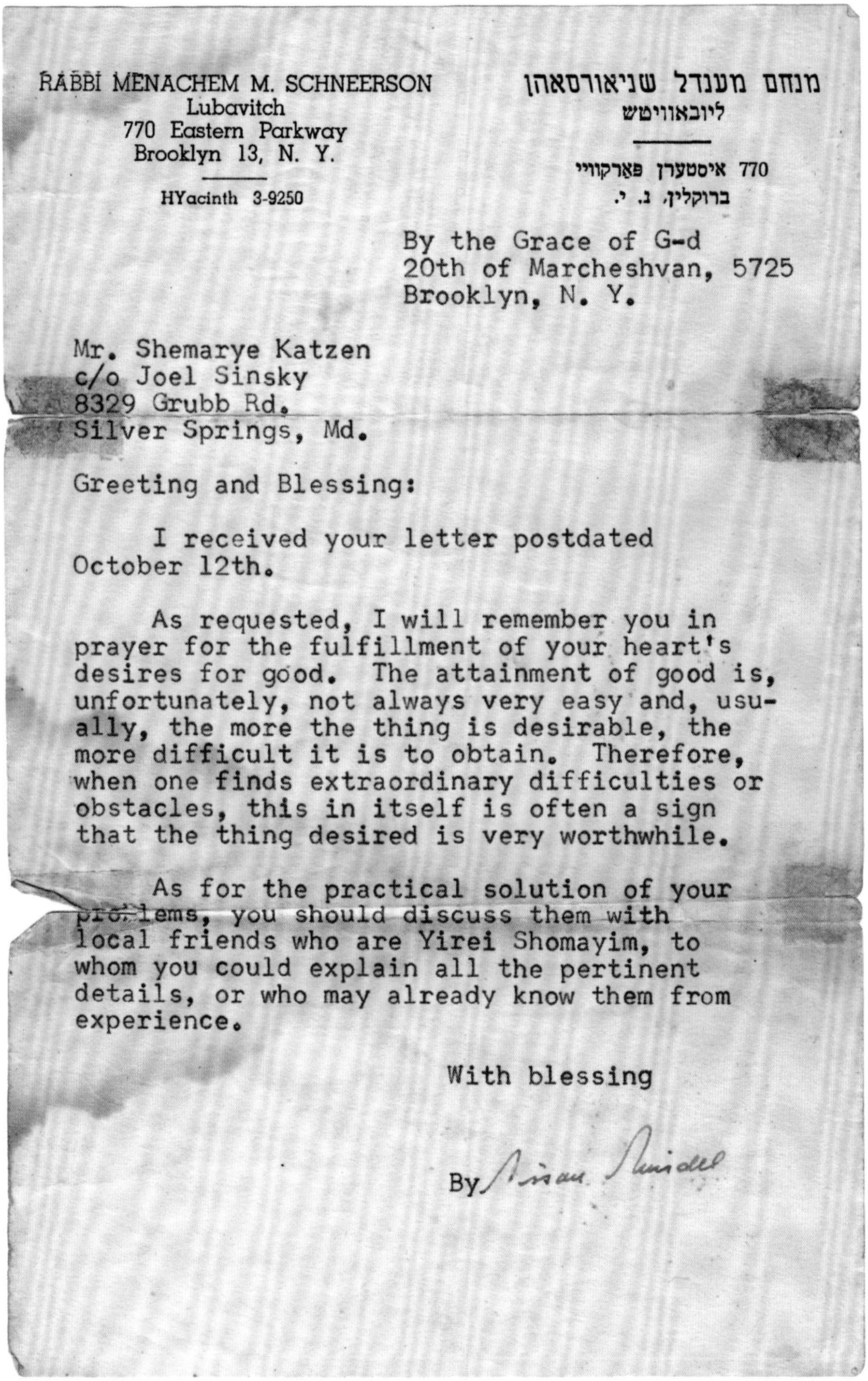

RABBI MENACHEM M. SCHNEERSON   מנחם מענדל שניאורסאהן
Lubavitch   ליובאוויטש
770 Eastern Parkway
Brooklyn 13, N. Y.

HYacinth 3-9250   770 איסטערן פּאַרקוויי
                                         ברוקלין, נ. י.

By the Grace of G-d
20th of Marcheshvan, 5725
Brooklyn, N. Y.

Mr. Shemarye Katzen
c/o Joel Sinsky
8329 Grubb Rd.
Silver Springs, Md.

Greeting and Blessing:

I received your letter postdated
October 12th.

As requested, I will remember you in
prayer for the fulfillment of your heart's
desires for good. The attainment of good is,
unfortunately, not always very easy and, usually, the more the thing is desirable, the
more difficult it is to obtain. Therefore,
when one finds extraordinary difficulties or
obstacles, this in itself is often a sign
that the thing desired is very worthwhile.

As for the practical solution of your
problems, you should discuss them with
local friends who are Yirei Shomayim, to
whom you could explain all the pertinent
details, or who may already know them from
experience.

With blessing

By

The Rebbe's letter to Rabbi Katzen. 1964.
Courtesy of the Katzen family

As I proceeded with my *yeshivah* studies, I wrote to the Rebbe many times, and it was amazing to me how the Rebbe tolerated so many letters from me, and how he always answered.

In one of my letters I complained that I was always very tired and that I didn't sleep well at night. This made it hard for me during the day when I attempted to study for hours on end, trying to absorb knowledge.

The Rebbe responded that I should see a doctor, and that I begin reciting *Chitas*—the daily selections from the *Chumash* (the Five Books of Moses), *Tehillim* (Psalms) and *Tanya* (the seminal work by the Alter Rebbe, founder of the Chabad movement). And finally, he urged me to be more careful when reciting the bedtime *Shema*. He was referring to the prayer when we acknowledge the oneness of G-d before going to sleep. I recall that he specifically underlined the phrase "be more careful."

And ever since—for the last fifty-four years—I have been. It helped me enormously to sleep soundly back then, and it continues to help me to this day.

AFTER ALMOST A YEAR IN *YESHIVAH*, my twenty-third birthday came around, and I got an appointment to come into the Rebbe's office for a birthday blessing, as was the custom. I took this opportunity to confide in him my worries about how I might earn a livelihood in the future. I had been considering taking night courses at a local college while studying in *yeshivah* during the day, because I felt I needed to begin acquiring some sort of professional credentials.

But the Rebbe didn't want me to take my energy away from Torah studies after only one year in *yeshivah*. And to allay my worries about the future, he added with a smile, "Right now, G-d is managing to take care of three billion people who have no college education. So probably He can take care of you also."

The audience ended with the Rebbe giving me a blessing to continue learning. And as I was walking out, the Rebbe looked at me sternly and said, "Don't worry. Everything will be alright." I took this message to heart.

I met with the Rebbe several times after that, and I also wrote him many more letters. I once asked for his help with my stuttering. The

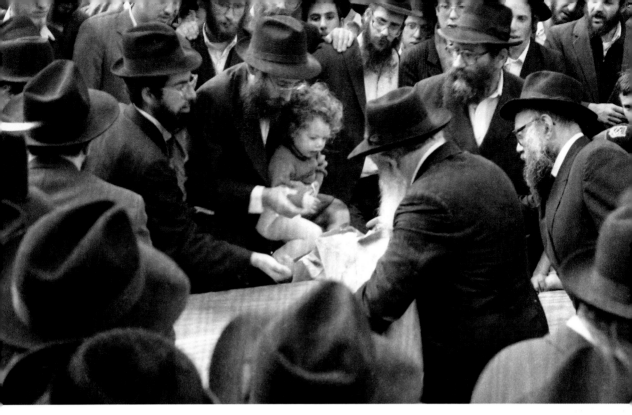

Rebbe responded — as he did earlier when I asked him about feeling tired and sleeping badly — to see a doctor. But he also wrote that it would be good "for you to strengthen your trust in G-d, who looks after every single individual constantly." And — wouldn't you know — as my trust in G-d improved, my stuttering improved.

At a different time, I asked the Rebbe what to do when traveling on New York subways, which often presented a challenge to a *yeshivah* student trying to avoid immodest sights. His advice was to memorize verses from the Mishnah or the *Tanya* and to recite them to myself when traveling. "This," he said, "will light up the darkness."

He often stressed bringing light into dark places, and he said this could be done by thinking or speaking words of Torah.

AFTER I HAD BEEN LEARNING IN *YESHIVAH* FOR A WHILE, I felt the need to go out into the work world, but I was not sure what I should do. As was my way by now, I turned to the Rebbe, who recommended I take an aptitude test, which would identify my natural inclinations.

I did so, and the test showed that I would most like to "help people." But I was not sure what that meant in terms of a profession: Should I become a social worker?

Rabbi Katzen and his children receive coins for charity from the Rebbe outside of 770. 13 Tishrei, 5745-1984.

Levi Freidin,
The Living Archive

Rabbi Katzen poses
with his students
in the late 1970s.

*Courtesy of the
Katzen family*

When I informed the Rebbe of the results, he said, "If you'd like to help others, you should consider becoming a teacher." He didn't say what kind of teacher I should be—neither what subjects I should teach, nor whether adults or children. He just said, "You can benefit others by teaching them love of G-d, faith, self-confidence..."—here he paused, adding, "and love for their fellow Jew." As I recall it, those were the items he listed.

So that is how I became a teacher, which was exactly right for me.

I remember the Rebbe once saying at a *farbrengen* that when you teach children, it is not only important how many pages of material you cover, but that you reach the *pintele Yid*, the G-dly spark inside each Jewish child. This was especially important in teaching Pre-1A, which is the equivalent of kindergarten in the Lubavitch day school system, where I have taught for over four decades. I have always tried to reach the *pintele Yid* and to instill in each child an awe of G-d. With the Rebbe's blessing, I believe I have succeeded. ∎

RABBI AVRAHAM CHAPUTA

See, Care, Act

*A casual conversation in New York leads
to astonishing results in Israel*

Rabbi Avraham Chaputa, an author of more than fifty books, serves as the head of the Kollel Midrash HaRambam in Petach Tikvah, Israel. Previously, he served as the head of Yeshivat HaRambam U'Beit Yosef in Tel Aviv for close to three decades. He was interviewed in his home in Petach Tikvah in March of 2013.

Yeshivat HaRambam U'Beit Yosef, a Sephardi *yeshivah*, was founded in Tel Aviv in 1955, and at that time I was appointed its head though I was only twenty. Of course, it was a small *yeshivah* back then, but it grew and grew. And, after a time, I was looking for a place where we could grow even more.

In 1972, I traveled to the United States to raise money for a building site and construction. At that time, a few donors to the *yeshivah*— businessmen who were Israelis and who happened to be in the United States just then—met me and said they had an appointment to see the Lubavitcher Rebbe. They asked me to join them and I agreed, although I knew very little about the Rebbe.

As I recall, the meeting was late at night. We went into the Rebbe's office, and my companions asked whatever they wanted to ask—as I recall they were seeking advice on business matters; the Rebbe blessed them, and we got ready to leave. Up to that point, I hadn't uttered a word, but suddenly, the Rebbe said, "The rabbi who is with you should stay." And then he rose from his chair and addressed me directly, "Are you Rabbi Avraham Chaputa?"

I was surprised that he knew my name.

I replied in the affirmative, and he asked me to sit down and began talking with me. This conversation lasted a long time, at least forty-five minutes. He spoke easily in pure Hebrew, smiling all the while. I would say it was a wonderful conversation, a very comfortable conversation as far as I was concerned.

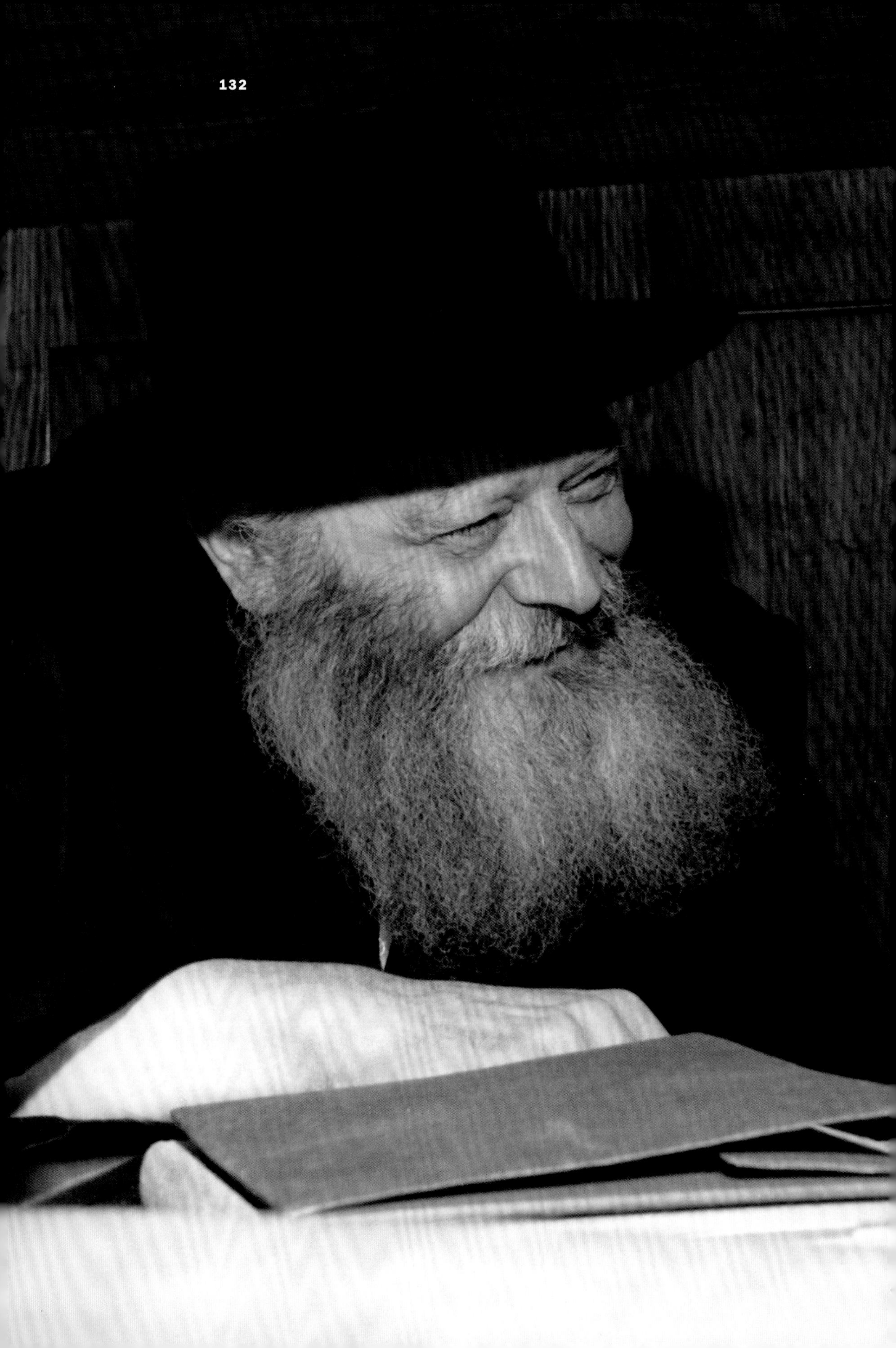

Every time one of the Rebbe's secretaries opened the door, they saw that the Rebbe was still talking with me, so they left us alone. They opened the door every few minutes, because there were a lot of people waiting outside; but, this didn't affect the Rebbe at all. He continued speaking with me, asking me all sorts of questions about the *yeshivah*, the students, the lessons, etc. I also mentioned that we were petitioning the city to obtain a new building site because the *yeshivah* had grown.

Before the meeting ended, he asked me to please include some Chabad teachings when I spoke to my students. I responded by saying that my talks were usually varied—in addition to Sephardic sources and teachings of Maimonides, they also included teachings from the various Ashkenazi schools of thought, including Mussar (the Jewish ethical movement), the Lithuanian *yeshivah* world, and the Chasidism of the Baal Shem Tov. However, I understood that he specifically wanted some Chabad teachings in my talks. As I had previously studied the *Tanya*, the seminal work by the founder of the Chabad movement, I agreed to do so.

As I was leaving, I mentioned that I had published many books, and he asked to read them, saying to his secretary, "Whatever book Rabbi Chaputa sends please bring to me right away. And any Chabad book that he wants, please give him before he leaves."

I RETURNED TO TEL AVIV AND —as amazing as it seemed at the time— within a short time the secular city officials gave us a plot to build a new *yeshivah*.

Around that time, I had been appointed to the Tel Aviv Religious Council, and I thought that the donation of this plot of land had something to do with my recognition by Rabbi Isser Yehudah Unterman, who had been the Chief Rabbi of Tel Aviv and who became the Chief Rabbi of Israel.

But I was wrong.

I only discovered what actually took place thirty-four years later, in 2006, when celebrations were held in honor of finishing the annual cycle of studying Maimonides's fourteen-volume *magnum opus* on Jewish law, *Mishneh Torah*. These cycles began in 1984, when the Rebbe instituted the practice of studying *Mishneh Torah* every day. As the leader of a *yeshivah* whose core curriculum focused on Maimonides, I was invited by Chabad to participate in beginning the new cycle of study. Of course, I agreed. But the night I went to speak there, I got a shock.

Someone showed me a copy of a letter that the Rebbe had written in October of 1972 to Yehoshua Rabinovitz, then mayor of Tel Aviv, which read in part:

> It is possible that my letter will surprise you, since we have never had the opportunity to meet or come in contact, etc., but as it is about a matter of public concern, I hope you will be receptive to my request, especially since the satisfactory resolution of this matter depends wholly on you....
>
> This matter concerns the Yeshivat HaRambam located in Hadar Yosef, Tel Aviv. As I have been informed, across from the *yeshivah* sits a plot of land which has been the subject of efforts by the *yeshivah* to acquire, but the formal permission for "a change of designation" has been dragging....
>
> Although I don't know the details and difficulties of the matter, I do know that this touches upon the foundational matter of public Torah study—particularly an institution of

Rabbi Chaputa at his son's Bar Mitzvah, seated between Israel's Chief Ashkenazi Rabbi Shlomo Goren (L.) and Chief Sephardi Rabbi Ovadia Yosef (R.). 1971.

Courtesy of Rabbi Chaputa

The Yeshivat
HaRambam building

*Courtesy of
Rabbi Chaputa*

the Sephardic community, whose youth have unique challenges: primarily problems with absorption after having been uprooted from the countries where their families have lived for hundreds of years and, now, after coming to the Holy Land, they must adapt to living conditions entirely different from what they are used to, etc. — certainly this issue is worthy of extra attention and your assistance beyond the letter of the law, and even more than that....

I am writing to support their request and to add my request as well, doubled and multiplied, to assist the aforementioned *yeshivah's* development in general — and in particular, that the desired plot be given to them, which, according to their request, is located close by....

I was astounded — the Rebbe was requesting that the mayor give us a plot for our *yeshivah*! In that meeting, he had heard me say that I needed a plot of land so that we could expand and admit more students. But I had not asked him to help me, nor did I expect him to. Yet he took it upon himself to do what he could to secure this plot for us.

Students of the
yeshivah, in front of
their new building.
Mid-1970s.

*Courtesy of
Rabbi Chaputa*

His eyes were open and watching over so many places—he was not just a Rebbe to his *chasidim*; he cared about the entire Jewish world.

It was really a wondrous thing. I have no doubt at all that the Rebbe's request played a pivotal role in our receiving the land.

We built a very large building, which accommodates hundreds of students.

And a good part of that I credit to the Rebbe's intervention. He saw the whole world before him. And he cared. And he acted. ∎

THINK BIGGER

RABBI DAVID LAPIN

A Nuclear Reaction

*A surprisingly scientific solution to
the limits of human endurance*

CEO of Lapin Consulting International in Los Angeles, Rabbi David Lapin is a specialist in strategy and leadership, a consultant to corporate CEOs and author of Lead by Greatness. *He is also the founder of the Keter Torah Community in Johannesburg, South Africa. He was interviewed in the My Encounter Studio in New York in June of 2015.*

From an early age, it was clear to me that I would become a rabbi. How could I not when so many of my ancestors were rabbis? Most notably, my great-uncle, Rabbi Eliyahu Lopian, was one of the leaders of the Jewish ethical movement known as the Mussar movement, in Poland, England and Israel; and my father was Rabbi Avraham Hyam Lapin, one of the prominent leaders of the South African Jewish community. The Gateshead *yeshivah* in England, where I was educated, was led at the time by other relatives of mine: Rabbi Leib Lopian, Rabbi Leib Gurwicz and his son, Rabbi Avrohom Gurwicz.

But, after receiving my rabbinic ordination, following studies at the Kfar Chasidim and Mir *yeshivahs* in Israel, I started to have my doubts whether this was the right path for me.

When I returned home to South Africa to get married and join the rabbinate there, I became concerned that I would not be able to retain my intellectual independence — something I have always been fiercely protective of. Serving as a community rabbi meant serving at the behest of the synagogue's board of directors, and I did not like what that implied. Therefore, I decided that I first needed to secure an independent source of income.

With that goal in mind, I went to work in 1975 for a commodities trading company and later founded the leadership consulting firm that I currently head, which is now known as Lapin Consulting International. In my consulting work I combined Torah wisdom with modern business strategies.

I also established a Torah academy, known as Beis Hamedrash
Keter Torah, where I gave classes
in Judaism. In the 1970s and 1980s,
this academy (along with Chabad
and Kollel Yad Shaul) became an
integral part of the South African
baal teshuvah movement — the
movement of unaffiliated young
Jews returning to their ancestral
roots and Torah observance.

Rabbi David Lapin. Circa 1981.
Courtesy of Rabbi Lapin

Although my colleagues
laughed at my idea of holding
Torah classes on Saturday nights
when most young people went to
the movies, I did it anyway, ensuring that these classes offered more
than movies ever could. It worked — these classes were attended weekly
by hundreds. On other days of the week, I tried another innovation,
conducting advanced Talmudic classes for bright young people who
could barely read Hebrew.

BUT I WAS NOT SURE I WAS ON THE RIGHT TRACK. Was this the best way
to bring people back to Judaism — especially since others were not using the same methods? Furthermore, was I right to divide my time between my business and my teaching? It seemed as if I had two full-time
jobs and my family was paying the price. I felt I needed the opinion of
someone much wiser than I; someone who had a global perspective
that embraced history, modernity and the future. This is why I decided
to seek the advice of the Rebbe, about whom I had heard so much from
my Chabad colleagues and acquaintances.

The occasion presented itself in 1976 when my wife and I visited
New York. However, I had not realized the extent to which the Rebbe
was in demand and that to see him one had to make an appointment
many months in advance. When I asked to see the Rebbe, I was politely
but promptly told that I would need to wait for several months; it was
not until I explained that my questions impacted the larger Jewish

community that I was invited to wait until the Rebbe finished his appointments for the night. "There's a slight chance we'll be able to squeeze you in," I was told. Deciding to take that chance, my wife and I sat down for the long wait.

The atmosphere in the Rebbe's waiting room was something that I will never forget. There was nothing grand about the space, yet I felt a sense of awe which I have never felt sitting in anyone else's waiting room—not the waiting rooms of other Torah giants, or those of industry heads or political leaders. As I waited, I felt sure that if I got in to see the Rebbe, something very important and life-changing was going to happen. I couldn't tell why I felt this, but the sanctity was palpable even in the waiting room.

As the night wore on, however, I was informed that it would not be possible to see the Rebbe. The hour was getting very late and the secretary in charge of appointments that night, Rabbi Leibel Groner, was concerned about overtaxing the Rebbe's health. (This was a year before the Rebbe suffered a massive heart attack.) But after a protracted (and very animated, I might add!) discussion, he agreed to deliver a letter with my questions and plea for an audience. I wrote the letter and waited for a reply. The response was quick in coming. The Rebbe would see me after all. I was given a long list of scholarly references on the subject

Visitors awaiting their appointments with the Rebbe recite psalms, as Rabbi Leibel Groner escorts a *chasid* into the Rebbe's study. 24 Tishrei, 5737-1976.

Levi Freidin,
The Living Archive

of my query and advised to use the waiting time in the library to look up these references before the audience began.

I WILL NEVER FORGET MEETING THE REBBE. I recall that he got up from his chair as my wife and I came in, looked directly at each one of us and greeted us warmly. His eyes were penetrating but kind. At that moment, I felt that he saw deep into me and knew me from the inside out. When he insisted that we sit down, I realized that we were going to have a real conversation—this was not going to be just a symbolic encounter.

The meeting lasted about fifteen minutes, during which time I felt that he was communicating with me on a level that transcends the mind, getting straight to the heart and the essence of my being. I was in the presence of an intellectual giant, a leader of the Jewish people, but also a grandfather who cared about me. In short, it was an experience like no other.

We spoke about the South African Jewish community and the phenomenon of so many young people returning to Judaism. In this context, I voiced concern that Chabad emissaries were allowing new returnees to Torah observance to teach others much too soon. I felt they didn't know enough and could be committing real errors in what they were communicating to those who knew even less.

"You are right that, in ideal times, this would not be the correct thing to do," he responded. "But, right now, there is a fire raging, and anybody who can carry a bucket of water must help put it out." He meant that in a time such as ours, with so much assimilation going on, the Jewish community is at risk, and *anybody* who can do anything about it needs to lend a hand.

This brought us to the topic of my own efforts, and the Rebbe brushed aside my worries about teaching Talmud to those who might not have the prerequisite skills. "The words which come from your heart will penetrate theirs," he said, "whether or not they have the skills."

"Don't underestimate what each person is capable of," he added, urging me to expand my efforts.

THAT'S WHEN I TOLD HIM ABOUT THE RESPONSIBILITIES that I faced and the limitations that I felt while trying to manage all the facets of my

The Rebbe shares a moment with an individual during a meeting of the Machne Israel Special Development Fund. 7 Tishrei, 5751-1990.

Sam Shlagbaum, The Living Archive

life without being totally overwhelmed. "In fact, I have been contemplating which to give up — my business or my Torah teaching. I am not sure where I should best direct my energies. I don't feel I can continue both at this pace."

His response stunned me. Not only was he of the opinion that I should give up nothing, but that I should *increase* all my activities. I do not remember his exact words, but the gist of his advice was that my business involvement increased my ability to bring people closer to Judaism; it increased my influence and was a vehicle for *kiddush Hashem*, for sanctifying the name of G-d. He stressed that I would have greater impact if I continued to be involved in both — business and Torah — and that I should do more in the rabbinate, more in the *baal teshuvah* movement and more in Jewish education.

I was still very young then, and I couldn't imagine how I could manage all this. So, I burst out with: "I feel very humbled and honored that you would even talk to me this way, but it just isn't realistic! I'm already up to here."

I remember what he said next very clearly: "I'll tell you what your difficulty is. You think that human interaction is like a chemical reaction. But it isn't. In a chemical reaction, there are two elements which

Rabbi David Lapin (R.).
Circa 1981.

Courtesy of Rabbi Lapin

interact with each other, and their interaction results in a third sub-
stance, a new chemical compound. But people aren't chemicals. When
people interact, the result is a *nuclear* reaction!

"A nuclear reaction occurs at the core and then it radiates in a spher-
ical, rather than in a linear way. As the outer rings of your sphere get
larger and larger, the number of people you are touching gets bigger
and bigger—indeed, there is no limit. This is because, when you touch
the heart of one person, that person in turn touches many other people.
Each person you touch—even for a moment—represents a nuclear
reaction in terms of impact."

He was right, of course, and way ahead of the research that since
then has proven his words to be true. For example, the Framingham
Heart Study showed that our mood affects people three times removed
from us—not only our friends, but our friends' friends; and we impact
people not just with our words but also with our moods and our energy.

Since then, I've kept in mind what the Rebbe said to me. Whenever
I've stood in front of a class, whether teaching ideas of ethical business
practice or teaching Torah, I considered that each individual could, in
turn, impact hundreds of others. The reach is exponential. In my work
as a rabbi and as a business consultant, I was affecting tens of thousands of people, week after week.

That's what the Rebbe conveyed to me—the huge amount of holiness
that I, and every person, could bring into the world.

And that's something that I've never forgotten.   ■

MRS. SARA RIVKA SASONKIN

Personal Treasure

*How to transform a
life, simply by taking interest*

*As a teacher, Mrs. Sara Rivka Sasonkin has guided pupils of Chabad
schools for forty-three years. She lives on Moshav Avital near Afula in Israel,
where she and her husband, Rabbi Avremel Sasonkin, have served as the
Rebbe's emissaries since 1962. She was interviewed in the My Encounter
Studio in New York in November of 2014.*

My memories of the Rebbe begin at about age twelve, when I first came to Brooklyn to study at the Bais Yaakov seminary in Williamsburg, which is not far from the Chabad Headquarters in Crown Heights.

I had been raised in a Chabad home, as the daughter of Rabbi Sholom Posner who for many years operated a Jewish day school in Pittsburgh. That's where I was enrolled until age twelve, but as there were no appropriate high schools for me in Pittsburgh, I transferred to Williamsburg.

Once there, every chance I got, I would walk to Crown Heights to observe the Rebbe's *farbrengens*. I always waited for the Rebbe to look in my direction as he was passing by, because if the Rebbe looked at me and smiled, his smile would light up my world.

Why this happened is very hard for me to put into words. I think only the people who encountered the Rebbe in person can really understand. The best way I can describe it is that, when the Rebbe was looking at me, I felt a connection with something beyond.

This could be sensed in the small encounters, when the Rebbe looked in my direction while I was sitting in a corner of the synagogue reciting psalms, or when he handed me a coin to give to charity, or when he inquired about my health.

One time I was battling a terrible cold, and my mother said to the Rebbe, "She caught a chill at the *farbrengen*." I wanted to drop through the floor from embarrassment when she said that.

But the Rebbe replied, "At a *farbrengen* one must become warm." Truth be told, I must have caught that cold trying to observe the Rebbe's *farbrengen*. In those days, the women used to go outside, to the back of the building, to see what was going on through the rear window. The neighbors were not happy about us being there. I once even caught a whole bucket of water over my head, which was definitely not pleasant. When it was freezing outside, we crowded close together to keep ourselves warm. Perhaps we were drawn to the Rebbe because he was so nice to us, even while his personality evoked the greatest awe.

One winter day, my mother took me to see Rebbetzin Chana, the Rebbe's mother. I recall that we were sitting in the Rebbetzin's dining room when the doorbell rang. Being the youngest in the room, I felt it was my duty to get up and open the door and, when I did, there was a man standing there with his collar up and hat down, smiling. It was the Rebbe, and I started to back away in awe. By that time the Rebbetzin had arrived and, seeing my reaction, she said, "You can wait in that room." She understood that I was uncomfortable intruding on this moment between mother and son. But the Rebbe tried to calm me down:"You don't need to hide from me," he said gently.

I HAD PREVIOUSLY ACCOMPANIED MY PARENTS when they went to see the Rebbe about the school they were running in Pittsburgh, but my first individual audience came in 1960, when I was finishing teachers seminary and was trying to decide what to do next. I had four options: one was to teach at my father's school in Pittsburgh; another was to accept an offer from another school in New York; the third was to travel to Israel; and the last was to join my sister Bessie in Milan, Italy, where she and her husband served as Chabad emissaries. I didn't know what to do, and I made an appointment with the Rebbe to seek his advice.

Sitting outside his office awaiting my turn, I was very worried about how I would even begin talking to him. Then the door opened and I walked in. The Rebbe was sitting behind his desk, writing something. As I approached, he lifted his head and said, "Good evening, Miss Posner." I wasn't expecting him to address me like that, and I just burst out laughing. My nervousness completely left me.

The Rebbe asked many questions about my life, making me realize that he cared about every aspect of it. Then he gave me a blessing that I should be successful in all my endeavors, telling me not to worry about what to do next year, just to take some time off and relax.

When the audience was over, I didn't want to leave. It was so good and warm to be in his presence. His kind, fatherly smile reassured me. When I finally walked out, I felt like I was walking on a cloud.

At the end of that summer, the Rebbe advised my parents to send me to Milan to help my sister. I was thrilled. At the time, only married couples were sent abroad as the Rebbe's emissaries, and I was just a teen-age girl, seventeen years old, so I saw this as a great honor. I was a little concerned about not speaking Italian, but the Rebbe said that I would be working with small children and language would not be a barrier.

Sara Rivka in 1961.

Courtesy of Sara Rivka Sasonkin

Sara Rivka and her sister Bessie Garelik, surrounded by campers of Camp Gan Israel in Italy. Summer, 1961.

Courtesy of the Garelik family

I WENT TO MILAN, WHERE I TAUGHT KINDERGARTEN and helped my sister and her husband. It was very hard at first. I was working seven days a week, and also trying to learn Italian. After a few months, I began to feel quite overwhelmed by the amount of pressure I was under. And so I wrote a long, very emotional letter to the Rebbe.

I got back a most amazing answer—sent "Special Delivery"—which I quote in part:

> I received your recent letter and ... was somewhat taken aback by the tone.... You have surely learned in [the ethical] books of Mussar and especially in *chasidus*, about the tactics of the *Yetzer Hara* [evil inclination] to instill a spirit of depression, discouragement and despondency in order to prevent a Jewish person from fulfilling his Divine mission.... This is exactly what has happened in your case, and I'm surprised that you do not realize it....
>
> You surely know of the saying of the Baal Shem Tov [the founder of the Chasidic movement] that a soul comes down to live on this earth for a period of *70—80 years* for the sole purpose to do another Jew a *single* favor materially

or spiritually. In other words, it is worthwhile for a Jewish soul to make that tremendous journey and descend from heaven to earth in order to do something once for a fellow Jew. In your case the journey was only from the USA to Milan and can in no way be compared with the journey of the soul from heaven to earth. However pessimistic you might feel, even the *Yetzer Hara* would have to agree that you have done not only a single favor, but numerous good deeds, and even only your work with the children of the Gan [kindergarten] would have justified it ... not to mention the fact that your arrival in Milan has undoubtedly considerably encouraged also your sister and brother-in-law and has inspired other young people on similar missions.

Ever since I got this letter, it has been one of my "rechargers." It's a letter that I read very often and quote from.

The Rebbe was so responsive to my feelings. He knew exactly how to speak to me, how to relate to my every emotion, and how to communicate his caring. And, of course, it made me feel very, very good.

On the envelope, "Express, Special Delivery" is written in the Rebbe's hand.
Courtesy of Sara Rivka Sasonkin

Sara Rivka and her
sister Keny Deren
watch as the Rebbe,
who is flanked
by several of his
secretaries, enters the
office building next
door to 770.
6 Kislev, 5739-1978.

*Courtesy of
Sara Rivka Sasonkin*

But even more than that, the letter revealed just how much the Rebbe understood people's foibles and how accepting he was of our failings. He didn't expect us to be angels. He didn't expect us to be perfect. He didn't expect us to always control our *Yetzer Hara*—he understood that it can get the better of us sometimes. And for me, personally, this long letter revealed a special concern—especially when he wrote how much he personally cared about my success.

> As for your mentioning the fact that no one seems to be interested in your work, etc., surely you will admit that G-d, Whose knowledge and providence extends to everyone individually, knows and is interested in what you are doing.... (I need hardly mention that I, too, am interested in your work.) If it seems to you that you have been left to "carry the ball" yourself, it is surely only because there is confidence in you, and that since you have been sent to Milan, you *undoubtedly* have the ability, qualifications and initiative to do your work without outside promptings, etc.

RABBI MENACHEM M. SCHNEERSON
Lubavitch
770 Eastern Parkway
Brooklyn 13, N. Y.

HYacinth 3-9250

מנחם מענדל שניאורסאהן
ליובאוויטש

770 איסטערן פּאַרקוויי
ברוקלין, נ. י.

By the Grace of G-d
28th of Teveth, 5721
Brooklyn, N. Y.

Miss Sarah Rifkah Posner
c/o Garelik
Via Giulio Uberti, 41
Milan

Blessing and Greeting:

I received your recent letter, and the previous one. Needless to say,
I was somewhat taken aback by the tone of your letter. It is a good
illustration of how it is possible for a person to read and to learn
and to receive instructions from books and teachers, and yet when it
comes to actual experience, all this instruction goes by the wayside.

I refer to the things which you have surely learned in books of Mussar,
and especially Chassidus, about the tactics of the Yetzer Hara to
instill a spirit of depression, discouragement and despondency, in
order to prevent the Jewish person from fulfilling his Divine mission.
This is the most effective approach, and if the Yetzer Hara would attempt to dissuade the person directly from fulfilling his mission, he
would not be easily misled. However, instead, the Yetzer tries to discourage the person in all sorts of ways, using "pious" arguments, which,
unfortunately, often proves effective, at least in some degree.

This is exactly what has happened in your case, and I am surprised that
you do not realize it. The proof is that from the information that I
have received, I can see that you have accomplished a great deal more
than you imagine. Incidentally, at the Annual Dinner of the Lubavitcher
Yeshiva last night, Rabbi Lookstein spoke of his visit in Milan and
how impressed he was with the Lubavitch work there, and his address
was one of the highlights of the Dinner.

Let me also add another important and essential consideration. You
surely know of the saying of the Baal Shem Tov that a soul comes down
to live on this earth for a period of _70-80 years_, for the sole purpose
to do another Jew a _single_ favor, materially or spiritually. In other
words, it is worthwhile for a Jewish soul to make that tremendous
journey and descent from heaven to earth in order to do something for/once
one fellow-Jew. In your case the journey was only from the U.S.A. to
Milan, and can in no way be compared with the journey of the soul from
heaven to earth, and however pessimistic you might feel, even the
Yetzer Hara would have to agree that you have done not only a single
favor but numerous good deeds, and even only your work with the children
of the Gan would have justified it. Considering further that every beginning is difficult, especially where there is a change of place, environment, language, etc., and yet the beginning has proved so successful, one is surely justified in expecting that as time goes on and the
initial difficulties are minimized and overcome, there will be a more

that if you do find yourself in such a frame of mind, you should try
to conceal it and not write about it. For our Sages have said "When
a person has an anxiety, he _should_ relate it to others," for getting
something off one's chest is in itself already a relief.

One should also bear in mind, as the Old Rebbe has stated most emphatic-
ally in the laws of learning and teaching Torah, that a person who is
engaged in teaching children should especially take care of his health,
since it directly affects the success of the work. I trust, therefore,
that you are looking after yourself in matters of diet and rest, etc.,
and that you will always be in a state of cheerfulness and gladness.

Hoping to hear good news from you,

With blessing

The Rebbe's letter to Sara Rivka.
Courtesy of Sara Rivka Sasonkin

These sentences made the letter a personal treasure to a girl who already admired and followed the Rebbe, and would have continued to do so even if he hadn't sent me any letters.

He continued, advising me how to handle the depressing thoughts I was having:

> Since one is only human, it is not unusual to lapse occasionally into a mood of discouragement. But, as has been explained in the *Tanya* and in other sources, such a relapse should only serve as a challenge to bring forth additional inner reserves and energy to overcome the tactics of the *Yetzer Hara,* and to do even better than before....
>
> The above should not be understood to mean that if you do find yourself in such a frame of mind, you should try to conceal it and not write about it. For our Sages have said, "When a person has an anxiety he *should* relate it to others," for getting something off one's chest is in itself already a relief.
>
> One should also bear in mind, as the Old Rebbe [the Alter Rebbe, founder of the Chabad movement] has stated most emphatically in the laws of learning and teaching Torah, that a person who is engaged in teaching children should especially take care of his health since it directly affects the success of the work. I trust, therefore, that you are looking after yourself in matters of diet and rest, etc., and that you will always be in a state of cheerfulness and gladness.

Although I only realized that later on, he was giving me guidance for life. It may seem that we can't change ourselves. A person who is an introvert is an introvert; an extrovert is an extrovert. We can smooth our edges a bit, but we can't remake ourselves into a different person. But one of the very few things we *can* truly change is our attitude—our "frame of mind," as he put it. We can decide to approach life's challenges with an attitude of "joy and goodness of heart." This is a choice, and it takes work.

The Rebbe was telling me not to allow all kinds of trivial things to take control of my feelings, but instead to keep looking at the other side

of things, because that's true *simchah*—true happiness.

This kind of attitude to life takes work. It's a choice. It's a constant effort. It's hard. But it's worth it.

IN 1962, I WAS MARRIED TO AVREMEL SASONKIN, and the Rebbe officiated at our wedding, which was an amazing blessing in itself.

By the time I met him, Avremel was already working as the Rebbe's emissary, teaching in the Reshet, the network of Chabad day schools in Israel, and this is where we made our home.

The conclusion of Sara Rivka's *Chupah*, at which the Rebbe officiated. The Rebbe can be seen on the left of the bride. 30 Sivan, 5722-1962.

Courtesy of Sara Rivka Sasonkin

Sara Rivka decorating
a wall with *mitzvah*
themes. Circa 1980.

*Courtesy of
Sara Rivka Sasonkin*

But, after eight years, in 1970 my husband decided to give up teaching and go to work for Bezeq, the Israeli phone company. That is when I felt compelled to return to New York to see the Rebbe and assure him that, even though my husband had given up teaching, we had not abandoned our mission as his emissaries.

When I saw him, the Rebbe inquired about my husband's new job, which he approved of. In response to my concerns, he said, "If Avremel is happy and spreading happiness, then he is my emissary. If he speaks to others about *Yiddishkeit*, then he is my emissary." And I remember thinking, "Thank G-d!" ■

PROFESSOR AARON CIECHANOVER

Marching to the Nobel

*An Israeli biologist makes an astonishing
discovery outside the lab*

Professor Aaron Ciechanover is an Israeli biologist who won the 2004 Nobel Prize in Chemistry for characterizing the method that cells use to degrade and recycle proteins. He is a member of the Israel Academy of Sciences and Humanities and the Pontifical Academy of Sciences, and is a foreign associate of the US National Academy of Sciences. Presently, he serves as a faculty member at the Technion Institute in Haifa, where he was interviewed in November of 2012.

For a time, my brother Yossi served as legal advisor to the Israeli Ministry of Defense under Moshe Dayan and, in this capacity, was appointed to head the Ministry's delegation to the United States and was put in charge of the IDF's military equipment acquisitions. He assumed the position in 1974, right after the Yom Kippur War, when Israel's military equipment was, for all intents and purposes, entirely wiped out, and the IDF needed to rebuild all its military hardware from the ground up. So his was a very important mission. While in the US, my brother grew very close to the Lubavitcher Rebbe and helped arrange for many important Israeli military leaders and government officials to visit with the Rebbe.

So, in 1977, when I came to see my brother in New York, he suggested we pay a visit to the Rebbe. We met the Rebbe in his private office, and it was a long meeting, lasting a couple of hours.

In the course of our conversation, the Rebbe asked me what I was doing, and I explained to him in very simple, layman's terms that I was studying how proteins in the human body are constructed and destroyed. We know that the human body self-destructs all the time for a very important purpose — because without destruction, there can't be new construction.

The example I like to use is of raw meat, which everyone knows is made of protein. If we leave raw meat on the table for several hours, the protein is destroyed and the meat becomes ruined. But while our bodies are basically made of the same kind of cells, they don't get ruined

because living bodies renew themselves all the time. So I told the Rebbe that I and my research team were interested, in particular, in the process of destruction and construction of proteins and, more generally, in the mechanism that is responsible for destruction and construction in the human body and in all life, including animals, birds, plants, bacteria, etc.

But the Rebbe was not at all satisfied with this explanation. He wanted to know the exact nature of my research, and he kept asking more and ever-deeper questions. Later, I realized that there had been a methodical progression to his inquiry—he wanted to know what this system is, how it functions, what role it plays in nature, why man needs it, and the benefit that will be derived from our exploration of it. And through this back and forth, we ended up discussing my work at a very high scientific level.

Of course, I knew that the Rebbe had studied engineering, and it was obvious that he had a good understanding of the fundamentals of science. Clearly, he had a wealth of experience, and clearly, he was intelligent in a most unusual way. While he wasn't a biologist and he didn't use the technical terminology that I use, he certainly understood the principles of biological mechanisms. This was evident from the order in which he posed his questions.

AT HIS INSISTENCE, I EXPLAINED CONCEPTS with which he was not familiar—how amino acids link up on top of each other to form proteins. I well remember going into considerable detail, telling him that a protein is made up of these links, and every link has a different color and a different name, and that when a protein is produced, these links must join in a correct sequence. If they don't, there will be a mutation and a genetic disorder.

I spoke mostly in Hebrew, switching occasionally to English. At first, I was concerned that I would lose the Rebbe, but he had a great command of Hebrew and had no trouble following. And he asked very insightful questions, but also very practical ones.

"What, exactly, do you do?" he wanted to know. "When you come to the lab in the morning, how do you go about solving a problem?"

The Rebbe greets Prime Minister Menachem Begin in front of 770. Yossi Ciechanover (R.) can be seen behind the prime minister. 2 Av, 5737-1977.

Velvel Schildkraut, The Living Archive

I answered that we take cells from animals and break them down in order to introduce a protein that we can track using radioactive marking. We then look for the disappearance of the marking, which is proof that the protein was broken down. He was very interested in how we set up such a tracking system, and he questioned me about it in great detail.

Suddenly, the conversation took a turn. He asked, "Why are you doing this? What is this research good for?"

This was a question I did not know how to answer. We had just begun our research, and we had a long way to go. The research process is like an onion—first you peel the outer layer and then another and then another. There is no end to the layers.

"If you finally discover something, how will it help people?" the Rebbe prompted.

Again, I had no answer. All I could say was that, in research, there are stages. First researchers discover a basic mechanism and its function in biology. And then other researchers come and discover the role this mechanism plays in disease, which might lead to pharmaceutical companies finding a cure. We can't find a cure for a disease without knowing its mechanism, and you can't know its mechanism without researching it.

Of course, the Rebbe understood that, but he was already

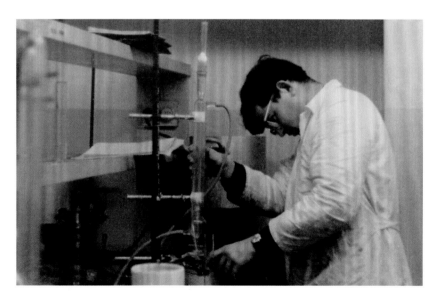

Aaron in the Hebrew University chemistry lab. 1966.

Courtesy of Aaron Ciechanover

anticipating the end result, which I had not even begun to consider.

All these years later, we know that our research has proven very beneficial. Based on our work, drugs have been developed against various malignancies and specific cancers, and I believe that, in the future, we will see drugs against neurodegenerative diseases, as well as others. Today, all the major pharmaceutical companies are interested in our research.

But, back then, I had no way of knowing what would be, so I simply answered, "There are stages in scientific research, and we are only at the first stage. We are part of a chain, and we are only at the beginning of this chain."

But the Rebbe was totally focused on purposefulness. With his questions, he took the discussion to the edge of where our research might lead—to the end of the chain, to the good that would come of it.

I REMEMBER THE END OF OUR CONVERSATION VERY WELL. The Rebbe posed a very philosophical question: "How does nature know to destroy exactly the same amount of proteins it builds?"

"If it were to destroy more than it builds," he continued, "then

Yossi Ciechanover approaches the Rebbe at a *farbrengen* marking twenty-five years of the Rebbe's leadership. 10 Shevat, 5735-1975.

Velvel Schildkraut, The Living Archive

Aaron Ciechanover

*Courtesy of Aaron
Ciechanover*

everything would be gone. And if it were to build more than it destroys, the proteins would accumulate. So how do these two processes communicate to achieve this equilibrium?"

I had no answer to this question (and I still don't).

But the Rebbe was ahead of me: "Don't you think that this is really the wonder of creation—that there is construction and destruction and that they balance each other so well?" I do not recall precisely the words he used but I believe that he quoted Ecclesiastes, saying that nature understands "there is a time to build and a time to destroy...."

I have to say that with this statement the Rebbe touched my weak spot. I am strictly a man of science—I try to explain occurrences in nature according to science and not according to religion. So I simply conceded that, yes, there is a mystery of creation at work here.

I believe that the Rebbe understood the tremendous complexity of nature, how destruction communicates with construction, and how it all fits together, occurring at the exact time it's needed. And I think that's what the Rebbe was trying to communicate to me. We ended the conversation on that note, in a very friendly way.

In parting, the Rebbe urged me to return for another visit. He said, "I would really like to see you again, and to hear from you about advancements in science and what you are doing." Unfortunately, that opportunity never arose.

I LEFT THE REBBE'S OFFICE in a state of astonishment. I don't think I'd ever had such a deep conversation with my supervisor, who understood everything I was doing but only spoke about the day's experiments. No one had ever taken me to such philosophical heights as the Rebbe had.

I had come to tell him about my work, but I ended up learning an important lesson from the Rebbe—something that has been with me my entire life, to this day:

Science is about the details, but there is also a bigger picture. If you want to succeed in science, you obviously need to know the details, but you have to be aware of the bigger picture also.

This became clearer and clearer to me as our research proceeded. We were met with a lot of skepticism. No one believed us, because we were going against the prevailing trend. Many predicted that we were marching directly to the academic graveyard, but we kept going for eight long years until we finally achieved success. And maybe there was something of the wonder of creation here again. Maybe G-d, the Creator—and I am not committing to belief in Creationism here, but I do think that something or someone was watching over us—enabled us to succeed.

The recognition came later. In the 1990s, when our research was finally recognized, there was suddenly a huge flood of interest from labs and pharmaceutical companies. By the millennium, it was already an explosion. And in 2004, Professor Avram Hershko, Professor Irwin Rose and myself received the most prestigious of

Aaron at work with his Nobel co-laureate, Professor Avram Hershko.
Courtesy of Aaron Ciechanover

Aaron receiving the
Nobel Prize from
the king of Sweden.
December 10, 2004.

*Courtesy of Aaron
Ciechanover*

all scientific awards, the Nobel Prize in Chemistry.

By then, of course, I had an answer to the question the Rebbe had posed: what my research was good for and whether it would help people.

He had zeroed in on the essence of the process, beyond the details. He was a person who could look at the forest, without needing to look at the individual trees, and understand the essence of its composition. And because he did, our conversation reached heights that I don't remember reaching, before or after, with anyone. It was as if he took me up the mountain and made me look at the view from there.

Afterwards, I descended to the forest floor and continued to look at one tree, at another tree, at the details. But the experience left such an impression on me that thereafter, when I would reach a milestone in my work, I would stop and say, "I've arrived at this point here; now let me go back up the mountain and see from above where I stand."

Today this is a routine part of what I do. It's something called "process reset." It works like a GPS screen: you zoom in to see exactly where you are on the road, but then you zoom out and say, "Now let me see how far along I've driven—let me see the complete map."

This is what I learned from the Rebbe. He taught me to look at the big picture, and this is a very important skill.

MRS. DEVORAH KLAR

Lost and Found

An ageless educator and her dramatic
journey to the classroom

Since 1980, Mrs. Devorah Klar and her husband, Rabbi Boruch Klar, have served as Chabad emissaries in New Jersey, where they presently operate the Shabbat House of West Orange. She was interviewed in the My Encounter Studio in November of 2018.

My parents — Rabbi Pinchas and Alta Chaya Klein — were Holocaust survivors from Poland. But by the time I was born, they had immigrated to Canada and that is where I grew up. We used to visit the Chabad Headquarters in New York almost every year, at the end of Sukkot usually, when we would have a private audience with the Rebbe. The Rebbe, who always seemed very kind, would ask me about the Torah portion that we were studying in school, so I would always make sure to know it well before the trip.

By the time I was twenty-one, I had graduated high school, gone to France to study at the Beth Rivkah Seminary there, then went to Israel for two years before moving to New York. While I was in Israel my religious observance lapsed, and my parents felt I needed direction. They urged me to ask the Rebbe for advice, but I refused.

I was sure that the Rebbe was going to tell me to be a teacher, something which I was vehemently against. I said that I'd rather beg for money on street corners than become a teacher, because I had always hated school. So, I didn't want to get his advice, which I was certain I would not follow. Furthermore, I was not really religious anymore — I had my own universalist philosophy, which did not include keeping Torah. I was proud of the fact that I was not a hypocrite, pretending to be religious when I was not, and I felt I was very liberal-minded.

Before long, however, a series of events conspired to make me seek

The Rebbe distributes nickels for charity.
29 Elul, 5750-1990.
Levi Freidin, The Living Archive

his advice after all:

At age twenty-one, I was admitted to St. John's University in Queens to study criminology. I thought this field would suit me—it would be exciting. I was interested in eventually doing police work or criminal rehabilitation, which would allow me to actualize my beliefs in justice and in the inherent goodness of man. I was so enthusiastic about this prospect that I invested all the money I had saved from my previous jobs working in hotels to enroll.

But my very first class was a disappointment—the professor seemed more interested in cracking jokes than teaching. My second class was not much better—it was criminal law, yet it was also not very satisfying because the subject matter was so dry. What really tipped the scales, though, was my third class. St. John's was a Catholic university where religious studies were mandatory, so I had to listen to some priest in a long black frock as he pontificated on the scriptures.

I felt like dropping out—every day that I stayed, my hard-earned savings were going down the drain—but I was not sure what to do.

And that is when I finally asked my brother-in-law, Rabbi Yankel Eckhaus, to arrange an audience for me with the Rebbe, and he obliged. It coincided with my twenty-second birthday, which was in November of 1974.

When I walked in, the Rebbe invited me to sit down and I did, forgetting that sitting before the Rebbe was not considered respectful for a *chasid*—I had been out of the system for a long time—and I handed him the letter in which I explained my dilemma.

After he read it, he began to speak. And it struck me that he spoke to me in a language that was most clear to me—Yiddish mixed with English. Obviously, he spoke fluent Yiddish, a language which I also spoke until I was five. But as I grew up, my Yiddish became Yinglish. He had somehow intuited that this mixture suited me best, and he found just the right balance—if he had used more Yiddish words, I would have been lost, yet if he had only spoken English it would have been unnecessary.

What he told me was that when a Jew in my specific situation is surrounded by non-Jews, two things can happen—either the Jew develops an inferiority complex, or the Jew becomes like the non-Jews.

Devorah on a trip to
Scotland. 1974.

Courtesy of
Devorah Klar

His assessment resonated with me. Some of my friends who were living
in non-Jewish environments had complained of feeling like outsiders
and I had noticed that they developed the inferiority complex the Rebbe spoke of. As for me, I was likely to fall in the second category and
become like the non-Jews.

Then the Rebbe spoke about my career path. He did not outright tell
me to abandon it, but he said that perhaps, in my future life, I wouldn't
be happy working with criminals. "For you it would be better to work
with healthy people rather than sick people," he advised.

"But if everyone works with healthy people, who will work with the
sick ones?" I countered.

Maybe it was a bit nervy of me to ask such a question but he didn't
seem offended. Instead, he proceeded to give me a very long answer,
none of which I remember. But what I do remember is that, after I left
the Rebbe's office, the realization dawned on me that the answer was
simple: He wasn't talking about anyone else — his advice was intended
for me, Devorah Klein, alone.

In convincing me of this, the Rebbe was completely right. At the time
I thought of myself as a kind of a tough person — I even applied for a job
with the NYPD — and I wanted to work with people who had difficult

pasts and had made bad choices. But, truth be told, my personality was not at all suited to that kind of occupation because I have a sensitive temperament and I tend to absorb other people's emotions. And the Rebbe understood that. He understood me better than I understood myself at the time.

"It would be good for you to study education," the Rebbe said. "Maybe go to a teachers' seminary." This was the advice that I had feared getting, but now, when the Rebbe was gently making the suggestion, it didn't scare me. In fact, it felt right.

For so many years I had not been open to hearing anyone telling me what to do. But I was open to the Rebbe. He changed the orientation of my compass, so to speak—pointing me in a direction I wanted to go even though I didn't know it.

That didn't mean he was about to run my life for me, though. As I was leaving, I asked him whether I should live in New York or Montreal, but he wasn't going to hand all the decisions to me on a silver platter. "It doesn't matter—you decide," he said, and it was obvious from his tone that I shouldn't press him further on this question.

THE DAY FOLLOWING MY MEETING with the Rebbe, I pulled out of St. John's University, managing to salvage some of my money. And I accepted a Shabbat invitation from a friend.

I was moved to do so because, for some time before this, I had been aware of an emptiness inside of me—I often felt as if my soul was dead. Although I had allowed my religious observance to lapse two years earlier while living in Israel, I at least felt spiritually connected just from being in the Holy Land. So I was totally unprepared for the emptiness that descended on me when I found myself without Torah in the United States, where I didn't even know who I was. I had thought that pursuing a career in criminology would give me back my sense of self, but it had just proven disillusioning.

Now, following the meeting with the Rebbe, something shifted.

The friend who invited me for Shabbat lived in Far Rockaway, which I found to be so much more peaceful than noisy Manhattan where I was living. She was studying at the Ayelet HaShachar Teachers' Seminary run by Rebbetzin Sarah Freifeld, whose husband, Rabbi Shlomo

Freifeld, was the head of the Sh'or Yoshuv Yeshivah. The Freifelds and the members of their community were warm, kind and genuine — they really lived what they believed. And so I enrolled in the same seminary, beginning a dual process of returning to Judaism and developing a career in education.

From that point on, I never looked back. I went on to teach in Jewish day schools, afternoon programs, camps, and other experiential educational environments, and I found the work very

Rabbi Shlomo and Rebbetzin Sarah Freifeld
Courtesy of Benjie Brecher

satisfying. Children are works in progress, and they are malleable, so a good teacher can avert many problems that would later require the intervention of a criminologist or social worker.

It was also good for me in another way. I found that working with children of all ages strengthened me personally and spiritually. Being in the position of a mentor meant I had to set an example, and that responsibility had a lasting effect.

LONG BEFORE I CAME TO THE REBBE TO ASK FOR DIRECTION, the Rebbe knew that this would be my true calling.

When I was about eleven or twelve, he asked my father to tell me that I should be a positive influence on my less-observant classmates, which came as a surprise to me, since I was a rebel and troublemaker at the time. For most of my life I liked to do things my own way, and I certainly didn't like being told what to do. From an early age, I hated school. I wasn't interested in my studies and I was always questioning my teachers, which they interpreted as trying to make trouble, so I was often asked to leave class.

So when my father came back from a meeting with the Rebbe and conveyed the Rebbe's message, I remember thinking "Who — me?! Like

I'm going to make somebody else more observant?"

But, in truth, I *was* a bit of a leader, and others followed me. I also had a gift for speaking so that others would listen. And while the Rebbe's message did not have an immediate impact, it remained etched in my memory.

The Rebbe read me correctly again in 1969 when, after completing the seminary in France, I wanted to go to Israel to work on a kibbutz. My parents were concerned and went to ask advice of the Rebbe, who said, "What's wrong with going to *Eretz Yisrael*?"

The two years I spent in Israel proved to be the best years of my life, and not a day goes by that I don't think about that time. I discovered what it means to be connected to the Holy Land in a way that can never happen in America, which in the 1960s was a turbulent place. I had an intense feeling of aliveness—of belonging and connection—which I did not experience anywhere else. But I also discovered that my *Yiddishkeit* was superficial, which is why I jettisoned it so easily, only to reclaim it

Devorah on a trip to London. 1974.

Courtesy of Devorah Klar

again as my own when I matured. And I have to say that I might not have valued my Jewishness as much if I had not had the Israel experience. The Rebbe must have understood that about me also.

AFTER I RETURNED TO TORAH OBSERVANCE, taking the Rebbe's advice to become a teacher, there were many things I had to sort out—such as how I should behave, what I should wear, and whom I should date. At the time I was still meeting men who were not observant, but, as I found my way and things came together, I started seeing men who were observant but not Chabad *chasidim*. I was trying to be open, yet I wasn't getting anywhere.

After a while, I felt frustrated and very sick of the dating game. It was wearing me down, and it wasn't enjoyable in the least. My sister, who was trying to help me, added up how many potential matches had not worked out for me, and the count was one hundred and nineteen! By then, I was twenty-four.

At this point, I wrote to the Rebbe. I was seeing Mr. 119, and I was not sure what to do.

The Rebbe answered, "If you are in a state of doubt, then you are not able to come to a decision." (In other words, he was explaining to me why I was finding it impossible to make any sort of commitment.)

His take was so refreshing. Other people were telling me the opposite—that if I didn't decide soon, I would forever regret that I had walked away from my soulmate. Instead, the Rebbe advised that maybe I should take a break from dating. Perhaps after a break, things would become more clear for me. But the most important thing he said was, "It all depends on you."

After dating unsuccessfully for so long, with everybody giving me advice, my inner voice had been silenced. I no longer trusted my own feelings. When the Rebbe told me that it all depended on me, he gave me the gift of trusting myself, of listening to myself. After that, I stopped forcing myself to meet the expectations of others, and that's when I met my husband Boruch—Mr. 120!

Boruch and I dated for nine months, which is a long time in the religious world. The reason was distance. He was living in Morristown, New Jersey, and by then, I was back in Montreal, Canada. So while our

dating periods were intense, they were few and far between.

As well, there was another problem. Unlike me, Boruch had not been raised in a religious home. He had found *Yiddishkeit* on his own and, by the time we met, he had spent less than two years in *yeshivah*. When I mentioned the high standard of learning in my family, his response was: "I guess there is no point in us dating further." And instead of arguing with him, I said, "Yes, you're right."

I had wanted to continue seeing him, but when he said what he said, my pride weighed in, and I refused to try to convince him otherwise.

That night I found that I couldn't sleep—I felt that I had lost something precious. And that's when I realized that your soulmate may not necessarily be the person who is most similar to you, which was a big revelation to me.

My mother saw how downcast I was the next morning, and she suggested that I write to the Rebbe. He immediately responded, "It's worthwhile to continue."

And so we did.

The Rebbe greets Devorah on the "Sunday dollars" receiving line. 16 Cheshvan, 5751-1990.

Chaim B. Halberstam, The Living Archive

We were married in 1978, and shortly thereafter we went on to serve as emissaries of the Rebbe in Morristown, New Jersey. This was just the right place for us and we have been very successful, launching many outreach projects such as the Jewish Renaissance Fair; Café Devorah, a Saturday night kosher nightclub; grand Purim balls and Chanukah *menorah* lightings.

More recently, we created the Shabbat House in West Orange, which is perhaps our most promising project ever. There are only so many Jews who will attend a synagogue, but Shabbat speaks to everyone. The Shabbat House is a home built only for Shabbat. Thousands of people have experienced the warmth of Shabbat there to date, though we are measuring our success not by numbers, but by the effect — by people who were touched deeply inside.

AFTER A BREAK FROM WORK to raise a family, I have continued with my career as a teacher, but some years after the Rebbe passed away, I found myself feeling dissatisfied. I had been teaching in a Modern Orthodox day school, but this particular job was not for me. I felt frustrated by the rigid curriculum; I needed my students to connect with what I was teaching rather than simply absorbing information at a rapid pace, so I quit. The problem was that I did not know what to do next — and I

The Klars teaching students of Fairleigh Dickinson University in Teaneck, New Jersey, about Shabbat. 1979.

Courtesy of Devorah Klar

The Klars in
Morristown with their
children Yehoshua and
Tzemach. Circa 1982.

*Courtesy of
Devorah Klar*

was just turning fifty. On my birthday, I went to the Rebbe's resting place
where, in the reception room, there are always videos playing of his talks.

On the video screen, an address of the Rebbe was playing. The Rebbe
was saying: "The main objective of education is not the transmission of
a large amount of information to the pupil.... The true purpose of education is to imbue the pupil with the ability to utilize the knowledge for
the benefit of introducing justice, integrity and peace into society. The
main idea of education is to nurture the character of the pupil until he
becomes a true *mentsch* in all the aspects of his day-to-day conduct...."

He totally validated my innermost thoughts!

And then the Rebbe continued with something that pertained to me
even more directly: "This country has developed the custom that when
a person becomes forty-something or fifty-something years of age, he
or she earns the privilege to think about retirement, to decrease his or
her activities that benefit humanity—the true purpose for which he
was created."

"Wasn't 'man created to toil'; to spread goodness in G-d's world?"
the Rebbe asked.

"The age on one's birth certificate cannot be used as an excuse to do
less. On the contrary, if G-d gives a person fifty, sixty or seventy years,
that's proof-positive that they have more to accomplish."

The Rebbe hands copies of a Chasidic discourse to Tzemach and Rabbi Boruch Klar. 24 Cheshvan, 5751-1991.

Yossi Melamed, The Living Archive

Here I was, on my fiftieth birthday! It was exactly what I needed to hear in order to take the next steps in my life with confidence—to continue to teach, but with a different set of goals in mind.

Many of us lock ourselves into a little pigeonhole defined by how old we are. I hear people say all the time, "I can't do that anymore, now that I'm older." To them I quote the Rebbe:

Are you going to let a number on your birth certificate dictate who you are? You have a job to do in this world. You alone can impact your community, your city, your country, the entire world!

TODAY, I HAVE TO ASK WHAT MY LIFE would have turned out to be if I had not gone to see the Rebbe way back when. He spent ten minutes with me—maybe fifteen, but no more than that. And I walked out a different person and never looked back.

What made the difference?

He truly cared. He made time stop for me in those few minutes. He never tried to tell me what to do—he just gave the right advice at the perfect moment and he inspired me to be all I could be. ■

Making Waves in the Holy Land

The radio personality with a hidden tape recorder

Beginning in 1979, Moti Eden forged a broadcasting career in Israeli radio and television, serving as director of Israel's television station, Channel One, from 2003 to 2006. He was interviewed in March of 2010 in Haifa, Israel, where he works as the spokesperson for the Port of Haifa, the country's largest seaport and shipyard.

Following my service in the Yom Kippur War and a stint at Hebrew University, I began working as a reporter for the radio station, *Kol Yisrael*. Initially, my areas of responsibility were covering the Ministry of Interior, the Ministry of Public Security, the Municipality of Jerusalem and the Office of the President. But after I covered a funeral in Jerusalem of a leader of the ultra-Orthodox and anti-Zionist faction, Edah HaChareidis, I saw that religion could be an interesting topic as well.

This topic was natural to me as I had come from a religious home and studied in *yeshivah*. (Indeed, members of my family descended from the Munkatch and Spinka *chasidim*.) And it was while covering religion that I came in contact with Chabad and learned of the role that the Rebbe was playing on the world stage.

I had to meet this man for myself.

Through the intercession of Rabbi Berke Wolf, Chabad's spokesman in Israel, I managed to arrange an interview with the Rebbe, which was scheduled for July 1, 1980.

At that point, I had been working for *Kol Yisrael* for a little more than a year, and I knew that, for a novice, I had just landed a big scoop. So I prepared for this interview very carefully, learning more about Chabad and the protocols of speaking with the Rebbe. I brought along a small tape recorder, but I didn't know if I would be allowed to use it, so I hid it from the Rebbe's secretaries. But when I went in and began to speak with the Rebbe, I brought it out in the open. He saw it of course. I assumed that he didn't mind that I recorded him since he didn't object. So the interview was taped.

The Rebbe spoke about many things — especially about Israel — and he gave me advice how *Kol Yisrael* could best serve the public. He pointed out that radio has a big advantage over print media. Whereas the reader can flip pages and omit articles, the listener can't. A responsible broadcaster needs to take advantage of that fact to not just inform but to educate.

The Rebbe urged me to focus on stories that pertain to all Jews, stories that people will be interested in hearing on the radio, that would intrigue the listeners as well as the general public. He believed that Jewish ideas could be news and should not be relegated to some largely-ignored religious program.

But I wasn't convinced that such a thing could work. "How can we make news from everything?" I asked. "Not everything is news! The Torah is not news!"

He replied, "Our sages teach us that every day we must approach Torah anew, as if it were given today. So when you say that this week's Torah portion is news, you are stating the truth. You only need to find some

Moti interviewing Colonel Motti Mizrachi after a clash with Hezbollah in South Lebanon.

Courtesy of Moti Eden

way to tie this in with the events that just happened in the world."

He was giving me a basic lesson in newscasting! He was trying to guide me and explain how people, who had tuned in to hear interesting news, could also hear Torah that was no less interesting.

This goes to show the importance that the Rebbe gave to utilizing all means of communication. At the time, other rabbis wouldn't go near radio or television, but the Rebbe was saying, "Use it and make the most of it."

Indeed, the Rebbe understood the value of radio, and he spoke to me about the prospect of broadcasting for the whole world to hear. In those days—before cellphones, before the internet, before social media, even before TV was available in undeveloped countries—there wasn't any device that could reach the *whole* world except for radio.

But the Rebbe saw that this fantastic device was underutilized by the Jewish people. How much good it could do to bring people closer to one another—indeed, to bring the Final Redemption!

The Rebbe in his study. 30 Cheshvan, 5744-1984.

Yossi Melamed, The Living Archive

THE MOST STARTLING PART OF THE INTERVIEW was the Rebbe's assessment of the situation in Israel. Remember, it took place in 1980, seven years before the first intifada.

He said, "According to the intelligence I have received from Washington, the situation is extremely grave. But after thirty-two years of tension, the world is simply tired of facing reality." And he spoke to me about a growing extremism that was brewing among young Arabs.

He went on to note that in the past—thirty or forty years ago—Israel could easily bribe the senior Arab sheik, and this solved the problem as the younger ones would do nothing on their own. Now the situation was changing to the other extreme. The younger generation was more fanatical both about politics and about religion, and they couldn't be bribed, because for them there was nothing more glorious than self-sacrifice for "Allah."

The Rebbe said that it caused him pain to realize that the attitude of much of Jewish youth toward self-sacrifice was the opposite: "Thirty years ago in Israel, no one needed to be convinced that self-sacrifice was needed. Everyone wanted to be a pioneer. But today's Jewish youth are saying 'Enough already! We've lived with stress and tension for thirty years. Now we deserve to live a peaceful life, a fun life.' ... This attitude is a weakness that is obvious to all the surrounding nations, and they are exploiting the situation. There is simply no time for Israelis to come to a full cognition of the changing attitude of the Arabs." He emphasized that he didn't want to cause panic, but it was urgent for people to recognize what was happening.

He was so right. Within a few months, the tensions that would lead to the Lebanon War of 1982 began. In retrospect, seeing what happened, it should have been

A negotiation between Abraham Shakarczr of Kibbutz Be'eri and Sheikh Hadj Ibrahim of the Muslim town of Ikhzaa. 1950.
Fritz Cohen, Israel Government Press Office

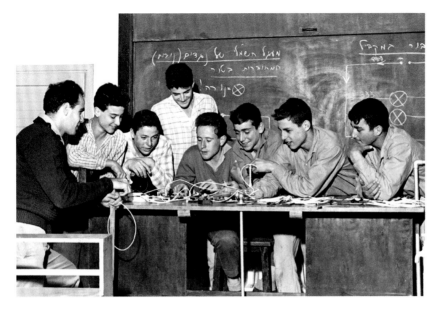

Israeli high school students participating in a physics lesson in Kibbutz Givat Brenner. 1964.

Fritz Cohen, Israel Government Press Office

obvious. But no one saw it except the Rebbe.

He said, "I cannot express how dangerous the situation is for Israel. And the current government in Washington is not strong at all…. Politicians in Washington are just looking for the easiest way. They just want to sleep soundly."

The Rebbe urged me to do what I could to effect change, beginning with changing the outlook of Jewish youth regarding their personal connection to the Holy Land. They needed to understand that they were an essential link in the chain of forty generations of their ancestors — Jewish men and women who settled the Land that was given to them by G-d as an eternal inheritance. Nothing has been stolen; no injustice has been done. The Arabs were latecomers to the Land of Israel, arriving long after the Jews.

"These are simple facts that every Jewish boy and girl has to understand," he stressed. "And this is where you and *Kol Yisrael* come in. Because you can teach the Israeli youth that the verse in the Torah, 'Hear O Israel, the Lord is our God, the Lord is One' wasn't just addressed to someone named 'Israel' who stood at Mount Sinai three thousand years ago. It was meant for every Avraham, Moshe and Shlomo who lives in Tel Aviv today!"

The Rebbe wanted me to take the events related in the Torah and, through the news, link the past with the present. He understood that the best way to connect Israeli youth to their history was to make them see how it relates to current events. And that knowledge would give them the strength to deal with the upcoming dangers.

The other thing that they can never forget, the Rebbe said, is who they are in essence—part of the Nation of Israel to whom G-d gave the Torah: "Even those who consider themselves secular cannot change this fact any more than they can change the color of their eyes or the size of their heart. People can only choose whether they will damage their heart or whether they will make it more healthy. So too, every Jewish son and daughter can choose whether they will act in accordance with their essence or whether they will fight their nature."

AT ANOTHER JUNCTURE IN THE INTERVIEW, I asked him about the Jewish children's rallies, which I knew were critically important in the Rebbe's eyes. That summer he had begun urging people to organize such rallies, something he had also done earlier, before the Yom Kippur War. "Why?" I asked him.

Moti broadcasting
from Beirut.

Courtesy of Moti Eden

He said, "Children have the power to avert danger. It is written in the Book of Psalms, 'Out of the mouths of babies and infants, You have established Your might ... to silence the enemy and the avenger.' A seventy-year-old, even though he is sitting in the Knesset, cannot avert danger the way an innocent child can."

A children's rally in Israel. Lag B'omer, 5746-1986.

Levi Freidin,
The Living Archive

In this and the many other things he said, the Rebbe was conveying to me the idea that strengthening Israel spiritually will automatically lead to strengthening Israel physically. And this inner strength will radiate to the surrounding countries that currently perceive Israel as weak.

In a similar vein, the Rebbe spoke about strengthening Jerusalem.

I had told him that I lived in what was then called Mishor Adumim—this was the original settlement upon which Maaleh Adumim was eventually built—and the Rebbe immediately went to the crux of the matter:

"Mishor Adumim is fine; settling there is fine," he said, "but more important is the heart of Jerusalem—the Old City. When the Arabs see that Jews are settling all around Jerusalem but the government of Israel is too afraid to give Jews permission to settle the entire Old City, they make the obvious inference. So it is not enough to feel satisfied to live *near* Jerusalem—that should be just the prelude to saving the Old

City and restoring it to its original glory as the Great City of King David."

AT THE VERY END OF THE MEETING, the Rebbe said, "Don't let this conversation go to waste. See that it brings action."

I left the Rebbe in awe. He was, in my opinion, an outstanding leader, and his foresight was tremendous.

This is why, as I was going out the door, I asked the Rebbe for his autograph. I know that this seems like a childish thing to have done, but I did it anyway. I said, "Please autograph my copy of the *Tanya*." The *Tanya*, written by Rabbi Schneur Zalman of Liadi, is a fundamental book of Chabad, and I wanted the Rebbe to sign it.

The Rebbe said, "I will give you a small *Tanya* of mine, but I won't sign it, because then everyone will ask me to do the same." I promised to keep it a secret, but he just smiled, "There are no secrets among *chasidim*. And besides, the main thing is to study what is written in it."

He was right of course about there not being any secrets, because no sooner had I left the room than word was out that I had brought a tape recorder into my meeting with the Rebbe. This cassette was quickly borrowed from me and duplicated, and within a half hour it was out there, playing on Chasidic radio all over New York, and everyone was talking about it.

That's when I understood the dramatic importance of every word uttered by the Rebbe.

When I returned to Israel, I immediately edited the recording down to the most essential ten minutes and, during the Friday program, *Afternoon Journal*, I played it.

In that extract, the Rebbe was speaking to the people of Israel in very strong terms, using words like "I can't describe how grave the situation is …," warning us that great dangers were being ignored, and that our leaders were falling asleep on the watch. It was a truly frightening message.

The Rebbe was issuing a wake-up call to the nation.

The response was amazing. There was a tremendous uproar. All the media were quoting the Rebbe, even foreign correspondents based in Israel.

Jerusalem
Courtesy of Yanky Ascher

Afterwards, we excerpted more in subsequent broadcasts on *Kol Yisrael*, and even today, they sometimes use clips from that recording.

When I went out to cover the Lebanon War, my interview with the Rebbe followed me everywhere. I recall in the middle of the Beirut-Damascus Highway meeting *chasidim* who asked me about it.

I covered Lebanon for the next eighteen years, and all the while the Rebbe's words guided me, encouraged me and gave me strength. During that time, I switched from radio to television, broadcasting on Channel One—eventually becoming its head of operations and general manager—and although the conflict was still in progress, I did not neglect the Rebbe's instructions to me. I also covered all of Chabad's activities—the campaigns, the children's parades, the work with soldiers, etc. Everything in the field that had to do with Judaism found its way on to Israeli television because I didn't forget what the Rebbe had told me to do.

Moti, together with a group of *chasidim* who had come to print *Tanya*s in Beirut.

Courtesy of Moti Eden

The Rebbe greets
Moti, his wife Tamy,
and their children,
Dotan and Shira, at
the "Sunday dollars"
receiving line.
23 Nissan, 5751-1991.

Chaim B. Halberstam,
The Living Archive

SOME YEARS LATER, after the end of the Gulf War, I took my wife and children to New York, as part of the celebration of my son Dotan's Bar Mitzvah.

We came to see the Rebbe as he was giving out dollars for charity — on Sunday, April 7, 1991 — and it proved an intimate meeting even though it lasted only a few minutes.

Being the mischievous journalist that I am, I asked the Rebbe what will happen in the future: "When will Mashiach come? How close is he really?"

"When I know, I'll give you a call," the Rebbe joked, adding, "until then we must await him."

But I persisted, "A short time? A long time?"

To which the Rebbe replied, "I believe, as Jews affirm daily [in accordance with the Thirteen Principles of Faith], in the coming of Mashiach, and I expect his arrival today."

At another point in the exchange when it became clear to me that the Rebbe was very much up-to-date on my work, I remarked, "The

Rebbe knows everything!" He shot back, "But I don't yet know what you will do tomorrow."

"Do you have a good suggestion?" I asked.

"I have the confidence that you will make the right decisions," he replied. "You must evaluate your abilities. You can aim high, because you have much greater abilities than you realize."

"In what direction?" I asked, searching for a hint.

"In the direction of spreading Judaism," he replied, "so that Israel is not only *called* the Land of Israel, but that anyone who looks at any part of it should see that it *is* the Land of Israel."

But I didn't quite understand what he meant by this until much later.

There came a time in 2002 when I applied for the position of director of Channel One. I thought there was little chance of my being selected because I was out in the field and not connected politically; as well, there were a dozen other candidates running against me. But what do you know? One day, as I was going about my job, I heard someone shouting my name, "Moti, Moti, get over here!" And then I heard, "You've been chosen!"

That's when I remembered the Rebbe telling me that I didn't yet know my true abilities, that I didn't know what I was capable of. He had the confidence that I would rise to the challenge. I gave it my all, and I hope he's pleased.   ■

The 2 AM Debate

The couple that came hoping for a present
and left with a future

Rabbi Chaim Brovender is the founder of Yeshivat Hamivtar, Midreshet Lindenbaum and WebYeshiva.org. He resides in Jerusalem where he was interviewed in March of 2010.

Mrs. Miriam Shulamit Brovender is a former teacher who for the past thirty years has worked as a marital counselor. She was interviewed in her home in August of 2020.

Rabbi Chaim Brovender

I was born in Brooklyn, where I attended Modern Orthodox schools, namely the Yeshiva of Flatbush—both elementary school and high school—and then I went on to Yeshiva University, where I received my rabbinic ordination. After I got married, I made *aliyah* to Israel, continuing to learn at Hebrew University, and received a Ph.D. in Semitic languages.

While in Israel, I felt myself drawn to learning Torah and, after that, to teaching Torah, and that's basically what I've done my whole life.

In 1968 my wife Miriam and I were on a visit to New York from Israel, and we decided to request an audience with the Lubavitcher Rebbe. Everybody understood that a blessing from the Rebbe was something worth grabbing onto, and my wife especially wanted a blessing for children—because we didn't have any children yet—so we got an appointment to see him.

To be honest, I was less than enthusiastic. As a confirmed *litvak*—that is, far from a *chasid*—I went just to please my wife and her parents, who came along. In fact, when Rabbi Leibel Groner, the Rebbe's secretary, asked me why I had come, I answered, "I'm just the driver."

The appointment was for the wee hours of the morning because the Rebbe learned and worked all day and would only see people at night.

We came into his office and were astonished to find it in perfect order. His desk—a very big desk—was absolutely clean. There was nothing on it, except maybe one piece of paper and, I think, a small Book of Psalms. That's all.

The Rebbe in his study.
18 Cheshvan, 5735-1974.

Velvel Schildkraut,
The Living Archive

It was almost as if the Rebbe wanted to convey a message: "Right now, I have nothing else on my mind except for the two of you sitting in front of me." And that was quite startling to me.

I have been in the presence of some very busy people who would be multitasking while speaking to me. Of course, I assume that such people are very clever and able to do two or three things at the same time, but I hardly feel like the center of their focus. But with the Rebbe, it was nothing like that. His attention was totally on us, as if he had no other concern in the world, which was remarkable.

The conversation that followed was conducted in Yiddish, a language in which we were all fluent. The interesting thing was that the Rebbe didn't start with, "What do you want?" or "What's the purpose of this meeting?" Instead, he asked us our names, where we were from, what we were doing … that sort of thing.

When we mentioned that we were from Israel, he wanted to know the particulars. So I told him that we had made *aliyah* two years prior, and that I learned in a *kollel* in Jerusalem.

"Where do you live?" he asked.

"Kiryat Moshe," I replied, referring to our neighborhood in Jerusalem.

"On what street?"

Now, everybody knows that the Rebbe never set foot in Israel, so this was a peculiar question. Like somebody asking, "Oh, you come from Mongolia? That's so interesting. What street do you live on?" as if that would matter.

But, being polite, I answered the Rebbe, "I live on Rechov Reines, number 13."

And then he asked, as if he was clarifying something for himself, "Is the vegetable store still there?"

I didn't know what he was talking about, but Miriam immediately understood his question. "Yes," she said, "there is a vegetable store downstairs, in the basement."

I couldn't believe it.

Everybody knows that the Rebbe had a good memory; everybody knows that he remembered all kinds of things that other people forgot. But to remember that there's a vegetable store at number 13 Rechov Reines in Kiryat Moshe, when he had never been to Jerusalem —when he had never even been to Israel—*that* seemed quite extraordinary!

Perhaps the Rebbe knew about that vegetable store because he had met the owner and remembered the address. Maybe that is why he was checking to see if the store was still there. All I can say is that, at the time, I was floored, and although I had come reluctantly, I was suddenly eager to hear what he had to say.

LATER IN THE CONVERSATION, the Rebbe asked me what I was going to do with my life.

I didn't have a clue about what I was going to do, because I was pretty happy not doing anything other than learning Torah. And that was just fine with me. So this is what I told the Rebbe.

But he said, "You shouldn't just learn Torah—you should also teach Torah."

"Well, in a sense I am also teaching Torah," I replied. "After all, learning and teaching are closely related. And everybody in the *yeshivah* learns with a partner, so sometimes my partner knows less than me and I end up teaching him something, and sometimes I know less and he teaches me something."

"No, that's not what I mean," the Rebbe said. "You should set up a school for people who aren't in *yeshivah*, who don't have an opportunity to learn Torah like you do. A great many people are searching right now and it would be a great *mitzvah* to guide them. You have the talent to do this."

"You should leave Jerusalem," the Rebbe continued. "Go somewhere like Ashdod or Ashkelon, or any place where they have no *yeshivah*. Go where they can really use your talents."

I responded, "The rabbis in my *yeshivah* all think I should stay where I am and keep on learning."

When he heard that, the Rebbe smiled and said, "The rabbis in *yeshivahs* aren't always right. Think about what I said."

I promised to do that.

ALTHOUGH I HAD NOT ANTICIPATED THIS, upon my return to Israel, events were set in motion that ensured that my promise to the Rebbe was fulfilled.

As soon as I got back, Rabbi Mordechai Elefant, the head of my *yeshivah*—Israel Torah Research Institute (better known as Yeshivas Itri)—asked me to start a night program for foreign students. This proved so popular that, after a year, Rabbi Elefant asked me to expand it.

From there, I decided to branch out on my own and I opened a *yeshivah* in Jerusalem for American Jews who were new to Judaism. It was called Yeshivat HaMivtar. But, while I was able to start the *yeshivah* without a problem, I hadn't realized how difficult it would be to raise the money to sustain it. I was a little naive about that.

Because of financial issues, I was forced to move the *yeshivah* out of Jerusalem and I ended up taking it to Efrat—a new settlement about twenty kilometers from the city. There, I was able to keep it going for twenty-five years, up until I retired.

Rabbi Brovender (R.)
with his students at
the Tomb of Samuel.
1972.

*Courtesy of the
Brovender family*

The *yeshivah* had a philosophy similar to Chabad, in that each student
was asked to do something good for the Jewish people after graduating—
to go out into the world and teach others. Indeed, most of our graduates
ended up becoming rabbis or teachers. Today, I have alumni all over
the world dedicated to spreading Torah, and some of them have even
become emissaries of Chabad.

I myself also branched out. I went to Moscow for a year to head up
a *yeshivah* there, and then I went to London for a couple of years to do
the same thing. Today, I run WebYeshiva.org, in order to spread Judaism even further and allow people in far-flung places where there is no
Torah learning to access it online.

So it turned out that I did exactly what the Rebbe asked of me. He
had wanted me to leave Jerusalem and open a *yeshivah* in a place where
there was no such thing.

Thinking back on it, what he said turned out to be more of a predic-
tion than advice. Although he said, "It would be *good* if you did this," he
implied, "This is what you are *destined* to do."

I have no way of knowing for sure if that was his intention, but I do

Rabbi Brovender
(R.) with students
of Yeshivat Hamivtar.
1976.

*Courtesy of the
Brovender family*

believe that this was a distinct possibility, because the Rebbe didn't waste words.

And as for the blessing to have children, very soon thereafter my wife became pregnant and, as time went on, we became the parents of six children. So there, too, the Rebbe didn't waste words.

Mrs. Miriam Brovender

After I married my husband, Rabbi Chaim Brovender, in 1962, I found that I could not have children. I went to see a fertility expert in Brooklyn, who conducted a series of tests over several months and then sat me down and said, "Your test results are not good. I am quite certain that you will never have children, so I think you should consider adopting."

I was twenty-two years old at the time, and to me this verdict was unacceptable. "You are not G-d," I told him. "You are just a doctor. You have no right to pass such a judgment."

He didn't respond and I started to cry. I demanded the results of all the tests he had done and I left. I never went back to him again.

A short time later, we made *aliyah* to Israel — this was in 1965 — and I started treatment at the Tel HaShomer Hospital in Tel Aviv. It took three buses to get there from Jerusalem where we lived, but I felt it was worth it. Following a series of tests, I met with three doctors and asked them straight out, "Tell me honestly: What are my chances of having children?" Two gave me a bleak prognosis, but one — Professor Shlomo Mashiach, who continues to practice in the field — had a completely different attitude. Professor Mashiach said, "You have to pray to G-d so that He can help us help you."

This time I cried again, but they were tears of joy, as I was so moved by the sensitivity with which Professor Mashiach said these words. He was there to help me — but he also knew that he needed help from Above.

Nonetheless, his treatments initially did not yield results. During this time, we came to visit family in New York and decided to go see the Rebbe for a blessing. For years, I had wanted to go see him and I was excited that I finally had the opportunity.

Our appointment was for two in the morning, and I made sure to submit a letter in advance, stating that I was coming specifically to receive a blessing for children. The very moment I entered the Rebbe's office, I felt sure that my request would be granted because I felt enveloped in warmth. Suddenly, I was calm and comfortable.

My parents and my husband were present, and the Rebbe first spoke to them. I recall that he tried to encourage my husband to do outreach work. My husband demurred, but the Rebbe pressed him, even saying to my father, "I want you to be my lawyer and convince your son-in-law that he should do this."

After a few minutes, the Rebbe's secretary knocked on the door, signaling that our time was up. Before I knew it, we were taking our leave, and I was on the verge of tears. The Rebbe had seemingly forgotten to give me the blessing that I had requested in writing.

But, of course, the Rebbe did not forget. He looked at me and said, "May we hear good news this coming year."

Those few words jumped out at me, and I left exhilarated. He said it with such compassion and sincerity that it was all I needed.

All throughout our trip back to Israel, I kept hearing his words in my mind, and upon return, I resumed the fertility treatments, certain that this time they would work. And they did.

Only three months after I received the blessing from the Rebbe, I

Rabbi and Mrs. Brovender surrounded by their children and grandchildren.

Courtesy of the Brovender family

found myself pregnant for the first time — after eight years of marriage! Of course, I informed the Rebbe and received a blessing for an easy birth, which helped me remain calm when I went into the delivery room.

I gave birth to Na'ama Chana, my oldest, and then I asked the Rebbe for more blessings, and he blessed me again and again. I gave birth to Eliezer Menashe, Efrat Freidel, Shira Beila, Batsheva, and Bruria Liba, my youngest.

Mrs. Brovender with her first daughter, Na'ama Chana.
Courtesy of the Brovender family

They are my gems — gems that were given to me by G-d through the Rebbe's blessings.

But my story continues.

We have since been blessed with grandchildren and great-grandchildren. And all of them are here because of the blessings I received from the Rebbe so many years ago. Each birth is a gift. Each birth is a miracle. Each time we witness a birth of another one of our descendants, we witness another miracle.

ENDURING ADVERSITY, DISCOVERING SERENITY

RABBI EPHRAIM STURM

Dining Clubs against Assimilation

The best solutions are always the doable ones

Rabbi Ephraim Sturm served the National Council of Young Israel for forty-five years, including thirty-six years as the organization's Executive Vice President and Chief Executive Officer. He also served as a chaplain in the New York State Guard and taught medical ethics at the New York College of Podiatric Medicine. He was interviewed in his home in October of 2007.

I first met the Rebbe when I went to him to discuss my mother's illness.

I did so, not because I was a *chasid* — in fact, I was educated in schools of opponents to Chasidism. But when my mother fell ill, and no one in the academic world, of which I was a part, could help me, I went to the Rebbe.

We all knew that the Rebbe was the best address for problems like this and his door was never closed to anyone. Indeed, it was common knowledge in the Jewish world — it was in the public domain, so to speak — that to get good advice, to get a compassionate answer to a difficult question, to hear a solution to a complex dilemma, you went to the Rebbe. And that's why I went.

My mother's doctors could not agree on whether they should operate or not. An operation offered a possibility of a cure, but it also carried risks, which were much greater in the 1960s. Yet, doing nothing meant that things would go on as they were, with the inevitable ending.

As a son, I was torn. And my mother couldn't make the decision. So I went to the Rebbe.

The Rebbe didn't know me, didn't know my mother, didn't know anything about my family, but when I told him my dilemma, he looked at me and I saw tears in his eyes. He reacted as if he was my brother.

I want to describe the expression on his face — how his intense blue eyes filled with tears — but I can't do it justice. He had a holy look and such an air of compassion about him. I felt an immediate heart connection — as they say, "words that come from the heart, enter the heart" — and I felt that this was a man of truth, a man of G-d. And even if he said nothing to me, I would have gone out with something, just having seen him.

He advised that they should operate, but his advice was not as important as his reaction and his sensitivity.

I must stress that I didn't go representing Young Israel; I said nothing about being the chief executive officer of Young Israel. I was just a Jew asking for his blessing and advice on a personal matter. And for him to show such empathy, such emotion, such care and concern — that, in itself, was amazing.

It's really remarkable how he could relate to every individual, to every community, with the same intensity. I'm sure that decisions made by the Rebbe on the world scene were made by him with the same depth of understanding that he showed to every individual who came to see him about a minor issue and with the same depth of concern that he showed me.

Rabbi Sturm and his parents walk down the aisle at his wedding.

Courtesy of the Sturm family

AND THEN THERE CAME A TIME — in the late 1960s — when I went to him in an official capacity. This was because I had discovered that too many Orthodox boys and girls who were going to out-of-town colleges were dropping *Yiddishkeit* and intermarrying. At first the number was three percent, but it was rising rapidly and this alarmed me.

Young Israel was founded as an organization dedicated to making Orthodox Judaism more relevant to young American Jews, and here was an issue that went to the core of our mission. So I called together all the officers of Young Israel and I said to them, "We have a problem!"

We agonized over it, and we decided to go ask the top American Jewish leaders what we should do. Now I can't tell you exactly what each one said because I don't remember. But I do remember that one of them said we have to make sure that colleges hire more Orthodox professors. Well, that was not in our power. Another said that we have to make sure that the Jewish high schools imbue *Yiddishkeit* in their students so that they are able to withstand the pressures of college.

The Rebbe stops to speak with an individual as he heads out of the synagogue.
17 Tishrei, 5737-1976.

Levi Freidin,
The Living Archive

How could we do that? Another said that Young Israel should issue a proclamation that nobody is allowed to go to an out-of-town college. We did not have that kind of clout.

And then we went to the Rebbe, who was already playing a significant, behind-the-scenes role in our organization, with many members of the executive board seeking his sage advice. Indeed, the Rebbe's advice proved the wisest and most fascinating.

The Rebbe had the ability to speak to the individual while considering the broad issues involved — to look past the symptoms and go to the heart of the problem. He made us see that we had to find a way for Orthodox Jewish boys and girls to congregate on the college campus while at the same time allowing them to be part of the university.

He didn't force his solution on us. He merely said what he thought without claiming that this was "the" answer. His was just a suggestion, and he made it clear that he would not love us any less if we rejected it.

"Consider the American educational system," he began, as he went on to explain the specific character of US campuses and how they differed from German ones with which he was personally familiar:

"In Berlin, a religious Jew had to defend his religion; he had to be able to answer Germans who challenged him, and in order to do that he had to know the philosophy of his religion. But Americans are not interested in religious philosophies. They are more interested in consistency. The average American wants sincerity and honesty in religion, whatever religion anyone chooses to follow. And if a Jew is consistent in his beliefs and actions, the average American will respect him."

The Rebbe then explained what consistency means for the average Orthodox Jew in America. Religious boys and girls start out wanting to be consistent — to follow the precepts of Judaism. Before leaving home, they promise their parents: "Don't worry. When I'm away at college, I'll observe Shabbat and I'll keep kosher. I'll have cornflakes every day for breakfast, cottage cheese every day for lunch, and salad for dinner.... I'll manage for four years." Maybe they mean it, maybe they don't. But, even if we assume that they *do* mean it, can they do it?

The Rebbe painted a picture of a young man sitting in a college dining room with his non-Jewish peers. For how long is he going to eat cottage cheese every day and keep his *yarmulke* on his head? What is

Rebbe's Plan for Cornell

FORWARD
FOUNDED APRIL 22, 1897

...Reform Seder").

It would be worthwhile for your readers to know the history of the National Council of Young Israel's more than 40 years of college kosher dining clubs, so that they may judge if it is worthwhile.

In the 1950s we noticed that the rate of intermarriage on the college scene was reaching the then-alarming rate of 3%, with the vector indicating a rising tendency. Even those opposed to intermarriage were tolerant of or even encouraged inter-dating. The national officers, after I alerted them to this creeping danger, agreed with me that we should consult with the foremost religious leaders for suggestions and guidance.

We met with such notables as Rabbi Moshe Feinstein, Rabbi Aaron Kotler, Rabbi Joseph B. Soloveitchik, the rebbe of Lubavitch, and other rabbinic leaders, in addition to some Orthodox professors.

Some religious leaders said that we should use the influence of Young Israel to strengthen the religious commitments on the high school level so that later the college student could withstand the temptation of campus life. Others suggested that we urge more Orthodox academics to become involved with the daily life of the Jewish college student. Another religious leader asked that we campaign against young men and women going to college, and to Ivy League colleges in particular.

*   *   *   *   *

As worthwhile as these three major lines of suggestion may have been, Young Israel did not perceive itself as the organization qualified to undertake any of them. Young Israel had no input in local yeshiva curriculum, which was in the purview of Torah Umesorah. Not being an academic organization, Young Israel did not have the format to relate to college professors. Knowing its membership and their drive to send their children

---
How long could a student live on lettuce, tomatoes and cottage cheese?

---

to college, Young Israel reasoned that it would be useless to advocate raising a non-college-educated generation.

Young Israel was frustrated until we met with the rebbe of Lubavitch, who is alleged to have been a graduate of the Sorbonne. The rebbe analyzed the dynamics preceding inter-dating, which can and usually did lead to inter-marriage. He stated that unlike the European university students who challenged one another's philosophical and theological commitments, the American student was extremely liberal with deep respect for the religious belief of others. He added that the American college student respected integrity and consisten-

cy in the observance of religious belief and abhorred hypocrisy and waffling.

The projects therefore called, according to the rebbe, for a method whereby the student could fulfill his/her religious need with the least amount of obstacles. Having ruled out that philosophy and social pressures were the most salient hurdles, the rebbe stated that food became a pivotal issue. The rebbe asked rhetorically, How long can a student subsist on lettuce, tomatoes and cottage cheese purchased at the college cafeteria (even assuming the unlikelihood that these products were kosher)? Furthermore he asked, could a male student wear a yarmulke in the cafeteria? Remember this was in the 1950s, when even the most Orthodox Jewish lawyers, doctors and accountants did not wear their *kippot* in court, in the hospital or in their private offices. The rebbe continued to point out that in the cafeteria Jewish boys and girls would be eating with non-Jews, which in itself was a step toward inter-dating.

The Lubavitcher rebbe then extolled the virtues of the establishment of a kosher dining-club, which would provide kosher food in addition to the Jewish atmosphere conducive to the observance of mitzvot, such as washing, benching, *zmiros* and *divrei torah*.

When this suggestion was approved in principal by the other *gedoylim*, Young Israel proceeded to implement its kosher dining-club project.

For the record, an outstanding Talmud student and former rabbi in a Young Israel synagogue came to his Orthodox commitment through a chance atten-

An article written by Rabbi Sturm for *The Forward*
about his meeting with the Rebbe.
Courtesy of the Sturm family

he going to do when a girl says to him, "Take a taste of my lunch, it's delicious!" How can he reject her offer? After a while, the non-Jewish peer group will pressure him—not because they *mean* to pressure him, not because they are opposed to what he is doing, but because that's just how life is. And in the liberal atmosphere of a college campus, it is difficult not to yield to such pressure.

And then came his advice: "What you have to do is create a program to bring together all the young Jewish students in one place at their most vulnerable time. That vulnerable time is not in the classroom when they are each occupied with their own notes and their own marks, but outside of the classroom. So the best thing you can do is establish kosher dining clubs on college campuses."

When he said that, a lightbulb lit up in my head. This was the answer I had been looking for. This was a practical solution and something

Members of the National Council of Young Israel, including Rabbi Sturm, embark on a trip to Israel.

Courtesy of the Sturm family

that we were able to do. We could bring the Jewish boys and girls together in the kosher dining rooms, and thus ensure that they would meet and date and marry each other.

Our first club was at Cornell, and it became the flagship of our operation. It was in a B'nai B'rith building and served only kosher food to Jewish students. On Shabbat, about 200 people came for services and meals, and on Passover, we had to have two *seders* to accommodate all the participants. And the kosher dining clubs multiplied from there until,

Rabbi Ephraim Sturm
Courtesy of the Sturm family.

when I left Young Israel, we had seventeen of them.

Of all the advice that we were given, the only one that was practical and workable, the only one that we could really tackle, was the advice to start the kosher dining clubs that came from the Rebbe.

Today people might make the case that it's viable to go to an out-of-town college because there are so many kosher products available in every American supermarket. But thirty or forty years ago, it was not so. Back then things were quite different, yet the Rebbe understood that generation and knew what had to be done. The proof is that his solution worked!

YEARS LATER, when I taught medical ethics at the New York College of Podiatric Medicine, I learned that sometimes the doctor knows the correct medicine that will cure the patient, but the patient can't take it. So he must find a solution that will both enable a cure *and* be compatible with the patient's system and medical situation. That is something the Rebbe knew very well, and that is what he taught me — if you are going to give advice, give advice that is doable. The Rebbe understood that.

Rabbi Sturm
participating in a
farbrengen in 770.
19 Kislev, 5744-1983.

Yossi Melamed,
The Living Archive

When he advised a certain course of action, he did so knowing that the person would be able to carry it out.

But even more so, he had a way of empowering the person.

When I came to talk to him about my mother, I left feeling empowered to deal with the problem. When I came to talk to him about the problem of assimilation on college campuses, I left smiling from ear to ear because he didn't just give me good advice, he empowered me to act on it. Had someone asked me before I walked in if I could build seventeen kosher clubs on college campuses, I would have said "No way!" But after I saw the Rebbe, I knew I could do it. He told me what to do and he gave me the courage to do it. ■

MRS. RHODA FRIEDLAND

Would You
Do Me a Favor?

*Sometimes the greatest miracles happen
when you do nothing*

Mrs. Rhoda Friedland was one of the founding members of the Jewish community in Monsey, New York, where she organized an outreach group for Jewish women. She also was a frequent contributor to various publications of the National Committee for the Furtherance of Jewish Education. She was interviewed in her home in August of 2015.

My family was living in Crown Heights—an upscale Jewish neighborhood of mostly nonobservant residents—when the Previous Lubavitcher Rebbe, Rabbi Yosef Yitzchak Schneersohn, arrived in America in 1940 and established the Chabad Headquarters at 770 Eastern Parkway. His settling in Crown Heights caused some consternation among those who had been living in the area for many years, as they feared the changes that might be brought about by the new Chasidic community.

Unlike many of his neighbors, my father, Benjamin Horwitz, was more interested than affronted. He decided to walk over to 770 to see for himself what the Lubavitchers were all about. He returned later in the day and announced to us, "This is the kind of Judaism I've been seeking all of my life." Thereupon, he began learning Torah and Chasidic teachings with Rabbi Meir Greenberg and with Rabbi Menachem Mendel Schneerson, the Previous Rebbe's son-in-law, who would later become the Rebbe.

My father also became a supporter of the National Committee for the Furtherance of Jewish Education (NCFJE), an umbrella organization for a number of educational initiatives, among them the Release Time program for public school students, anti-missionary activities and summer camps. I myself volunteered to write for NCFJE and did so for many years.

Working with the head of the organization, Rabbi J. J. Hecht, led to a close friendship between our families. At one point, my husband

The *sheva brachot* celebration after Rhoda and Everett's wedding. July, 1947.

Courtesy of the Friedland family

and I confided in him that, due to a medical condition, I would not be able to bear children, and we were considering adoption. Hearing this, Rabbi Hecht insisted that we meet with the Previous Rebbe to ask for his advice and his blessing before making any decision.

I vividly recall the moment when my husband and I, together with Rabbi Hecht, entered the Rebbe's room. Although he was wheelchair-bound due to the travails he had endured in the Soviet Union, his face was shining with a special radiance.

During our audience, which took place on a Thursday night in January of 1950, just two days before the Previous Rebbe passed away, Rabbi Hecht spoke into the Rebbe's ear and explained our problem.

"Did they go to doctors?" the Rebbe asked.

"Yes, they did," Rabbi Hecht replied, "but the doctors said they probably won't have children."

At that the Rebbe laughed. He actually threw back his head and laughed. And then he said, "They will have children, and they will have healthy children."

When we left the Rebbe, Rabbi Hecht slapped my husband on the back and said, "I'm going to be the *sandek* and hold the baby for his *brit*."

But nothing happened for a time.

MEANWHILE, I WAS EXPERIENCING A SERIES OF HEALTH PROBLEMS, and the doctors insisted that I must have an operation that would end any hope of my having children.

I reported their prognosis to Rabbi Menachem Mendel Schneerson, who took over the leadership of Chabad a year after the Previous Rebbe's passing. (In those days it was possible to just knock on the Rebbe's door to enter and speak with him.) And each time I went to him, his answer was the same, "If my father-in-law said that you will have children, you will have children. No operation! Get another opinion."

The Previous Rebbe at his US citizenship ceremony, with his son-in-law the Rebbe at his side. 16 Adar, 5709-1949.

The Living Archive

On one occasion the Rebbe sent me to see his wife's doctor, who also adamantly insisted that I needed surgery. I reported this to the Rebbe. While I was speaking to the Rebbe, this doctor called him and reiterated what she had said to me, telling the Rebbe that I would lose my life if he prevented the operation. The Rebbe hung up the phone, looked at me and simply said, "See another doctor."

I made an appointment with a prominent Manhattan doctor. After examining me, this doctor picked up the phone and made arrangements for my surgery at Mt. Sinai Hospital. "In two weeks you're going to have this operation," he declared. "No arguments!"

This finally convinced me that I had no choice, so I went back to the Rebbe to thank him for all of his advice and concern, and to inform him that I'd be having the surgery. After he heard me out, the Rebbe said, "Would you do me a favor?"

"Of course," I replied, "How can I help you?"

Benjamin, Lenny and
Sammy Friedland. 1957.

*Courtesy of the
Friedland family*

"See one more doctor," the Rebbe said. "Any doctor you choose, as long as he is a professor."

AS A FAVOR TO THE REBBE, I called my cousin who had recently had a baby to ask for the name of her doctor who had been highly recommended, and I made an appointment within the next few days.

After his examination, this doctor said, "I understand that there are problems, but I must tell you that there is also a possibility that you're pregnant. I want you to go home and begin bedrest, while I study the results of your tests in my lab." Two days later he called me and confirmed that I was pregnant.

I stayed in bed for most of the pregnancy. At one point, Dr. Avrohom Seligson, whom the Rebbe had asked to see me frequently, said that there was a chance that the baby was lost. He called the Rebbe to tell him that. A few hours later, the phone rang and, when my husband answered, it was the Rebbe, who said, "Don't worry. You will have this baby, and it will be a healthy baby."

I gave birth to my eldest son, Binyomin Mendel, on Passover of 1952. And after that, we were blessed with two more sons — all because I did the Rebbe "a favor."

DR. YITZCHAK BLOCK

The Reluctant Philosopher

*Revelations from the great thinker
who was too humble*

A professor of philosophy at the University of Western Ontario in Canada, Dr. Yitzchak Block also served there as the Chabad campus emissary. He was interviewed in his home in February of 2008.

I grew up in the 1930s in Nashville, Tennessee, during the Great Depression, in a Jewish environment that was predominantly Conservative. None of my peers—no child my age—came from a home that observed Shabbat, although some homes (like ours) kept kosher.

It was not until 1943, when my father passed away after a protracted illness, that I was introduced to something else. I was thirteen years old, and hardly anyone in the family attended my Bar Mitzvah because they were at my father's bedside in the hospital—although just how serious his condition was had not been revealed to me. The rabbi tried to make me feel better about the poor attendance, promising, "We will have a proper Bar Mitzvah ceremony for you when your father gets out of the hospital." But that never happened because shortly thereafter, my father passed away.

There was something that everybody in my community held by, and that was saying *Kaddish* for the departed. This meant I began attending the local Orthodox synagogue for the daily prayers to recite this special text in memory of my father. But something interesting occurred: I came to enjoy the synagogue, so I continued to participate in the daily prayers even after the eleven months of reciting *Kaddish* ended. I started keeping Shabbat, and by the time I was fourteen, I had become fully Torah observant, which meant that I was seen as a fanatic by my peers. But I didn't care.

Being Torah observant proved a challenge, however, when I had to miss the basketball tournaments held on Shabbat, especially since I was the star of the team and a lot of pressure was put on me to participate.

I was torn—and I still consider it the biggest test of my life—but, thanks to my mother, I was able to stand up to the pressure. She herself was not Torah observant, but when she saw me wavering, she said to me, "You have to make up your mind: either you are going to keep Shabbat or not. You can't have it both ways." And that did it. I stuck to my resolve, and I have her to thank for it.

In 1949, Rabbi Zalman Posner, a Chabad emissary, came to town—an unusual sight with his uncut beard and *tzitzit* hanging out. And yet, to me, he seemed like the real thing, a Jew totally

Yitzchak Block playing baseball in the yard of his house in Nashville. Circa 1940.
Courtesy of the Block family

dedicated to the truth of Torah. He ignited within me an interest to seriously study Torah texts at a time when I was, instead, seriously studying philosophy at Vanderbilt University.

I managed to combine the two, and that is where my story really begins.

AT VANDERBILT I WAS INTRODUCED to the philosophy of Kant and Plato, which mesmerized me, and I was swept up in the study of their ideas. It was a pure pleasure for me to study philosophy. At the time, I had the good fortune to learn under Professors Christopher Salmon, a visiting scholar from Oxford; and Arthur Smallion from Harvard, who also made sure that I was accepted to his alma mater for graduate studies in philosophy.

However, I wasn't sure that I should go there. The University of Edinburgh in Scotland had also accepted me, and that exotic location appealed to me more. Meanwhile, I decided to spend my summer vacation—this was the summer of 1952—at the Chabad *yeshivah* in New York.

When I first got there, I thought it wasn't for me. I had been used to academic study in the silence of the library, but in the *yeshivah*, the students were yelling at each other as they passionately debated the Talmud. It was a foreign world to me, and I decided to go home to Nashville instead. But when I called my mother to say I was coming home, she talked me out of it. I'm sure that she wanted me to return—she was lonely with her children living far from her. But she also sensed what was best for me and, for the second time at a crucial point in my life, she stepped in to make sure I made the right choice.

I decided to give *yeshivah* a try, and I came to like it very much. While there, I had the opportunity to get an audience with the Rebbe, who had taken over the leadership of Chabad-Lubavitch only the year before. He was a young man then, just fifty years old, and I vividly remember that he still had a black beard. I also remember his amazing blue eyes.

A lecture at Vanderbilt University. 1954.

*Vanderbilt University Special Collections and
University Archives*

Yitzchak Block. 1948.
Courtesy of the Block family.

We talked about Plato, and I was very impressed that the Rebbe called him "Platon," which is how the Greek scholars refer to him, and it struck me that the Rebbe must have a deep knowledge of the subject.

He said that the philosophy of Plato was very cruel. I was shocked—I had never heard anybody say that about Plato before. He was obviously referring to Plato's belief that you had to take children away from their parents and train them to be subservient to the state which, I had to admit, is a cruel approach to raising children.

Although I never discussed philosophy with the Rebbe again, his view of Plato influenced me, and eventually I abandoned the study of Plato and become a student of Aristotle instead.

During that summer I attended an amazing *farbrengen* over which the Rebbe presided, and I remember that he offered me a piece of cake from his table. I said, "No, thank you, I had cake already," but, judging by the reaction of the crowd, I realized that I had been wrong to refuse. I just thought I was being polite when I demurred. After all, who was I to take the Rebbe's cake?

The Rebbe smiled and put the cake back on the plate, but afterwards, Rabbi Posner came to me with another piece from the Rebbe and said, "I suggest you make a blessing and eat it." I did and thought nothing much of it. Only years later did Rabbi Posner tell me something which the Rebbe said at the time. He was supposed to tell it to me then, but he didn't; I guess he felt I wasn't ready to hear it. The Rebbe had said, "*Zog em az sof sof vet er veren ah chasid. Er darf nit farshpilen di tzeit*—Tell him that sooner or later, he will become a *chasid*. He shouldn't waste time."

When the summer ended and I was leaving the *yeshivah*, I was still unsure where to go. So, I wrote to the Rebbe asking whether I should

pursue graduate studies at Harvard or at Edinburgh. The Rebbe responded that it should be Harvard, and he underlined the word for emphasis. So that is what I did.

Studying at Harvard was difficult. When I enrolled, I thought I knew philosophy, but I quickly saw that I didn't know anything. At Harvard there were graduate students who knew more than some of my professors at Vanderbilt, and this is no exaggeration. I was studying ten hours a day, and I was still unable to keep up.

This depressed me terribly, and I began to lose interest in philosophy, especially as I didn't think I'd be able to pass the exams at the end of the course. These exams were brutal; they were administered over a period of two weeks, and only a third of the class was expected to pass. I knew I would not be one of the lucky ones.

I began to yearn to return to *yeshivah*, and one day I got on the bus and came back to Brooklyn. My *yeshivah* buddies were all very happy to see me, and I felt great—until I saw the Rebbe, that is.

Yitzchak Block lifts the Torah in 770 as the Rebbe looks on.
3 Tishrei, 5743-1982.

The Living Archive

"I've decided to return to *yeshivah*," I told him proudly. But he seemed unimpressed. "I think you will come to regret that you gave up your profession," he replied.

He must have seen the crestfallen expression on my face because he smiled and said, "You must have courage."

I walked out stunned, but I got back on the bus and resumed my studies at Harvard. It was very hard, but I qualified for a Master's Degree in philosophy, although I failed the exams for a Ph.D.

I wrote to the Rebbe, again telling him that I wanted to return to *yeshivah* because I failed my exams, but the Rebbe would not agree to that. "Take them again," he responded. "You are smart, and there is no reason you shouldn't pass." And sure enough, I passed the second time and went on to write my dissertation on Aristotle. But this was also difficult for me, and I might not have finished it were it not for the Rebbe nudging me all the while, "Finish ... finish your dissertation."

So, finally, I did—in 1958. It was called "Aristotle's Theory of Perception," and it proved quite an original dissertation in many ways. The Rebbe urged me to write an article based on my novel ideas, which I did. But I had trouble publishing it in an academic journal because my interpretations went against the accepted thinking of Aristotelian philosophers of the day.

I confided in the Rebbe how difficult it was for me to publish, and he responded with a brilliant suggestion: "Ask one of your Harvard professors to intervene on your behalf."

I would never have thought to do that in my wildest dreams, because I knew that what I had written was very controversial, and it was absurd to think that any professor would stick his neck out for me. But, because the Rebbe advised it, I asked a top professor at Harvard, Dr. Roger Alderman, who had liked my ideas, for help. He agreed to take up my cause and convinced Dr. Ludwig Edelstein, the editor of the *Journal of Greek Theology* at Johns Hopkins University, to publish my article.

That article got me a lot of attention. Indeed, I became famous because of it, and I was able to publish many more papers. This was all because of the Rebbe's foresight. I was a nobody, and the Rebbe turned me into a well-respected scholar. But it was not until later that I understood why he did it.

The Rebbe shares a word with Yitzchak Block as he distributes *lekach* at the door of his *sukkah*. Hoshana Rabbah, 5748-1987.
Yossi Melamed, The Living Archive

Rose Block, Yitzchak's mother.
Courtesy of the Block family

HAVING FINISHED MY PH.D., I once again returned to *yeshivah* and, finally, the Rebbe let me stay for a while. During this time, my mother came to visit and I arranged an audience for her with the Rebbe. She later told me that in that meeting she confided to the Rebbe just how lonely she felt — she was a widow, with all of her three children living far away. She said that when she lit Shabbat candles on Friday night, she felt so terribly alone.

The Rebbe heard her out and said, "You don't have to feel lonely, because G-d is with you all the time."

His words were like a balm to her. From that point on she stopped feeling lonely. It utterly amazed me how the Rebbe turned her entire outlook around with just a few simple words.

Another thing that utterly amazed me was that, although the Rebbe met my mother only once, he never forgot about her. I recall an instance years later when he was giving out *lekach*, honey cake, on Hoshana Rabbah. He called me over and gave me a piece to send to my mother. "How is she feeling?" he asked. Truly, his level of caring was hard to fathom.

I CONTINUED IN THE *YESHIVAH* with the aim of getting my rabbinic ordination. But when I told the Rebbe about my plan, he responded, "*Lo mit an aleph!* — Under no circumstances whatsoever!"

That is not to suggest that he discouraged my Torah studies. Far from it. I vividly recall three times that I came to see him when he told me to learn the *Kitzur Shulchan Aruch* (the abridged Code of Jewish Law). I got the message and, believe me, today I know it better than most rabbis. What he didn't want me to do is go around with the title "Rabbi." He wanted me to be known as "Professor."

Yitzchak Block
addresses a group of
Jewish college students
in Crown Heights.

Courtesy of Jay Rochlin

It was only after I started teaching that I began to grasp his reason. When Jewish students would see me wearing a *yarmulke*, many would come over to me to discuss doubts about religion that were troubling them. Some of these young men studied in *yeshivah* during the day and pursued secular studies at night in local schools such as City College, Brooklyn College, or Rutgers University, all places where I taught for a time in my early years as a philosophy professor. They had questions they were afraid to pose to their *yeshivah* teachers, but they felt comfortable asking me because I had obtained a Ph.D. from Harvard, yet I had remained Torah observant.

And now I finally understood what the Rebbe knew all along—that with my degree and my reputation as an Aristotelian scholar, I was in a position to have a major impact on other Jews, particularly young Jews. I would never have been able to do that if I had quit graduate school and returned to *yeshivah*; even if I had become a rabbi, I would not have had as much influence on others as I did in my capacity as professor. I didn't even have to open my mouth—just being who I was, a respected philosopher who was religious, spoke volumes to all those who met me. And I do believe that quite a few secular Jews came closer to Torah

Yitzchak Block with
a student. 1965.

Courtesy of
Michael Cole

because they saw, through my example, that there was no contradiction between being observant and being respected in academia.

The Rebbe knew that this was how it would be. He wanted me to become as important in the world of philosophy as I could possibly be because, the more important I was, the more influence I could have on my students. In retrospect, I have no doubt that that's what he had in mind all along.

DURING THE TIME THAT I WAS TEACHING PHILOSOPHY at Brooklyn College, I arranged, in conjunction with the Brooklyn Hillel Foundation, for some of the students to meet the Rebbe.

It was a very special audience with about thirty or thirty-five students attending. One among them asked him, "What is it that you do? What is the function of a Rebbe?"

The Rebbe smiled and answered (and I am paraphrasing):

"Do you see that switch over there? The light fixture is connected to the power plant through a network of wires that run through that switch.

"The Baal Shem Tov, the founder of the Chasidic movement, made it his mission to proclaim that every Jew, without exception, is connected to the power source and that, if one searches, that connection will be manifest." One can never know what will complete the circuit, the Rebbe explained, but when the switch is flipped, the soul will be activated and it will come to life.

"Some people need help to locate that switch. And the function of a Rebbe is to help every Jew find their switch, express their connection to G-d, and connect with the power source."

THE REBBE WAS CONSTANTLY ENCOURAGING ME to put myself out front — to show myself to people as a *chasid* who was a force in philosophy. This meant that I had to write papers, attend conferences and give guest lectures. Without his prodding, I would not have done any of it, but this is what made my career.

There came a time when I was invited to speak at an important conference at Brown University, but, to my chagrin, after I agreed to do it I discovered that I had been scheduled to speak on Shabbat. I had managed to do that in the past without violating Shabbat when conferences were held in hotels, but on this occasion the conference was held on campus, which meant traveling a considerable distance, and I did not know what to do. I wrote to the Rebbe asking his advice but did not hear back. I wrote again and again heard nothing. I called — no reply. It was not until it was almost time for the conference that I got the Rebbe's answer, advising me to tell the conference organizers that, for urgent reasons, I needed to return to New York the day before, so could they please switch my speaking time to Friday morning.

"Oh, my G-d!" I said to myself. "How do I do something like that? It's a week before the conference!" However, by then I had known that if the Rebbe says something I'd better listen.

When I called the person in charge, he said, "I was just about to call you! I wanted to ask you to switch to Friday morning because the professor scheduled to speak at that time has come down with the flu."

I was amazed! Later I would joke that the Rebbe had to give that other professor the flu to get me out of that predicament. This way, I got to speak at an important conference, and I made it to New York in

Yitzchak Block with
his children. 1970.

*Courtesy of
Michael Cole*

time to spend Shabbat with the Rebbe.

At another conference at Yale University, I met someone from the University of Western Ontario, and this meeting led to my being offered a prestigious position there. I was not sure if I should accept it because I was worried that, as a lone *chasid*—indeed as the lone Jew on the faculty—I would not fit in, but the Rebbe convinced me to take that job and move to London, Ontario. And this is where I have been ever since, doing my part as the Rebbe's emissary, in addition to my professorial duties. Among other things, I took over the Hillel House there and organized Passover *seders* and holiday meals for the Jewish students on campus, while my wife started a Jewish nursery school and then a Jewish elementary school in town.

I have said it before, and I will say it again—the Rebbe is entirely responsible for my professional success.

From the very moment that I set foot in Lubavitch, the Rebbe was working overtime to make sure that I would become a famous professor. And he pulled it off—even against my will, so to speak.

Exactly how he did it, I am not sure. But here I stand as proof. And, because he did, hundreds of people who have looked to me as a role model are Torah-observant today. Just as he had envisioned. ■

RABBI DAVID H. HILL

The Unforgettable Chickens

The heroism of Russian Jews and the Americans
who joined the fight to help them

Rabbi David H. Hill served as vice chair of the National Conference on Soviet Jewry and ran Operation Lifeline, which sent American Jews behind the Iron Curtain to teach Torah and distribute religious articles during the 1960s and '70s. Rabbi Hill also headed the National Council of Young Israel from 1961 to 1965. He was interviewed in his home in Queens, New York, in December of 2010.

At a very young age, I joined Young Israel, an organization that sought to make Judaism relevant to young American Jews and to welcome those who were estranged from their religion. As an adult, I became active as a volunteer and, after a time, I became a delegate to the National Council of Young Israel, the body that governed all the Young Israel branches; later, I became an officer and, in 1961, I became national president.

As president, it was my goal to figure out what the best thing would be for Young Israel to do for the Jewish people—not only in America, but also in the Soviet Union. The latter issue was particularly close to my heart because I had been born in Latvia, although my family immigrated to the US in 1930 when I was nine. Nonetheless, I identified with the Jews stuck back there.

In trying to figure out the best way to guide Young Israel, I decided to seek counsel of the sages of the generation, and among those I met with was the Lubavitcher Rebbe.

When I came into the Rebbe's office—a simple room filled with books—I sat across from him, while he sat behind his desk never taking his eyes off me. When he spoke, he was very direct. "In which language would you like to converse?" he asked, and when I answered, "If you don't mind, in Yiddish," he seemed surprised: "How did it come about that the American president of Young Israel speaks Yiddish?"

"It is my native language," I responded, and then I asked him, "What do you think should be the primary focus of Young Israel for the next ten years?"

The Rebbe's office today.

Courtesy of Yanky Ascher

The Rebbe expressed support for our work and encouraged us to do more. As he spoke, it became apparent to me that he knew everything that was happening in Young Israel. For example, he knew that we had only one kosher kitchen—at Cornell University. And he said to me, "Your primary focus for the next ten years should be Jewish college students who have little Jewish background. You have to give them a place to congregate—a place that not only has kosher food, but also educates them in Torah. So, you should organize centers like this on at least ten college campuses."

"Excuse me, Rebbe," I countered, "but where am I going to find the money for this?"

The Rebbe replied, "When I ask my *chasidim* to collect money for one of my activities, they get it done. You don't have those kind of *chasidim*?" And when he said this, he had a big smile on this face.

His other advice was that we should find a common denominator that Reform, Conservative and Orthodox could rally around—some issue that everybody agreed on. One such issue that the Rebbe suggested was opposing missionary activity aimed at the Jews. Another, which he said should be at the top of our list, was supporting Israel.

(The common denominator was very important to him and, much later, when a Sephardi synagogue in Brooklyn—Congregation Magen David—wanted to join Young Israel and we insisted that they change their prayer service to conform with Ashkenazi customs, he objected. He immediately sent a message telling us that there was no basis for rejecting Sephardi customs, and that we should accept the Sephardim without such a condition. We heard him, and we followed his directive.)

At the end of the audience, I asked him, "What can I do for the Jews of the Soviet Union?" I explained that I had asked that question because of my family's roots, adding, "I remember my mother telling me that one of the members of our family was Mordechai Dubin, who made heroic efforts to save the Previous Rebbe when he was arrested in Leningrad." (I was referring to the Rebbe's father-in-law and predecessor, Rabbi Yosef Yitzchak Schneersohn.)

Upon hearing this, the Rebbe invited me to come another time so that we could specifically discuss the subject of Russian Jewry.

Rabbi Mordechai Dubin (R.)

Courtesy of the Kramer family

The Rebbe shares
a moment with an
individual at the door
of his office.
Erev Yom Kippur,
5741-1980.

Levi Freidin,
The Living Archive

WHEN WE MET AGAIN, the Rebbe said, "Because of the danger to the Jews
in Russia, I never give out any information to people outside Lubavitch
concerning the way we are helping them. But I will give you some names
and addresses, and I will open other doors for you. However, I have two
conditions. The first—if you are going to send them rabbis, send rabbis
with beards. Why? Because the average Russian Jew who remembers
a rabbi, remembers a rabbi with a beard. If you send in people who are
clean-shaven, the Russian Jews won't accept them. The second—you
are dealing with life and death over there, so you can't give any interviews to the press. Otherwise, you will be putting people's lives at risk.
It must be *bli pirsum*—without publicity."

I gave him my word. And then he gave me between forty and fifty
names of people throughout the Soviet Union.

At that time, there was no other underground apparatus in Russia
except for Lubavitch, and the only teachers of Judaism in most places
were Lubavitcher *chasidim*. They all worked under the Rebbe's direction,
and they reported to him. These were the people whose names the
Rebbe gave me. He also gave me advice on how to train my volunteers,
each of whom would go over there for about two weeks.

My task was to teach these volunteers how to get through Soviet passport and customs checks, what to take with them, what they could or
could not write down, what they had to commit to memory, how to
make a phone call from a phone booth, how to hail a taxi. For example,
I taught them: "Never take a taxi in front of your hotel, and when you
give them the destination, never give the correct house number."

Along the way, I was also asked to train volunteers from the Agudah,
an organization that was opposed to the secular government in Israel
and that didn't want to encourage the Russian Jews to make *aliyah*.
Since this organization was controversial with Israelis, I didn't know if
I should train their volunteers or not. So I asked for the Rebbe's advice.
His answer came back, "If they are going to teach Torah, then absolutely.
The more people teach Torah, the more Jews will return to Judaism."

Each of our volunteers was debriefed upon return. Each one had
to write a summary for the Rebbe of everything that had happened
during his stay—what he had done, whom he had met, what were the
particular needs of the Lubavitcher *chasidim* he spoke with. The latter
was most important because the Rebbe's office kept a list of what was
needed and, as people came and went, they would be asked to smuggle
these things into Russia.

An underground
wedding in Soviet
Russia.

*Courtesy of Nathan
Brusovani (Bar)*

Mrs. Abbie Teitz, Rabbi Elazar Teitz, Rabbi Mordechai Pinchas Teitz, Rabbi Yitzhak L. Hechtman and Rabbi David Hill stand in front of the first Soviet-authorized shipment of kosher food and religious articles to Moscow. 1966.

Courtesy of the Hill family

Come Sukkot 1968, the biggest need was for the items that would make the observance of the holiday possible, especially *etrogim*, the citrons needed for the *mitzvah* of shaking the *lulav*. These tropical fruits were not available in Russia so they had to be imported, but how? The Rebbe advised, "Write a letter to the Russian Embassy and tell them you would like to send 'fruits of the season' to the Soviet Union."

I did that, but they knew what "fruits of the season" meant, and they turned me down.

Then, a person I knew, Dr. Maurice Sage—who, incidentally, studied at the Sorbonne the same time as the Rebbe—said he might find a way of smuggling the *etrogim* in diplomatic pouches. Another former student of the Sorbonne, who was now an ambassador representing an African country in Moscow, was willing to do this. I went back to the Rebbe, who advised me, "Make the most of this opportunity. Take small *lulavim* and *etrogim* and fill up valises with them." It worked like a charm.

I USED TO TELL MY VOLUNTEERS BEFORE THEY SET OUT, "No matter where you have traveled in your life, you will always remember what you saw in Russia." Indeed, I will never forget some of the poignant scenes that

I witnessed on my trips there during the 1960s and '70s.

The incredible level of self-sacrifice of the Russian Jews I met was very inspirational to me and to everyone else who was part of Operation Lifeline. I recall spending time in Leningrad with Rabbi Yitzchak Kogan—whose name the Rebbe had given me—and seeing chickens running around his house on Shabbat. When Shabbat ended (and it ended very late over there), two of the young men present said to him, "Yitzchak, Yitzchak, slaughter the chickens already, because we have to make the train for Moscow!"

This intrigued me. What were these two doing traveling with freshly-killed kosher chickens on a midnight train to Moscow?

They explained that they were going to be circumcised the next day, and they felt that, at a proper circumcision feast, chicken should be served! Their answer stunned me. These young men were willing to be circumcised at their age without painkillers and, what's more, they were willing to go to such great lengths in order to bring kosher food for the feast. This impressed me to no end, and it gave me even more incentive to help them in any way I could.

But the fact is that my whole operation could never have been the

Yitzchak Kogan (C.) in Leningrad, Russia. Early 1980s.

Courtesy of Chabad.org

success that it was without the Rebbe's guidance and help. And I say this publicly wherever I go.

For sure we had other key supporters—among them: Alexander Schindler of the Reform movement, Label Katz of B'nai B'rith, and the Satmar *chasidim* of Williamsburg, New York. But the Rebbe opened the door at a time when only Lubavitch was involved with Russian Jewry. From the time of the Russian Revolution in 1917, when the Yevsektsiya— the Jewish section of the Communist party, whose stated mission was the destruction of traditional Jewish life, the Zionist movement and Hebrew culture—shut down synagogues and *yeshivahs*, and all rabbis were forced into retirement, Lubavitch refused to submit. Lubavitch kept the flame alive. And it all had to do with the leadership of the Lubavitcher Rebbe—both the Previous Rebbe and the last Rebbe.

Chabad emissaries followed the Rebbe's directives and drew strength from his guidance, even if that meant risking their lives. This is where the strength of the *chasid* comes from—his faith in the Rebbe— in knowing that the Rebbe knows best which path he should follow. As the Rebbe certainly did.   ■

MRS. HENY KARNIEL

Currency Exchange

*A lifetime of caring for children and a marvelous
moment with one of her own*

Mrs. Heny Karniel, a veteran educator, has served—together with her late husband, Rabbi Amos Karniel—as a Chabad emissary in various locations in Israel, beginning in 1961. She was interviewed in her home in Kfar Chabad in May of 2014.

From the time that my husband Amos and I married, we have been connected to the Rebbe. The first time we wrote to him was to request a blessing on the occasion of our marriage, and from that point on, we were guided by his wise counsel.

Back then—that is, in 1961—we were both teachers working in Jerusalem, but when we asked to become the Rebbe's emissaries, he advised us to go to Kfar Maimon, an agricultural settlement in the Negev that belonged to Hapoel HaMizrachi, the religious Zionist movement. On the one hand, this was a natural fit for us because my husband had roots there and both of us had once been affiliated with this group; on the other hand, it was challenging: the people of this settlement felt they were already religious enough and they didn't see the need to grow spiritually—certainly not through the study of Chabad teachings.

But, following the Rebbe's directives, we found a wide range of possibilities for activities there. The Rebbe always said to lead by example, so we tried to do that without imposing on others.

When I discovered that there were complaints that the *mikveh* was not open as needed, I volunteered to be a *mikveh* attendant. I brought in a teacher whom the women respected to give classes in *Taharat Hamishpachah,* the Laws of Family Purity. Eventually, I became involved in building a new *mikveh* for the women.

My husband gave Torah classes to the community on Shabbat, beginning with the Talmud and then adding in the *Tanya,* the seminal work of Chabad Chasidism. Considering that initially the residents were suspicious of our ways, it was gratifying to see how excited they were to learn the *Tanya*.

Our children took our mission just as seriously as we did. When our oldest son, Benny, was getting ready to start first grade, he wanted to go to a more religious school where the children were like him, instead of the one in Kfar Maimon. But when he wrote to the Rebbe about it, the reply was: "Your task is to study in this school so that you will inspire the other children. Ask your parents to spend time with you after school to teach you additional Jewish subjects."

So he went to this school and announced to his teacher, "It is my job to inspire others" and, in the end, he had quite an effect even on her. After school, he studied with my husband as the Rebbe had advised, and he also made it a habit of bringing friends home so they could join in. These study sessions became so popular that we ended up having two classes—one for boys and one for girls. And the community even opened a library of Jewish books for the children, such was the demand.

Residents of Kfar Maimon head to a communal celebration.

Lehava Netivot via PikiWiki

Amos Karniel teaching
in Kfar Maimon.

*Courtesy of
Heny Karniel*

AS OUR FAMILY GREW, we needed to expand our house. But we were renting and didn't want to sink money into a place that didn't belong to us, because we would never be able to recover our investment. But the Rebbe said to do it. "You should build with joy and gladness of heart," he instructed us. So we did.

Shortly thereafter — this was in 1974 — I gave birth to our youngest child, and when I returned to teaching after maternity leave, I was informed that the Department of Education wanted to transfer me to a new school. Apparently, I had been recommended by my principal to teach a special education class in Tkuma, a Negev farming settlement located about five kilometers from Gaza. The position called for teaching boys and girls, ages fourteen to sixteen, who couldn't learn in a regular classroom setting. These youngsters, some of whom didn't even know how to read, lived in foster homes in the community and had to be taught in a special framework due to their troubled backgrounds.

When this job was proposed to me, I was warned that it would not be easy; two other teachers had already tried it and quit. However, because

my principal attested that I had what it takes to handle such kids, I was
being offered this chance.

"Before accepting, I need to hear what the Rebbe says," I responded.

I contacted the Rebbe's office, and the Rebbe advised me to
take the job. He also gave me specific instructions on what to
teach these students—I was to tell them Chasidic stories and stories about righteous people; I was to try to engage them in Jewish observance and to encourage them to pray and give charity.
The Rebbe once quoted to me the saying of our sages, "Words that come
from the heart enter the heart," so I knew that if I connected to these
kids with love, they would be receptive to me.

When I accepted the position, I followed the Rebbe's instructions to
the letter. I taught the boys about *tefillin* and *tzitzit*, and the girls about
Shabbat candles, and I made a special effort to spend personal time

with each student. Thank G-d, it worked out well.

Because they loved hearing the stories so much, I used them as a reward for good behavior. If they behaved nicely, I'd tell them a story at the end of the day.

Just how well this worked was brought home to me one day when the kids decided to have a fight in class. During the melee, a chair went flying toward me. Just in time, I ducked, and it smashed through a window behind me. My table and chair were covered in shards of glass. I saw that this was a test of wills, so I continued teaching as if nothing had happened, while they stared at me. I didn't raise my voice and I didn't issue a punishment. At the end of class, I picked up my things and walked out, ignoring their pleas to tell them a story.

The next morning, I walked into a changed class. Their behavior was exceptional. One boy even blurted out, "We feel that you love us," or words to that effect. The Rebbe was totally right: Words that come from the heart enter the heart.

Heny addressing her students. 1997.

Courtesy of Heny Karniel

AFTER A YEAR, THE CLASS WAS DISBANDED, and I moved with my family to Kfar Chabad. The kids from that class all went on to religious high schools, except for one girl. She returned to Beer Sheva, to the home of her mother, who was living with her Arab boyfriend. In an attempt to get the girl out of what was a very negative environment, I went there. But I was rebuffed. The Arab boyfriend told me, in no uncertain terms, to go away. "If you try anything, I'll kill you," he threatened. "I know who you are and where you live."

I returned home quite shaken and, on my husband's advice, wrote to the Rebbe. In response, the Rebbe asked if I knew the girl's birthday. In fact, I did, because I made a point of celebrating all my students' birthdays in class. The Rebbe told me to recite daily the psalm corresponding to her age. Aside from that, I shouldn't get involved.

So this is what I did.

From that day, for fourteen years, I recited a psalm for her, each year advancing the number by one on the day of her birthday. Fourteen years! I figured that I'd be praying for her for the rest of my life. But then, something amazing happened.

In 1989, my husband gave a talk at a Chabad synagogue in Zichron Yaakov. When he finished, a woman walked up to him and asked, "Rabbi, are you the husband of the teacher from Tkuma?"

"Yes, I am," my husband responded. "And who are you?" He didn't recognize her, and even her name didn't jog his memory.

"I have been searching for your wife," she went on, "but you moved and I couldn't find her."

He gave her my number, and when she called me, she filled me in on what had happened in the intervening years. Yad L'Achim—an organization that specializes in rescuing Jewish girls from unsafe situations—saved her, got her on her feet and helped her get married. She told me that she and her husband are fully Torah observant and have one daughter.

I was very happy to hear this. More than anything, all that had happened to her proved to me the power of reciting psalms for the well-being of another person. And, of course, the power of the Rebbe's foresight!

HOWEVER, I'M GETTING AHEAD OF MYSELF. I need to explain how it was that we came to move from Kfar Maimon in southern Israel to Kfar Chabad in central Israel.

Already in 1974, the Rebbe told us that we should begin thinking about leaving this community and moving to a location that would be better for our children's education. My husband visited New York that year, and the Rebbe mentioned this to him, adding, "but only if your wife agrees."

Of course, I agreed. I knew that if the Rebbe suggested we do it, it was the best thing for us.

The Rebbe directed us to move to Kfar Chabad, where a new housing project had just gone up and an apartment was available. However, we did not have the down payment, which was 25,000 liras (the Israeli currency at the time). My husband did not want to bring this up to the Rebbe, because he firmly believed that if the Rebbe said to make the

Amos Karniel receives *kos shel brachah* from the Rebbe. *Motzaei* Simchat Torah, 5750-1989.

Mordechai Baron, The Living Archive

move, G-d would help us.

And G-d did.

A *yeshivah* decided to move into our house in Kfar Maimon and offered to reimburse us for the addition we had built some years before—which the Rebbe had told us to build "with joy and gladness of heart."

What was their offer? 25,000 liras!

So we moved, although the change was difficult for some members of the family. Our boys were thrilled, but our girls initially found it hard to acclimate to the new community and fit in socially. As well, I wanted to continue to be involved in outreach but did not see how to do this in Kfar Chabad.

We wrote to the Rebbe about it, who responded that we should first focus on our children's education. This surprised me because we were now living in a Chasidic community that was totally committed to Torah and to Chabad ways, and the schools were also of a high religious caliber. Here I had to worry about my children's education?

But the Rebbe's answer made it clear to me that the children's education depends on the home. I couldn't abdicate my responsibility and rely on the community alone.

This gave me an entirely new perspective. If ever my kids were to waver in their observance, I could not complain about their schools or their teachers; I couldn't say "this one is at fault" or "that one is to blame." These were my kids and I was totally responsible for them.

I took the Rebbe's advice to heart and, thank G-d, all my children adjusted to the new surroundings after a time. Both my husband and I found great jobs in the field of education, and everything worked out.

ONE DAY, MY HUSBAND SAID TO ME, "You've never met the Rebbe in person. It's time to do something about this."

I was all for it, but we didn't have the money to make the trip. Still, there is a famous saying by the fourth Chabad Rebbe, the Rebbe Maharash, "The world says that if you cannot crawl under an obstacle, leap over it. However, I say, *l'chatchilah ariber*—leap over it in the first place!"

So, in 1976, we decided to make the leap.

Without knowing anything about travel agencies, we stumbled upon

Heny and Amos
Karniel traveling to
New York.

Courtesy of
Heny Karniel

one in Tel Aviv owned by a religious fellow who knew all about the Rebbe and was willing to let us pay for the trip in installments.

Toward the end of our three-week trip, the Rebbe received us in a private audience. When we walked in, I became so overcome with emotion that I felt the need to lean on something for support.

The Rebbe spoke to me in Hebrew. "Are you satisfied in Kfar Chabad?" he asked.

"It has been good for me," I answered. To which he responded, "Good has no limits. We always need to aspire for better and better."

(Later, I made sure to write this down, because this was a lesson that needed to stay with me for the rest of my life.)

The Rebbe asked me how the children were acclimating to the new environment. "Everyone is very happy, thank G-d, especially the boys," I replied.

"Make sure the girls are happy, too," the Rebbe said. "Are they all lighting Shabbat candles?"

I said they were.

But the Rebbe asked me again, "Do all the girls light?"

And, again, I said they did.

The Rebbe asked me the same question for the third time, and I didn't understand why he kept asking, so I just gave the same answer.

Hearing that, the Rebbe chuckled and took out five one-dollar bills and spread them out on the desk like a fan. "The girls should put money in the charity box before they light," he said. And then he laid down two more bills for the boys. "Here are two dollars for the boys to put in the box as well, so as not to differentiate between your girls and your boys."

Only when I left his office did the Rebbe's message concerning the girls register on me. *All five* of my girls were to give money to charity before lighting Shabbat candles, including the youngest. She was not yet three, so I hadn't taken her into account when I had told the Rebbe they were all lighting. But she was already reciting the various blessings fluently—as I had mentioned previously in a letter to the Rebbe—so she could certainly recite the blessing over the candles and light one with my help.

Once I realized this, I wrote to the Rebbe that I finally understood what he meant. The Rebbe responded with a note thanking me for writing.

THE STORY ABOUT THE DOLLARS that the Rebbe gave us that day—the five for the girls and the two for the boys—did not end there.

Because the children were young at the time, I put each dollar in a separate envelope with each child's name on it and hid the envelopes in a safe place. As they grew up, I would give them their dollar. I gave my daughters theirs on the day they got married, but I never gave the boys their dollars. I haven't the faintest idea why not.

In 2005, as I was cleaning for Passover, I found those two dollars and, as soon as my younger son—Aharon—came over, I gave his to him. Then I called my older son—Benny, a Chabad emissary in Gedera—and told him, "I'm really sorry, but the dollar that the Rebbe sent for you twenty-nine years ago is still here. So, at the first opportunity, you have to come over and get it."

He began to cry. I was astonished, but he wouldn't explain. "When

I come over, I'll tell you everything," is all he would say.

When he came, Benny told me that there was a man in his synagogue who had been married for a number of years but had no children. At one point, he asked my son what he could do, and Benny reminded him that the Rebbe would often advise people in his situation to be especially careful in observing the Laws of Family Purity. A while later, the man reported back that he had followed this advice, but his wife had still not become pregnant.

"Again, he asked me what he could do," Benny related. "I don't know what put this idea in my mind, but I said to him, 'Listen, you and your wife need to learn the Laws of Family Purity *properly*. The minute you tell me that both of you really took this heart, I will give you my most precious possession—a dollar that I received from the Rebbe.'"

The dollar was very important to Benny, but it was even more important to him that this couple should merit to have children.

"It seems that my offer proved the right incentive," Benny went on. "He and his wife did as I suggested, and she became pregnant. He informed me of this just the other day, which meant that now I had to part

Benny Karniel blowing the *shofar* at a children's event before Rosh Hashanah.

Courtesy of Benny Karniel

with my dollar—a very hard thing for me to do. I stalled and stalled until I could stall no longer. Last night, I finally gave it to him. No sooner had I done it when you called me, Ima—just about five minutes later—to say that you had been saving another dollar from the Rebbe for me! And that is why I broke down in tears."

Hearing that, so did I!   ∎

The Fabric of a *Chasid*

*Too proud to take charity,
too humble to take credit*

Mr. Mayer Zeiler is the owner of Flocktex Industries, manufacturers of Impala fabrics. The plant is located in the Nachlat Har Chabad neighbor-hood of Kiryat Malachi, Israel, where he resides with his family. He was interviewed in his home in January of 2008.

My story begins with the passing of my mother in 1951, when I was four years old. My father—a Holocaust survivor and a Bobover *chasid*—went outside his circle to get a blessing from the new Lubavitcher Rebbe. He was in dire straits, coping alone with three small children, and a friend told him that the new Rebbe was an extraordinary person.

The Rebbe gave him a blessing and also tried to give him fifty dollars, which my father refused because he was too proud to take the money. But the blessing proved priceless—it has followed our family to this day.

I married into a Chabad family. My father-in-law, Reb Dovid Deitsch, who was an especially devoted *chasid* of the Rebbe, had a prosperous business manufacturing plastics, and that is where I became employed.

After the devastating Yom Kippur War of 1973, my father-in-law asked the Rebbe what he might do to help Israel. He was sure that the Rebbe would tell him to write a check to some Chabad organization doing good works in the Holy Land, but the Rebbe's answer proved starkly different. "Open a business in Israel," he said. "The new immigrants need jobs. Build a factory. You will be very successful and it will benefit many families."

My father-in-law didn't think such a venture made business sense, and he didn't do anything about it at first. But the Rebbe persisted. Each time we went to see him as a family, the Rebbe would ask, "Reb Dovid, what's happening with the business in Israel?"

During a *farbrengen*, the Rebbe has a word with Reb Dovid Deitsch. 13 Tammuz, 5735-1975.

Isaac Berez

Truth be told, none of us — not my father-in-law, not his children, not his sons-in-law — were interested in this project. Our advisors told us it would be a total loss. Indeed, those whom we consulted in the Israeli government also thought we would not succeed.

But the Rebbe insisted, so we tried. We tried to build a textile plant where he suggested, in Kiryat Malachi, a development town for Jewish immigrants coming mostly from Arab lands — a very poor place in the Israeli Negev. We opted for a textile plant because we had begun trading in the new synthetic flocked fabrics and thought it was a good idea to produce these fabrics ourselves. But despite our best efforts, we faced one bureaucratic stumbling block after another — we were told that we needed permits from the government, that we needed approvals from the ministries, that we needed to conform to obscure customs rules and satisfy other unreasonable demands.

It was an impossible project, but my father-in-law asked me to try to get it off the ground anyway. I was flying back and forth, making no headway, and becoming very weary of it all. So, I tried very hard to convince my father-in-law to convince the Rebbe that we should walk away from it.

In fact, during an audience in the summer of 1976, I myself discussed these issues with the Rebbe, but instead of accepting my argument that we should give up, he said, "How do you expect to run a business if you're not there on the spot?"

That was not—by any means—the response I was anticipating. But the Rebbe insisted that the solution was for me to base myself in Israel for a year. And since it was summer, now was the ideal time to move my family there, so the kids could begin school in September.

This was a very tough thing for me to accept. I thought of living in Israel for such a long time as a jail sentence. My wife, however, took it well. So, following the Rebbe's directive, we did it—we moved to Israel.

At first, I hoped the Rebbe would allow us to rent an apartment in Jerusalem, but he urged us to move near to where the plant was being built, so we moved into an apartment in the Nachlat Har Chabad neighborhood of Kiryat Malachi. By Israeli standards it was a roomy apartment, but it was a fraction of the size of our home in Crown Heights. And that's not the only thing that was a shock to my system—the neighborhood had no paved roads, no working telephones, no proper sewers. Buying staples like bread or milk meant standing in line from early in the morning.

Mayer and Ella Zeiler, with their children Shaya, Mendel and Zevi. 1971.

Courtesy of Mayer Zeiler

After a year, I told the Rebbe that I'd had enough—I wanted to come back to the United States.

"Is your wife not happy?" the Rebbe asked.

"No," I had to admit, "my wife is happy."

"And your children—are they unhappy?"

"No," I had to admit again, "my children are happy."

"So what is the problem exactly?"

"It's me—I just can't take it," I said. From where I got the guts to tell the Rebbe that, I don't know. I went on to explain that I felt my every effort in building the factory was being frustrated, and this entire enterprise was just not going to work. All I wanted to do was come home.

But the Rebbe refused to accept defeat. With a smile, he promised me, "The hard times are behind you; from now on, it will be easier."

And don't you know—that's exactly what happened!

SUDDENLY, DOORS WHICH WERE PREVIOUSLY SHUT BEGAN OPENING UP—it became easier to deal with the ministries, with customs, with banks. Wherever I went, I was making new friends.

Where before Yigal Horowitz, the Israeli minister for industry, had no time for me, now he actually paid a surprise visit to our plant. And then Moshe Katsav, the mayor of Kiryat Malachi who was elected to the Knesset in 1977, offered to introduce me to the new prime minister, Menachem Begin, at an event in the Knesset. At first Begin waved me away, but when Katsav said that I was a Lubavitcher, he turned towards me and asked, "Are you the one whom the Rebbe sent to open up a factory in Kiryat Malachi?"

I replied that I was, and then Begin amazed me by saying, "When I last visited the Rebbe, he spoke to me about you and your problems with the government. I hope you won't have any more problems from now on." He even instructed Katsav to make sure that I didn't.

I imagine that the Rebbe had much more important things to discuss with Begin than my troubles with the Israeli bureaucracy, and yet—for whatever reason—he brought it up. The Rebbe never forgot me and the task he set before me.

The Rebbe greets
Mayer and his son
Yitzchok Noach.
26 Tishrei, 5745-1984.

Levi Freidin,
The Living Archive

AT LONG LAST, our factory—Flocktex Industries—got off the ground.

It was hardly an immediate success, and I told the Rebbe so: "Yes, we are finally up and running. And yes, we finally have the machinery in place. But I can't get it to produce first-quality goods; I'm only producing seconds."

The Rebbe didn't seem to get the problem: "But the machine is working!"

"That means nothing," I argued. "So far it's produced a couple of containers of second quality fabric."

"Do you have good samples?" the Rebbe asked.

"Good samples I have," I responded.

"Well, you're a salesman. Take your samples, and go out and sell." And he gave me a blessing to succeed.

Assuming that I was meant to sell the second-rate goods, I started going around Europe, from city to city, trying my best to find buyers for what I had to offer. In my quest I found myself in Tilburg, Netherlands, in the offices of a company selling to Africa. I thought maybe they wouldn't be that picky.

However, when I met with the manager, he said, "I like your samples, but I don't want seconds. I am in the market only for first quality goods." He was willing to order more than twenty thousand meters of fabric, or about a hundred thousand dollars' worth, which back then was a tremendous amount of money, like almost half-a-million dollars' worth today, but I had no idea how we would manufacture it.

Still, that kind of deal I couldn't pass up. So I said to him, "When do you need it?"

He needed the goods by the end of the year, which was five weeks hence.

We agreed on the terms, and I walked out of his office thinking, "I don't know how I'm going to make this happen, but the Rebbe gave me his blessing to succeed." So I called up the plant and told the manager about this order.

His reaction was, "Are you crazy? We can't produce anything of that quality!"

I said, "Run the machine and keep running it until it does."

To make a long story short, the machine kicked in. The goods were produced, and they were first quality. They were delivered on time. The customer was satisfied, and we got paid.

From there our business grew. And it grew at a time when the textile industry was going out of business in the Western Hemisphere. All over Europe and the US, textile plants were closing down in the face of competition from Asia, but we bucked the trend.

The Rebbe made it all happen. Because of his constant prodding and support, because of his blessings, we became the first manufacturers in the world making a velvet-type fabric for curtains, a special dense fabric that would not admit light and did not require a lining. Not only that, it was a soft fabric, a unique product which became very much in demand in Europe and, eventually, the world over.

INITIALLY, WE GOT A LOT OF ATTENTION AT TEXTILE SHOWS in Germany, Belgium and England and were approached by a very big customer, the Christie-Tyler Group, furniture manufacturers out of Wales. But they required that all the upholstery fabrics they bought be flame-retardant. Applying the flame-retardant chemical made the fabric stiff, but we figured out a way around it. We conducted tests in our laboratory and

Mayer giving a tour of the factory to Knesset Member Uzi Landau. Circa 1995.

Courtesy of Mayer Zeiler

our fabric met all the standards, but Christie-Tyler was still not satisfied. They wanted a certificate from an English laboratory, which failed our fabrics repeatedly.

Three times, I asked the Rebbe for his blessing that we should pass the lab test, but we failed each time. I then visited the Rebbe as he was handing out dollars for charity, and he asked me if everything was okay now. I answered, "If the Rebbe says so, I am sure it will be."

The Rebbe gave me a puzzled look and said, "I don't understand."

That's when it dawned on me that the English test was not being done properly, for whatever reason. So I sent our head chemist over there to stand and watch, and finally we passed.

AS THE GLOBAL DEMAND GREW, we built a second plant, and then a third plant in 1981, increasing production all the while. Today, although we are not the largest company in Israel, we are one of the country's most successful textile producers; our velvet is considered the best velvet in terms of quality control and being the latest in design, and this has built our reputation the world over.

Would any of this have happened without the Rebbe's insistence? Absolutely not.

Our financial advisors told us this venture would not work. They said, "Go back to your Rebbe and explain to him that he doesn't understand industry and he doesn't understand financing. You can't make money in Israel. You can't have a successful industry in Israel. What he is telling you doesn't make any sense."

Though we all thought that we were going to be a failure—as did the Israeli government—we followed the Rebbe's advice, and today we are running a business that provides a livelihood for over one hundred families in Israel. Our company is a success not only by Israeli terms, but in American terms and in global terms. For this the Rebbe gets all the credit. And I mean that in every sense of the word.

Because we are an Israeli success story, everyone who is anybody in the government—and even visiting foreign dignitaries—have made a point of stopping by our plant. And when they've come—as the *chasid* of the Rebbe that I am—I've always invited them to put on *tefillin*. I have put *tefillin* on Shimon Peres, on Ehud Rassabi, on members of the

Mayer helps Prime Minister of Israel Shimon Peres put on *tefillin*. 1980s.

Courtesy of Mayer Zeiler

leftist Shinui party, and on Lord Marcus Seiff, the chairman of Marks and Spencer.

Whenever I've met these people, I've always let them know that the only reason I'm in Israel is because the Rebbe wanted a factory in Israel. I didn't want to come, but he ordered me to.

And the only explanation that I have for why it succeeded, when logically it should have failed, is that the Land of Israel is especially blessed by G-d (something that the Rebbe understood better than any businessman), and that — in addition — this particular venture was directed and blessed by the Rebbe himself.   ■

THE POWER OF A *MITZVAH*

The Longest Layover

A mother rescues her son from enemy territory

Mr. Menachem Ben Mashiah is a diamond dealer and real estate developer who lives in Savyon, Israel. He was interviewed in his home in February of 2018.

My family originated in Hamadan, Iran, where my grandfather, Rabbi Menachem Shmuel Halevi, served as a rabbi in the 1920s before immigrating to Jerusalem and establishing a Torah academy for young boys in the Bukharan Quarter. This school had some illustrious students — for example, Rabbi Ovadia Yosef and Rabbi Mordechai Eliyahu, both of whom went on to become Sephardi chief rabbis of Israel, and Rabbi Ben Zion Abba Shaul, who went on to head the famed Porat Yosef Sephardi *yeshivah*.

I was born in 1944 in Jerusalem, but as an adult, I made my home in New York from where I operated my family's business, dealing in pearls.

One of my clients was a Lubavitcher from Montreal by the name of Meir Plotkin. While he was visiting my office one day in December of 1973, I mentioned to him that, on the following Sunday, I would be flying to the Far East. In those days, this required multiple transfers. I had to travel from New York to Los Angeles, from Los Angeles to Hawaii, from Hawaii to Okinawa and from Okinawa to Tokyo. On the way back, I had to stop in Israel to visit my sick mother, which meant going from Hong Kong to Bombay, from Bombay to Tehran, from Tehran to Tel Aviv and only then to New York: a very complicated trip!

At that time, hijackings were not uncommon on international flights. When Meir heard how complicated my travels would be, he said, "I will call the Rebbe and ask him to give you a blessing for a safe journey."

I didn't know what to make of this. "I don't know if you should," I said. "I never met your Rebbe; I don't know him, and he doesn't know me."

But Meir insisted that I could not make this trip without the Rebbe's blessing and he made the call to the Rebbe's office, giving my name—Menachem, son of Shoshana Chaya—along with the request.

A short while later, after Meir had already left my office, the phone rang; it was the Rebbe's secretary, conveying a message:

"The Rebbe understands you are going to the Far East, and he wishes you a successful journey. But you should return by the same route."

"I can't!" I objected. "I have a sick mother in Jerusalem. I must stop in Israel."

"If you must travel by that route, then the Rebbe advises that you check all the *mezuzot* in your house before you leave," he said, again wishing me a successful trip, and he hung up.

I was very puzzled. I had just bought a big new house and affixed a new *mezuzah* to every door, nearly forty new *mezuzot* in all. Furthermore, it was a Friday and I was leaving on Sunday, so there was no way I could have all these *mezuzot* checked before my departure. However, I immediately contacted the scribe who wrote these *mezuzah* scrolls for me, telling him what the Rebbe had said. I figured that my wife would be able to oversee this matter in my absence and that, by the time I

Menachem and his wife at their wedding. Menachem's mother (R.) is seated next to the bride. 1972.

Courtesy of Menachem Ben Mashiah

Menachem (C.) at a
mine in Zambia, Africa.

*Courtesy of Menachem
Ben Mashiah*

would be flying back, all the *mezuzot* would have been checked and, if need be, they would have been fixed.

Still, the Rebbe's instruction left me with an uneasy feeling, so I removed the *mezuzah* from my bedroom door and examined it myself. Imagine my shock when I saw that the Hebrew letter *daled* was missing from the phrase *uvilechtecha vaderech*, meaning "and when you travel on the road…"

I immediately took a *mezuzah* scroll from one of the rooms in my basement and affixed it to the bedroom door, leaving strict instructions for the scribe — who was just as upset about this as I was — to take care of the rest.

I STAYED IN THE FAR EAST for over three weeks, during which time I forgot completely about my conversation with the Rebbe's secretary. Returning home, I boarded my flight, and I made all the scheduled transfers until the leg from Bombay to Tehran, which was via Air France. As we were approaching Tehran, where we had to refuel, the pilot announced that we could not land there due to heavy snow. Instead, we would be landing at a military airport in Kuwait.

2   DAILY NEWS, SATURDAY, AUGUST 30, 1969

Arabs Hijack Israel-Bound U.S. Jetliner

Damascus, Syria, Aug. 29 (Combined Services) —An Arab couple hijacked a Trans World Airlines jetliner bound from Rome to Tel Aviv today and forced it to fly here.

Six Israelis aboard were detained by the Syrian police. The cockpit of the empty plane was wrecked by a bomb blast after those aboard had disembarked.

The airlines said the craft carried 163 passengers and a crew of 12. Syrian officials said the passengers and crew — presumably with the exception of the hijack couple and the arrested ... said it had engineered the hijacking to seize a passenger responsible for the "death and misery of many Palestinian men, women and children." ... fied as Shadia Abou Ghazala and ... tional piracy" and urged the ...

Passengers and crew of hijacked TWA jetliner await lodging assignments in Damascus, Syria, yesterday after their plane was seized by Arab man and woman and forced to detour from Tel Aviv run.

UPI Radiophoto

The undesired trip, said the hi-

The *New York Daily News* reports on a hijacking.

Now, at the time, Iran was not as hostile to Israel as it is today. It was ruled by the Shah, who was friendly with the West. But the neighboring Arab countries were all sworn enemies.

Not only that, recently we'd had a spate of airplane hijackings by Palestinian terrorists. In 1968 and '69, two flights out of Rome were hijacked. Both flights were diverted, and the Jewish passengers were held hostage, to be swapped for terrorist prisoners. In the second case — a TWA flight diverted to Damascus — some of the Israelis were held for two full months.

The worst incident was the coordinated hijacking of five planes in September of 1970. Three were flown to Jordan, where the hijackers demanded the freeing of Palestinian terrorists from Israeli prisons; again, the majority of the passengers were released except for the Jews who were held as hostages. The fourth was flown to Cairo, where it was blown up. Only the fifth — an El Al flight from Tel Aviv to New York — managed to evade its captors because the pilot refused to accede to the hijackers' demands and somehow landed the plane safely in London.

The year before my trip, there was another similar incident where a Belgian Sabena airliner was hijacked on its way to Tel Aviv. As in every other instance, the hijackers separated out the Jews with the intention of trading them for hundreds of Palestinian terrorists in Israeli prisons. But the Israeli commandos stormed the plane and killed the hijackers.

In the event of a worst-case scenario, my odds were not great.

With all that in mind, I was scared stiff, and I finally understood why the Rebbe didn't want me to take this route.

Frantically, I informed a stewardess that as an Israeli citizen traveling on an Israeli passport, I faced grave danger landing in an enemy country. She promised to tell the pilot, who shortly thereafter made an announcement that we would not be landing in Kuwait, but in Baghdad, Iraq. We would stay on the ground less than an hour — just enough time to refuel — and then continue on to Tel Aviv. The pilot also came over to tell me personally that I was invited to sit in the upper deck with the crew, and that they would not abandon me — I shouldn't worry.

But it didn't go that smoothly.

Once we landed in Baghdad, we stayed there for eleven hours!

All the passengers were taken off the plane, except for the crew, who stayed on the plane with me. I was too scared to put on my *tefillin* because an Iraqi security guard came on board and remained there, watching us. I was also too scared to eat, because my food was clearly marked "kosher." I would not eat the nonkosher food either, so I ate nothing. Every minute on that plane, under the eye of that Iraqi guard, felt like a lifetime.

In the end, we were permitted to take off, and we landed in Israel. By then my ordeal was well known, and there was a pack of press people

An Air France aircraft.

waiting for me at Lod airport, but I was spared a confrontation with them. Instead, security rushed me off the plane so I could get to my mother's home in Jerusalem in time for Shabbat. All the while I couldn't stop thanking G-d for taking me out of this nightmare in one piece.

SOMETIME AFTER RETURNING TO NEW YORK, I contacted a friend, Rabbi Shalom Ber Hecht, and I asked him to arrange an audience for me with the Rebbe.

I will never forget walking into the Rebbe's office and seeing him seated at his desk, smiling a radiant smile at me. I ran over and kissed his hand. "Rebbe, do you know what happened to me?!" I began.

"I know, I know," he replied. "You were in danger, but what saved you was your devotion to the commandment to honor one's father and mother. It was because you wanted to see your sick mother that you were saved."

After that, I developed a long-standing relationship with the Rebbe, meeting him many, many times through the years. But without fail, whenever I see in my mind's eye that beautiful, serene smile he gave me when I rushed into his office, I break down in tears. ∎

DR. JOEL SINSKY

Penny Power

*The best, cheapest solution
to electromagnetic interference*

Dr. Joel Sinsky is a physicist who worked as a research scientist for the US Navy for more than twenty-five years and then went on to teach at the University of Maryland and Towson University for the next twenty years. He was interviewed in his home in Lakewood, New Jersey, in September of 2018.

I was born and raised in Baltimore, in a nonreligious home, but in my early youth I was exposed to authentic Judaism. I started putting on *tefillin* from the time of my Bar Mitzvah and increased my knowledge of Torah until age eighteen when I became totally committed to a religious lifestyle.

I attended the University of Pennsylvania, which at the time had just a handful of Orthodox students, and associating with them further strengthened my observance. When I returned to Baltimore to continue graduate studies at the University of Maryland, I prayed in a little *shtiebel* frequented by refugees from Eastern Europe, and that is where I met and befriended a Chabad *chasid* named Yitzchok Springer. Even though his English was not very good and my Yiddish was nonexistent, we managed to communicate—we forged a strong, affectionate connection. Rabbi Springer had a big influence on my outlook on life in general and on my religious practice in particular.

He often spoke about his Rebbe—about all the great things his Rebbe did—and he urged me to go to New York to meet his Rebbe for myself.

At that point I knew little about Chasidism, but I liked Rabbi Springer so very much that if he wanted me to meet the Rebbe, I would go meet him.

As I recall, it was in the summer of 1963 that I went. Rabbi Springer arranged for me to stay in the home of Mendel and Nechama Baumgarten, very warm and wonderful people who truly cared about their guests.

My audience with the Rebbe took place in the wee hours of the morning, and it proved to be an incredible experience.

Rabbi Springer had given me strict instructions on proper comportment before the Rebbe — I was to come prepared with my questions all written out and hand the note to the Rebbe at the beginning of the audience. This is exactly what I did.

The Rebbe read my note in silence and then asked me if I spoke Yiddish. I shook my head because I was too scared to speak. And then he began to answer my questions in English and in the order that I had written them down. I just listened.

My first question was: What should I do after I finish school? At the time, I was studying for my Ph.D. in physics, but more than anything I wanted to go into Jewish outreach. I saw the good work that Chabad did, and I felt that this was what I should also do.

The Rebbe replied that I should become a professor at a university that has many Jewish students. As a religious person, he explained, I'd be able to influence them and help them return to their Jewish roots. In this way I could best accomplish my goal.

I suggested in my letter that perhaps I should teach science in a *yeshivah* high school, but the Rebbe countered that I would have a stronger impact as an observant Jew in a college environment than teaching secular subjects to *yeshivah* students.

I also wanted to know if I should immigrate to Israel, but the Rebbe referred back to his previous answer and explained that his reasoning was the same: In the United States I could have a real impact, but in Israel I'd be treading water, at best. I was obligated to do my part to prevent American Jewish youth from going astray.

Finally, I had asked if I should begin dating for marriage, and he inquired how old I was. When I said, "twenty-six," he smiled and said, "It's high time."

Rabbi Springer had wanted to fix me up with a young woman from Kfar Chabad, Israel, but the Rebbe disagreed with this choice. He said that I should look for an English-speaking girl with a background similar to mine.

When he finished responding to my questions, he made two unrelated comments:

First, he advised that every morning, after formal prayers, I should re-cite the daily portion of psalms. I have done this ever since.

Second, he advised that I give money to charity from the heart and not out of a sense of obligation.

Initially, I didn't understand what he meant by this, but after a few hours of thought, it hit me like a lightning bolt.

I kept a small charity box into which I regularly put money. Because I felt a great debt of gratitude to Rabbi Springer and what this *chasid* had done for me, I intended for the money to go to Chabad. I felt I owed him. But the Rebbe didn't want my charitable giving to be a payback of some kind. He wanted it to be purely for the purpose of fulfilling the commandment of *tzedakah*.

When I left the Rebbe's office, I sat down and wrote a report of my meeting for Mendel Baumgarten, stating: "I am absolutely convinced that our Rebbe is, in intellect and spirit, of such a high level that it is impossible for me to comprehend it. His power is beyond belief, and

Rabbi Yitzchok Springer dances in front of Joel and Rebecca Sinsky at their wedding. February 20, 1966.

Courtesy of Joel Sinsky

ב"ה   כ"ז אלול תשכ"ג

1963

Dear Mendel:

Please let me first thank you most sincerely from the bottom of my heart for a wonderful and inspiring weekend. Please also relate my thanks to your wife and truly remarkable children.

I went into the REBBE at 4 AM. Actually I was next to last because someone else had missed his turn and so he decided to wait and go in after everyone else. I am absolutely convinced that our REBBE is, in intellect and spirit, of such a high level that it is impossible for me to comprehend it. His power is beyond belief and his insights are touched with divinity. I suppose I don't have to tell you this but I was firmly convinced of it last night. I first handed him my questions and he silently read them all without a word. He asked me if I spoke Yiddish and I wagged my head no because I, frankly, was too scared to speak. Then he began answering my questions in order. I only said 12 words during the whole interview because I decided to hold by whatever he said without question. The 12 words were "Yes Sir", "26", "Joan with a J" and "He didn't know it."

My first question was what I should do after I finish school in light of how important I think the work of Lubavitch is. He replied that I should get a job in a university as a professor and make an accomplishment in my chosen field because a religious person in such an environment can do a great deal of good by bringing young people to Yiddishkeit. I mentioned to him the possibility of teaching science in a Yeshiva and he said that this is a negative factor. That in a Yeshiva, the first duty is for the boys to learn Torah etc. and that secular subjects are only taught for special reasons and that they are a negative factor. He implied that a religious teacher of science in a Yeshiva is a waste. He said that such a teacher in a secular environment, though, is a positive factor. He said to choose a university where there are a large no. of Jewish students.

My second question concerned the Rabbi I learn with in Balti... He said that he knows of him and that he is a good person and that I should continue with him. (His name is R. Malin). I should ask a mutual friend about what to pay him

Joel's letter to Rabbi Mendel Baumgarten.
Courtesy of Joel Sinsky

his insights are touched with divinity."

I did not realize then just how accurate my first impression of him was, but a couple of years later, I received astonishing proof of how "touched with divinity" his insights were.

UPON RETURNING HOME, I became intensely involved with the Hillel House at the University of Maryland, bringing Chabad *chasidim* to lead the programs I helped organize there. The rabbi of the Hillel House was very happy to have them come because he saw what a tremendous influence they had on the students.

I received a great deal of satisfaction from my Hillel House involvement, but as far as my studies were concerned, it was a different story—after spending six years in graduate school, I was still struggling to get my Ph.D.

As part of the work for my doctoral thesis, I had to participate in a physics experiment which was so vast and complicated that it required erecting a building—equipped with vacuum chambers and suspension systems—just to house it. Supported by a grant from the US Air Force, this experiment was considered quite important, but I was not at all enjoying the frustration that it entailed, and I decided to revisit the Rebbe to ask for his blessing that I complete it once and for all.

In preparation for the audience, I wrote a letter explaining my work. I said that I was a member of a team working to develop a gravitational wave detector. Gravitational waves are disturbances in the curvature of "spacetime," and their detection allows for the observation of black holes and other objects in the distant universe that cannot be observed by traditional means such as telescopes, which is why this experiment was of interest to the US government. In brief, we were trying to conduct an experiment of dynamic gravitational interaction between two massive aluminum bars, but we were experiencing a lot of problems. (Incidentally, in 2017, a Nobel Prize was awarded for direct detection of gravitational waves, and what I was doing—under the guidance of Professor Joe Weber—was an early precursor of those prize-winning experiments.)

The letter ended up being four or five pages of scientific jargon. I knew that the Rebbe was very intelligent and had some background

Joel working on a lab experiment at the University of Maryland. 1968.
Courtesy of Joel Sinsky

in science, so I felt it would be insulting if I were to give him an overly simplified explanation of the experiment. So, I wrote just enough about my work to give him a feeling for the experiment but without getting into details of what the specific issue was — I only noted that I was having problems. And I asked for his blessing that I be able to bring the experiment to a successful conclusion, earn my degree at long last, and get on with my life.

When I handed this handwritten letter to the Rebbe, he started reading, and it took him just two minutes to finish it. I couldn't believe how fast he went through all my complex explanations.

When he got to the end, he asked me, "Do you have electromagnetic interference — is that what your problem is?"

I almost passed out from shock. That was exactly what the problem was! But how did he identify it so quickly? And he did it at four in the morning, when surely he must have been very tired after seeing people all night long! By the time I came to see the Rebbe, after investing much sweat and blood, we had figured out that our problem was interference; the trouble was that we couldn't find the solution.

Later, when I told my professor about this, he was so impressed that he exclaimed, "Why don't we hire him?!" The way the Rebbe instantaneously grasped this complicated conundrum was absolutely phenomenal.

Some of the others who heard the story tried to rationalize how the Rebbe caught on so fast by saying, "Well, he studied at the Sorbonne, so he must have known that." But that's just plain baloney. As a matter of fact, it would have been unlikely for even a learned physicist to reach that conclusion so quickly just from the brief description in my letter.

The Rebbe shares a moment with an individual during the
distribution of *kos shel brachah. Motzaei* Simchat Torah, 5737-1976.
Yossi Melamed, The Living Archive

It would simply have been too hard. And plain impossible for someone who doesn't work in physics every day.

But the Rebbe identified the problem. After he did so, he asked if my professor was competent in the field. When I replied that he was, the Rebbe instructed, "Bring a charity box to the laboratory and, every time you take a break, put a coin into that charity box. The amount of money isn't important, even a penny will do. When you go to lunch, put in a penny; when you go to dinner, put in a penny; when you leave for the day, put in a penny. Do this every time you go out of the room."

He didn't explain why I had to do this—he just blessed me to succeed, and I left. At the time, it seemed to me that he had simply changed the subject. After he knew my professor was well-versed in the field, he just checked to be sure I was fulfilling the commandment of charity.

Of course, I followed his instructions, making sure to give charity wholeheartedly and sincerely, like he told me to do the first time I met him. And, to my great amazement, just when the charity box was full—at Chanukah time of 1965—the experiment finally began to work.

Subsequently, I was able to finish my degree, get married and start a family. After a six-month hiatus in Israel, I got a job with the US Navy, where I worked as a research scientist for more than 25 years.

Over the years I've wondered a great deal why the Rebbe gave me those strange instructions—what connection was there between my putting a small coin in a charity box and my experiment?

The conclusion I reached was that I really needed to establish this *mitzvah* as *my mitzvah*—by doing it over and over, many times a day—and doing it properly, from the heart, each time. And, in the merit of that effort, I was rewarded with success in my work.

MR. MICHOEL MUCHNIK

Getting to the Heart of Art

An artist's tips for achieving maximum impact

Mr. Michoel Muchnik is a Chasidic artist and illustrator of children's books who is presently focused on developing bas-reliefs and murals. His works have been exhibited at the Brooklyn Museum of Art and other venues in the United States and abroad. He was interviewed in the My Encounter Studio in September of 2015.

As a young adult pursuing an art degree at the Rhode Island School of Design, I was caught up in the secular culture of the time. It was not until I was introduced to Chabad that things started to change for me. This happened in 1972, when I was twenty.

At a certain point after I enrolled in Tiferes Bachurim—the Chabad *yeshivah* in Morristown, New Jersey, for young Jewish men who were new to Torah observance—an opportunity came up for me and some of my fellow students to have a private audience with the Rebbe. As we went in one by one, I was very anxious because I did not know what to expect. Indeed, everything that followed was unexpected. Once I crossed the threshold into the Rebbe's study, I felt as if I had entered a different reality, and I remember thinking, "I have to take this spiritual feeling and somehow incorporate it into my art."

As I was standing there near the entrance to the room, not sure what to do next, the Rebbe said, "Come closer." So, I walked up to the Rebbe's desk and handed him the letter I had written listing my questions, and I also placed on his desk three small samples of my art because I wanted him to advise me what I should do with my artistic talent. I thought that perhaps I should become a Torah scribe, as I was good at Hebrew calligraphy and I believed that if I were to be religious this was probably a more suitable profession than becoming a painter.

The Rebbe said I should ask a scribe whether I should pursue that profession, but he offered another idea. He suggested that I design illuminated marriage contracts, *ketubot*, which have been the subject

The Rebbe hands
Michoel *lekach* at the
door of his study,
Erev Yom Kippur.
5748-1988.

Levi Freidin,
The Living Archive

of Jewish art for many centuries. I asked him if I might also illustrate
children's books and the Rebbe approved of that. At that point I was so
excited that he was giving me the green light to express my talent, that
I actually exclaimed *Baruch Hashem* (thank G-d!) out loud three times.

The Rebbe gave me practical advice for earning additional income
from my artwork. He suggested, for example, that I print copies of my
paintings. It also occurred to me that prints—which are much cheaper
and more widely distributed than originals—would allow more people
to see my work and learn from it.

At one point during the audience, the Rebbe fell into deep thought
and then said something like: "They will take advantage of you." It was a
scary moment to hear him say that. But then the Rebbe recommended
that I find a manager whom I could trust. He was warning me to be
careful and his advice was very wise indeed as I, like many artists, was
not well versed in the business world and could easily be victimized by
unscrupulous vendors.

WHEN IT CAME TIME FOR ME TO LEAVE AND, out of respect, I was backing out of the room, the Rebbe called me back and asked about the art samples I had left on his desk, "Are these for me?"

"If you would like them…" I answered, somewhat flustered.

He picked up each one and then selected a small watercolor of a winter scene in Russia, depicting a little synagogue with a Star of David on top and a crescent moon in the background. When he said, "I'll keep this one," I was so happy.

Again I started to leave, but again the Rebbe called me back.

"Is this an original?" he asked. I replied that it was, to which the Rebbe responded, "I can't keep an original, but if you make a print, please send one to me."

Of course, I made a print and sent it to the Rebbe. And I kept that little painting which he liked. I still have it, and it is not for sale.

Later on, whenever I made hand-signed limited edition prints of my work, I always tried to send the one numbered eighteen in the series to the Rebbe. I chose that one because eighteen is the numerical value of *chai*, meaning "life." Today, the prints I sent are housed in the Rebbe's library.

The watercolor painting selected by the Rebbe.

Courtesy of Michoel Muchnik

MUCHNIK, 1972   "SHUHL"

NOW, I DID NOT EXPECT IT, but the Rebbe proved quite the art critic. I recall sending him my first lithograph, which is a complicated form of fine art requiring a lot of handwork before the printing. It is called "The

Village of the Menchniks" and it depicts tiny Jewish people going about their lives—it's a very busy picture with a myriad of things going on.

After I delivered it, I got a response from the Rebbe that "if it can be done easily" a few things should be changed. The Rebbe noticed that I had depicted items which are related to each of the three spiritual pillars upon which, according to the Mishnah, the world stands: Torah, divine service (or prayer) and deeds of kindness.

He requested that I move these items to their appropriate places. For example, in the bottom left corner, there is a little house labeled "Free Loan Fund" and another labeled "Hospitality Hotel," and he asked that their location be moved to the right since these are deeds of kindness, the pillar which belongs on the right. As well, the Rebbe wanted the synagogue moved to the left since a house of prayer symbolizes divine service, the second pillar, which belongs on the left. And he suggested the Torah books and the *yeshivah*, an academy of Torah study, be both placed at the center of village life, where they belong.

The prints had already been made and I could not change them after the fact, but I learned from this. Afterwards, I would try to send the Rebbe a proof so any changes that he recommended could still be executed. And, of course, in future paintings I incorporated what he had suggested.

Later, it occurred to me that maybe the Rebbe was not only talking about my painting when he said these things were not in their proper place — maybe he was also talking about my personal characteristics and hinting that they weren't always in the right place.

This proved an invaluable insight. Once I caught onto that, it became a lifetime challenge for me to keep this in mind while I worked to better myself.

The Rebbe's instructions to Michoel written down by his secretary, Rabbi Leibel Groner. *Courtesy of Michoel Muchnik*

ANOTHER WORK OF MINE THAT THE REBBE COMMENTED ON was called "The Great *Mitzvah* Fair." It depicted a Jewish amusement park with rides made up of *mitzvot*. The Rebbe noted that the *mitzvah* of Sukkot — the *lulav* and *etrog* — was missing. Later, when I published a book with that title, I made sure that there was an illustration of a booth at the fair devoted to the *lulav* and *etrog*, and to another of the Rebbe's suggestions: a gift shop called "*Ahavat Yisrael* — Love of a Fellow Jew." This, of course, made total sense because a gift is a way of expressing love.

I must say that his comments were always insightful and his attention to detail astonishing. When I sent him a print of a kitchen scene that I called "Before Shabbat," featuring a family getting ready for the

The Rebbe hands a
dollar to Michoel's son
Gershon to be given
to charity. 14 Tammuz
5751-1991.

*Levi Freidin,
The Living Archive*

Shabbat meal, the Rebbe noticed that things didn't add up. He commented that I needed to add two more Shabbat candles for the women to light and one more *kiddush* cup as there were not enough cups for the men in the picture.

All that was in the early days, when I was still finding my path and my artwork took many forms. At one point, I started producing greeting cards; then I illustrated the revolutionary Chabad cookbook, *Spice and Spirit*; and then I created labels for charity boxes (that was at the Rebbe's suggestion). At another time, I was asked to design a button that was distributed by N'shei Chabad, Chabad's women's organization, as part of the Rebbe's Shabbat candle-lighting campaign. The button featured three candles—two to represent those the mother lights and an additional smaller one to represent the candle lit by the daughter—but when the Rebbe saw the prototype, he insisted that the daughter's candle be in the middle. He wanted the daughter's candle to be center stage because he very much wanted to encourage mothers to teach this *mitzvah* to the girls, and thus bring more spiritual light into the world.

At another time, I recall sending a set of little black and white prints of Jewish scenes for the Rebbe to comment on, and a short time later getting a call from his secretary with the message: "I have a check for you from the Rebbe for eighteen dollars."

The Rebbe had purchased a set! It gave me enormous encouragement at the time.

AS MY ARTWORK BECAME A BIT BETTER KNOWN, I was invited to exhibit it, and at one point I had shows scheduled in eight different Chabad Houses across California. I was very new at this and I badly miscalculated how much I would sell, so by the third stop I had sold almost everything. What was I going to exhibit on the fourth stop, never mind those after that? In a panic, I tried to paint some new things at night, but that didn't work out too well, and I had to borrow back the works I had already sold just to have something to show. By the end of the tour, I was a nervous wreck and I went home sick from the whole experience.

I wrote to the Rebbe for advice on how to avoid such anxiety in the future—what I should meditate on and what else I should do. He responded that I should focus on the concept of Divine Providence and that I should place on display at my exhibitions the following: a charity box, the Five Books of Moses, the Book of Psalms, and a prayer book. He also said that before every show, I should give to charity "eighteen times eighteen cents."

I did just that, and the Rebbe's advice helped me through many challenging situations.

Often exhibitions—especially in international venues, where one has to deal with customs, taxes, import laws and corrupt officials—can be very stressful. Then there are shows where hardly anybody shows up, or those where lots of people show up but nobody buys anything. But no matter what happens, meditating on Divine Providence and donating to charity even before making a profit helps to buttress my faith that G-d is watching and taking care of my livelihood. And that displaces a lot of the anxiety and fills me with peace. I am able to keep the real goal in mind, which is to touch other Jewish souls through my art.

Early on, I realized that this is what the Rebbe was encouraging me

Michoel at an art fair
in the early 1980s, with
charity boxes and holy
books on display.

Courtesy of
Michoel Muchnik

to do through my artistic talent — to spread the wellsprings of Chasidic teachings — because in this generation people are very much influenced by art.

But when I was first getting started, the art that was around tended to depict stereotypical images — like those one still sees of *chasidim* dancing. It didn't fully portray the beauty of *mitzvot* or the inner meaning of the Torah. It took the Rebbe to see that art could do more — that it could have a profound effect on people and draw them closer to Judaism.

Once I understood that this was my mission, I felt that I had a tremendous responsibility, and I believe that my efforts, as guided by the Rebbe, have borne a great deal of fruit. ∎

MAJOR GENERAL RABBI MORDECHAI PIRON

Defending the Defenders

What the chief rabbi and rebbetzin of the IDF
gave to those who give the most

Major General Rabbi Mordechai Piron served as a rabbi in the Israeli Defense Forces from 1948 to 1980 — the last nine years as chief rabbi. He authored six books on Jewish law, philosophy and history. He was interviewed in his home in Jerusalem in August of 2009.

By way of background—I was born in Vienna, Austria, to an Orthodox family. We were not the least bit Zionistic, and I was educated according to the approach that we Jews will return to the Land of Israel when Mashiach comes.

However, after Hitler annexed Austria to Germany in 1938 and the persecution of Jews began, that attitude changed. We knew we were in danger, although not one of us could have imagined in our wildest dreams the extent of the horror that would soon be visited upon the Jewish people. Nonetheless, my parents sought to protect me from whatever was coming by sending me to Israel—which was then called the British Mandate for Palestine. They tried to follow me, but failed to escape in time and perished along with the six million others. I was the only one of the family who made it out.

When I arrived in Israel, I was seventeen, and at first I learned to be a vineyard worker at an agricultural school called Mikveh Israel. But after a while, I moved on to study at the Mercaz HaRav *yeshivah* founded by the famed Ashkenazi chief rabbi, Rav Avraham Yitzchak Kook, who had passed away three years before my arrival there. I also joined the Haganah which, with the founding of the State of Israel in 1948, became the Israel Defense Forces (IDF).

During the War of Independence, I was wounded, and the IDF tried to discharge me because I couldn't fight any longer, but I wouldn't leave. So they offered me a position in the IDF rabbinate, where I served as

The Rebbe holds a *farbrengen* in 770. 10 Shevat, 5736.

Yossi Melamed, The Living Archive

a deputy to Rabbi Shlomo Goren; when he left in 1971, I became chief rabbi of the IDF.

While in the rabbinate of the IDF, I had many occasions to come to the United States on various missions. Indeed, Yitzhak Rabin used to call me "the flying rabbi."

The first time I came, in the late 1960s, I decided that I wanted to meet the Rebbe because I had heard so much about him. I recall arriving at Chabad Headquarters on the 19th of the Hebrew month of Kislev, not realizing that this was the day dedicated to commemorating the liberation from czarist prison of Rabbi Schneur Zalman of Liadi, the 18th-century founder of the Chabad movement. It was not the best day to make a visit, as the place was jam-packed. After a long wait, I almost walked away, but suddenly a *chasid* appeared and said to me, "Are you Rabbi Piron? Come with me."

He took me around back, into the synagogue crammed with several

thousand people and found me a seat. I recall that the Rebbe was midway into a talk, and though I had missed a great deal of it, his strong but pleasant voice penetrated my being. Somehow, it filled me with joy and a profound feeling of awe.

When the Rebbe finished speaking and singing began, another *chasid* appeared and urged me to come with him, bringing me straight to the Rebbe.

It's hard to describe what this moment was like for me. My knees were shaking, though I am not an excitable person—just the reverse; I have always been level-headed and rational. But in this encounter, I felt something special and unique.

As I stood there, the Rebbe poured me a small shot of vodka. No one told me what was expected of me, but I had a feeling that I should recite the blessing out loud, so that's what I did. I drank a little, and then shook the Rebbe's hand. As I did so, there was a tremendous feeling of joy in my heart. The Rebbe looked at me and said, "May everything that you want to achieve come true—both in the IDF and in your personal life."

That was my first meeting with the Rebbe, and ever since, I tried to see him whenever I came to the US; it became an emotional need for me.

THE NEXT TIME I CAME, I requested a private audience, and I spent four hours with the Rebbe. Outside, people were waiting. When I came out, I was besieged with questions: "What happened in there with the Rebbe? … Why so long?" But I was not at liberty to explain—only that, in general, we spoke about how I could fulfill my life's mission.

I came again after I had been appointed chief rabbi of the IDF in 1971. On this occasion, I was accompanied by my late wife. I wasn't sure if I

Rabbi and Mrs. Piron
Courtesy of the Piron family

could bring her to the Rebbe, but when I asked his secretary, the answer I received was: "The Rebbe says you *must* bring your wife!"

During that audience, the Rebbe spoke with her more than with me, discussing the importance of the Jewish woman, what that means in practice, how she might fill her home with a true Torah spirit, and how she should stand by my side—not simply to help me, but to work *together* with me. I recall that he said, "If a woman doesn't stand together with her husband, her husband cannot succeed."

He asked her, "How is it to live with a man who is the chief rabbi of the IDF, who is not at home very much—and when he comes home, he is very tired? How do you occupy your time without him?"

He suggested to her that she should take on her own projects—helping lone soldiers for example, or caring for the families of soldiers with problems. "A wise woman like you should be able to do a lot."

And, because of the Rebbe's advice, she did it. She had already been doing some of the things he suggested, but now she had more incentive to double her efforts. She worked with the definite feeling that the Rebbe was behind her.

During another audience—in 1973—he spoke about how I could instill the spirit of Torah into the soldiers of the IDF. He said, "By force, you will achieve nothing. The way to persuade people is by showing them the richness of the Torah." I recall that he also said, "The State of Israel exists today, but it faces many challenges, because so many of the gentile nations are not ready to accept the fact that the Jewish people have a state and that we will continue to flourish here."

In practical terms, he convinced me—because he was so adamant about it—that every unit in the IDF must have a pair of *tefillin* (in addition to a small library of Jewish holy books, as well as a charity box), so that whenever a soldier wanted to don *tefillin*, it would be available to him. As a result, we brought in Chabad *chasidim* to Tzrifin, the main IDF base, to stand there and offer *tefillin* to many soldiers, who accepted the idea good-naturedly, even happily, and were willing to do it.

A Chabad *chasid* helps IDF soldiers don *tefillin* in the Sinai Desert. November 27, 1973.

Levi Freidin,
The Living Archive

Chabad *chasidim* help
IDF soldiers fulfill
the *mitzvah* of *luvav*
and *etrog*. Sukkot,
5744-1983.

*Tzvika Friedman,
The Living Archive*

At that time, as now, there were many Chabad *chasidim* serving in the
IDF, and the Rebbe asked me more than once: "Did you meet Chabad
soldiers? How do these soldiers behave? How are they doing? How can
we help them?"

I was happy to report that the Chabad soldiers were sturdy, serious,
obedient, and that they wanted to continue in the spirit of Chabad.

When I did meet such soldiers, I would tell them, "I visited the Rebbe," and I could see how impressed they were by that — for them, this
was a tremendous thing. And they would ask me, "What happened?
What did you talk about?" So I would tell them what I could, and this
strengthened them.

THE *TEFILLIN* CAMPAIGN WAS VERY SUCCESSFUL, as was the Rebbe's campaign to affix *mezuzot* throughout the IDF. The Rebbe considered this very important, and he urged me to get it done. And so I did. In a joint effort with Rabbis Ephraim Wolff and Shlomo Maidanchik, I put up about 60,000 *mezuzot* throughout the IDF facilities. Afterwards, I got a letter from the Rebbe indicating that he was pleased.

One day during the thick of the *mezuzah* campaign, I received an urgent message that I must appear before the Chief of Staff. When I arrived, I found him sitting there with the head of the budget department. Both had very grim expressions on their faces. "We've discovered a major case of corruption in connection with the *mezuzot*," the budget head began. "We're paying a great deal of money for each of these *mezuzah* scrolls. This is excessive—we can get them printed through our vendors for a fraction of the price!"

I had been nervous going in, but now I relaxed. I proceeded to explain that printed *mezuzah* scrolls could never be kosher—they had to be hand-written by a scribe or they would be worthless.

I made sure to pass on that story to the Rebbe so he could get a chuckle out of it. But, in truth, it wasn't amusing—it was all very serious. This was an important, holy campaign which we launched on the Rebbe's insistence. The Rebbe made it clear to me that just as the *mezuzah* guards the Jewish home, it also guards the barracks where the soldiers live. It guards the guardians of the Nation of Israel.

AMONG THE ISRAELIS WHO HEADED VARIOUS MINISTRIES and departments, I was not the only one who would come to see the Rebbe. Indeed, I would venture to say that everybody who was anybody came.

I know for sure that there were officers at the highest level of the IDF, officials at the highest level of the Defense Ministry, and government ministers who were routinely in touch with the Rebbe. And they were impressed by him, just as I was. They asked his advice, which they took very, very seriously.

I assumed, though I cannot be sure, that from these visitors the Rebbe received his clear and up-to-date information of what was going on in Israel's armed services. He even had knowledge—which surprised me—about strategic and tactical matters. When I'd begin to explain to him some issue or another, he would already know all about it and would even add to my words. When I'd look at him in surprise, impressed by how much he knew, he would just smile.

Once, he asked me what was happening with the peace talks. In my answer, I explained that if we decide to retreat from some places, it's possible that, by way of compromise, the Arabs might agree to a peace treaty—the hope being that if we show good will, so will they.

The Rebbe was completely opposed to this approach. He held that this was downright dangerous from a security perspective, and that we had no right to give up any portion of the Land of Israel. He explained that the Land belongs to G-d, and He chose to give it to the Jewish people. So what right do we have to annul His gift?

ONE TIME I CAME TO THE REBBE to confide in him a problem I was experiencing. It related to an upcoming violation of Shabbat in the IDF, where I was told by the top brass, "Rabbi, we have to do this—don't get involved."

In the meantime, I came to see the Rebbe and I told him about it, because it bothered me very much. "According to my sense of truth," I said, "I should protest vehemently. I shouldn't let it happen. But my superiors are warning me to be quiet, to stay out of it. Perhaps, in this case, that is indeed the right way?"

The Rebbe looked at me. And I must say, the Rebbe's gaze had a way of communicating special meaning. It was as if the Rebbe had two expressions: the warm face of kindness, good-heartedness and friendliness, which was like a drink of water to a thirsty child; and a penetrating gaze, which felt as if he was looking right into my soul.

When I asked him my question, he gave me that second look. And then he said, "Do you know the story of Rabbi Eliezer ben Hyrkanus?"

The Rebbe was referring to the story related in the Talmud of the great 1st-century sage who refused to give in on a point of Jewish law even when his peers excommunicated him. His commitment to truth was absolute and he suffered to the end; it was only after his death that he was vindicated.

The Rebbe coming out of his office.
Purim 5731-1971.
Velvel Schildkraut, The Living Archive

"Do you know the story of Rabbi Akavia ben Mahalalel?" the Rebbe prodded.

Of course, I did. The story of Rabbi Akavia, another 1st-century sage, is also related in the Talmud, and it is similar to that of Rabbi Eliezer. He, too, stood firm in the face of opposition, and even though his peers offered to make him chief justice if he would change his mind on a point of Jewish law, he refused. "It is better for me to be called a fool all my days than become an evil man before G-d for even one hour," he said.

I got the Rebbe's point, but still I objected: "How can I compare myself and my dilemma with these great men?"

"A person should fight for the truth that is in his heart," he responded, "for in essence, this battle is with himself. And he should remember that he stands before the G-d of Truth."

He saw that I was shaken by the implication of his words, and so he added something to comfort me: "Sometimes, today's waves are very high and terrible, and one thinks that the storm will last forever, but suddenly the sea calms and everything is forgotten." That's what he said, and nothing more.

Wouldn't you know it—he was right. By the time I returned to Israel two weeks later, the whole issue had been forgotten. The struggle had been inside of me and I had become ready to stand up to it, but the issue had worked itself out.

MORE THAN A FEW TIMES, THE REBBE WROTE TO ME. Some of these letters have been published, some not. Again and again, he pointed out that the IDF can be a forum for instilling Torah values in the youth of Israel.

In one letter, written in the summer of 1974, the Rebbe wrote: "As we discussed many times, soldiers are inclined and ready to receive guidance in matters of Torah." He went on to explain that just as our ancestors declared at Mount Sinai, "we will do and we will hear," putting action before understanding, so too soldiers follow orders first before understanding the reason for them. Secondly, in the army, the commanders make determinations based on the needs of entire battalions, or even the needs of the country at large, rather than on the needs of individual soldiers.

Rabbi Piron (L.) with other officials of the IDF.

Courtesy of the Piron family

These are the prerequisites for receiving the Torah and its *mitzvot*: 1) putting action before understanding; and 2) knowing that all Jews are responsible for one another. In the words of Maimonides it is a matter of Jewish law: "A person should always look at himself as equally balanced between merit and sin, and the world as equally balanced between merit and sin. If he performs one *mitzvah*, he tips his balance and that of the world to the side of merit and brings deliverance and salvation to himself and others."

In his correspondence, the Rebbe always urged us to seize the opportunity we had to make a difference and supported all of our efforts.

His support meant the most to me after the Yom Kippur War, when I was responsible for burying 2,300 fallen soldiers. That was my fate; that's what Divine Providence wanted of me. It was a very difficult

Rabbi Piron reciting *Kaddish* at the funeral of President Zalman Shazar. October 7, 1974.

Saar Yaakov, Israel Government Press Office

period for me, as I had to visit many widows and mothers and tell them the catastrophic news.

It was a terrible time, and the Rebbe understood the toll this took on me. He tried to strengthen my spirits so that I shouldn't falter, telling me that what I did during the war was a very big *mitzvah*. And he predicted that Israel would continue to get stronger. After going through this horrendous war, in which we defied the odds and were victorious, we would become even stronger, with G-d's help, going from strength to strength. He emphasized this several times. To hear this was so important to me.

When the Rebbe passed away, I felt as if my own father had died ... really and truly. I was devasted and lost for a long time. I couldn't grasp that he was gone. For some reason, I had convinced myself that such a great Jew would live forever. And I have never visited his gravesite because, for me, the Rebbe isn't in a physical space — he dwells in my heart. ■

Don't Burn Your Bridges

Find out who needs a mikveh, *who needs a* Tanya,
and who just needs a bowl of fruit

Mr. Efraim Steinmetz was a businessman and community activist in Caracas, Venezuela. He was interviewed in Chicago in October of 1999.

The earliest images of the Rebbe that are lodged in my memory date back to when I was eleven years old and my family had just emigrated from Hungary to France. My parents knew we had to get out as anti-Semitism was exploding all over Eastern Europe, the Nazis were threatening Jews everywhere, and World War II was imminent. So my father devised a plan to take us to the Dominican Republic via Paris, where we stayed for several months before traveling on.

During our stay in Paris, my brother and I attended the Lubavitcher school on Rue Dieu. One day, my father told us, "When we first came to Paris, I had the privilege to meet a very fine man, the son-in-law of the Lubavitcher Rebbe. He is the one who told me about the school on Rue Dieu. I want you to meet him."

Of course, in 1939, the Rebbe was Rabbi Yosef Yitzchak Schneersohn—today known as the Previous Rebbe—and his son-in-law was Rabbi Menachem Mendel Schneerson who, some years later, would become the Rebbe himself.

The Rebbe (who was not yet the Rebbe then) made a deep impression on my brother and me. He seemed to love children, he talked to us as equals, and he also gave us candies. Although I am an old man now, I still remember that meeting vividly.

I felt at the time that there was a kinship between my father and him. My father was a deeply religious man but also an enlightened man who was well informed regarding what was happening in the world—he kept up with world politics, world events and the world economy. He was not the kind of Jew who sat learning Torah in the corner, oblivious to what is going on around him. And he felt that he found in the Rebbe someone with whom he could converse on an intellectual level. So their connection became very strong.

Later, my father told me how impressed he was with the Rebbe's humility, wisdom, and dedication to Torah learning. There were several pieces of advice the Rebbe gave him regarding migration that served us well—what to take with us and what to do once we arrived in the Dominican Republic.

My father followed the Rebbe's advice. He took a Torah scroll with him, and—before we left—he learned how to slaughter chickens in the kosher way. He had never done that before, but he learned, thanks to the Rebbe, who told him that there might not be any kosher food in the Dominican Republic.

We kept up a connection with the Rebbe ever since then. We visited him often in New York, especially after 1945, when we left the Dominican Republic for Venezuela. Through the years, he gave us many blessings and much good advice. Some of those meetings still vividly stand out in my mind.

Efraim (back, center) between his parents in the Dominican Republic. Circa 1940.

Courtesy of the Steinmetz family

The Rebbe in the 1930s.
Courtesy of Kehot Publication Society

IN 1960, I came to see him together with my wife to seek his guidance regarding the education of our children and whether their needs mandated that we move from Venezuela. We had three children at the time and we were expecting our fourth.

Efraim and Lore Steinmetz
Courtesy of the Steinmetz family

I recall that when we entered his office, the Rebbe stood up like a gentleman and greeted my wife warmly, inviting her to sit down. She did as he requested, while I stood next to his desk, since I knew that this was the proper way to behave in front of the Rebbe.

We explained that we were thinking of leaving Venezuela because our children were growing up and we were worried they could not get a good Jewish education in Caracas.

The Rebbe said, "Whenever possible I am not in favor of people moving away from their communities, because a person's location is determined by Divine Providence. Everyone has a mission to fulfill in the country of their residence, so you must be living in Venezuela for a purpose. There are things you must accomplish there, beyond just making a living. And there is a solution to your problem—you could hire a tutor now and when your children are a bit older you could send them to *yeshivahs* abroad."

As he was speaking, he must have noticed my wife's reaction to the suggestion that she part from her children, because he paused and turned to me, "I'll tell you the truth, Reb Efraim, I see a lot of sadness in your wife's eyes."

Then, he sought to reassure her: "Your husband is accomplishing important things, but if you feel you must move, you can try. Before you do, though, consider my suggestion—it will allow you to stay where you are, and it will do your children no harm; in fact, it will be good for them."

And then he shared this:

"When I was a little boy"—I think he said he was seven—"my father told my mother, 'Mendel can't stay with us anymore because he can't learn properly here.'

"My mother was very upset to hear this. She protested, 'My little Mendel?! You are going to send him far away to learn? He is so very young!'

"But despite her concerns, I was sent away. Where I stayed, I had to get up at four-thirty in the morning to reach my *cheder*. I had a little lantern and by its light I would walk in the night to the school to learn."

After he told that story, he addressed my wife: "It's not so bad to send your kids away to learn. You see? It didn't do me any harm!"

He laughed as he said that and my wife laughed too.

And then he said, "But if you do leave, don't burn your bridges behind you." He was implying that we should keep our friends in Venezuela in the event we needed to return.

As it happened, we moved to the US, but things didn't work out and, before long, we returned to Caracas. When I told the Rebbe that we were going back, he asked me, "You didn't burn your bridges behind you, did you?" And I was able to answer that we did not, as he had advised.

I CAN TESTIFY TO HOW MUCH THE REBBE CARED about every single Jew in every part of the world, whether in Caracas, or Hong Kong, or Tokyo, or wherever.

For example, I learned how much thought he gave to the Jews of the Dominican Republic. One day he said to me, "You know, they have no *mikveh* over there—not one in the whole country. I think you should build a *mikveh* for them."

I protested, "Rebbe, since we moved to Venezuela forty years ago, I haven't even set foot in the Dominican Republic!"

"That doesn't matter," he countered. "If you don't want to go, you can send people."

So that is what I did. I paid two young men to go there and they came back saying, "The community in S. Domingo doesn't want to build a *mikveh* because they don't have a place for it."

But the Rebbe wouldn't accept that answer. He sent over plans for a *mikveh* and I dispatched my guys there again. I told the Rebbe, "Although we can't build a *mikveh* in S. Domingo, we can build a *mikveh* here in Venezuela on the Margarita Island instead."

This is what we did and the Rebbe was happy, but he continued to insist that we build a *mikveh* in S. Domingo as well, and even sent blueprints for it. Unfortunately, many obstacles remained and it did not happen.

IN ANOTHER MEETING THE REBBE DEMONSTRATED how much thought he gave to the Jews of Caracas. He asked me to draw him a map of the city and show him where the Jewish population was located. So I explained to him that Sephardi Jews have their community here and the Ashkenazi Jews had their community there.

He then began to ask me detailed questions about the demographics of Caracas: How are things shifting? What are the trends with the movement of the Jewish population from one part of the city to the other? When he heard that the young professionals were moving to the eastern part of the city, he said, "That's very important to know. You have to establish a niche over there because with time the Jewish youngsters will find this a desirable place to live and they will need a Jewish community in place.

He was absolutely right. That is what happened. And, because of his foresight, that is where the first Chabad House—Hogar Jabad Lubavitch—was established, with Rabbi Moshe Perman at the helm.

I HAVE MANY MORE STORIES that I can tell about the Rebbe's care for Jews in far-flung places, all of which I witnessed firsthand.

I often made long international trips on business, and each time that I traveled from Venezuela through the US to Japan, I used to come to New York to see the Rebbe.

On one occasion in 1970, I called up and the Rebbe's secretary, Rabbi Mordechai Hodakov, told me, "I am very sorry, but this time I cannot give you an appointment. The Rebbe is simply too overbooked."

I said, "Just please ask him to give me a blessing for my upcoming

trip." He promised to do so and asked for my itinerary. "I'm leaving
Thursday for Chicago to spend Shabbat with my parents," I said. "And
on Sunday I'm flying to Japan, arriving there on Tuesday, and then I will
be spending Shabbat in Kobe."

"Very good. I have your father's number."

I went to visit my parents, stayed there through Shabbat and was
surprised when, as I was changing planes in S. Francisco, I heard an
announcement: "There is a phone call for Mr. Steinmetz." I went to the
phone, and it was Rabbi Hodakov.

I said, "How did you find me here?" He explained, "You told me
you'd be in Chicago, so I called your parents there. Your parents told me
you left already, but your father figured that by now you should be in S.
Francisco, boarding the plane for Tokyo. Listen, I need your address in
Japan. The Rebbe wants to send you something."

He didn't specify what it was and I was a bit puzzled, but I gave him
the name of the hotel where I'd be staying. He then added, "You have a

*Efraim on a business
trip to Japan.*

*Courtesy of the
Steinmetz family*

The Rebbe distributing Tanyas.

The Living Archive

blessing from the Rebbe for a nice trip and much success."

As planned, after I arrived in Japan, I went to Kobe for Shabbat. When I checked into my hotel, I was informed that there was a little parcel waiting for me, which had been sent by special delivery from New York.

I opened it, and it was from the Rebbe—there was a small prayer book and a copy of the *Tanya*, as well as a note that I should give this "to the one who may need it."

I didn't know what to do with these items, but I decided to take them with me to the synagogue that evening. When I arrived there, I met a good friend of mine, a pearl dealer from Jerusalem—Ben David—who had also come to Japan on business. He was very happy to see me, and he invited me to join him for a Shabbat meal, although I declined the invitation because I had already made other arrangements.

Then he asked me, "What do you have there?" indicating to the package from the Rebbe that I was holding in my hands. And so I told him the whole story.

When I did, he started to cry. He just completely broke down and couldn't stop crying.

When he composed himself, he explained: "This is the most wonderful thing that has ever happened in my life. You know, I have a custom since my youth to learn *Tanya* every morning after prayers. But by accident I left my *Tanya* at home and I have been without it for weeks now. I phoned my son and told him to send it to me; he promised to do so, but it never arrived. I have been very upset about this, and I didn't know what to do."

And then he said, his voice cracking again, "You know, the Rebbe sensed my predicament. He sensed my pain and he sent exactly what I needed."

It was an amazing sequence of events. I had called the Rebbe and said I was going to Japan, and the Rebbe sent these books, making sure they arrived before Shabbat, instructing me to give it to the one who needs it. And it was exactly what this man had been missing.

IN 1977, I WENT TO THE REBBE to ask his blessing for a speedy recovery on behalf of my father, who had just undergone an operation.

When he heard that, the Rebbe's face fell. He was usually smiling and happy to see me, and he used to say, "Many people come here to unload their baggage, but afterwards, I don't hear from them anymore. But you always bring me good news, and you follow up on the conversations we've had."

Unfortunately, this time, I brought him bad news — that a Jew he cared very much about was not well — and he said with a sad expression, "I'm very unhappy to hear that your father is not feeling well, and I wish him a speedy recovery."

Then he asked, "Where is your father now?"

"He is in the hospital, recuperating," I answered.

"You should bring him some Torah books," the Rebbe said. "And some fruit. I remember that, back in Paris, your father liked fruit very much."

Now, I repeat, this was 1977, almost forty years after the Rebbe first met my father in Paris. Yet the Rebbe didn't forget that my father liked fruit!

I don't know how he could remember such small details, but he did.

HIS MEMORY WAS JUST AMAZING, but truth be told, as far as I am concerned, the Rebbe was amazing in every way. In my opinion, he was the only Jewish leader in this century who worried about and was willing to help every single Jew, no matter who he was or where he lived. And I miss him very much.

These days, I find a lot of comfort in reading the Rebbe's letters in which he offers guidance to Jews dealing with so many different problems, and I always learn a lesson to live by. In this way, he continues to guide me.

Postscript by
Efraim's son, Binyomin

In 1939, my grandfather, Rabbi Chananya Yom Tov Lipa Steinmetz, together with his wife and their four small children, emigrated from Hungary to the Dominican Republic. They settled in the city of S. Domingo. At the time, there was a small Jewish community there, and my grandfather was soon appointed its leader.

During this time, my grandfather corresponded with the Previous Rebbe, and only recently have I discovered that correspondence. He requested *matzot* for Passover, as well as other essentials. In response, the Previous Rebbe, who had arrived in America only seven weeks earlier, expressed great interest in the S. Domingo community. He wrote:

> In response to your letter from this past *Erev Pesach*, I would like to know in detail about the number of families, may they increase, who are in your community; and their religious status ... when I receive a detailed answer to my questions then I will see how I can, G-d willing, help them.

In an addendum, the Previous Rebbe listed his specific questions, which indicated the level of his concern:

> 1) How many G-d-fearing families? 2) How many souls approximately? 3) How many middle-aged? 4) How many young adults? 5) How many children? 6) Is there a *mikveh*? 7) A rabbi? 8) A *shochet*? 9) Schools, teachers? 10) How do they make a living? 11) What is the conduct of the youngsters? 12) Is Shabbat observed? 13) What about kosher food? 14) What is the name of the institution helping the war refugees? 15) Have they turned to anyone for help? 16) What help do they need?

After receiving my grandfather's reply, the Previous Rebbe—in a letter dated six weeks later—focused on the need for a *mikveh* and the need to prepare a budget in order to raise the necessary funds.

Unfortunately, the *mikveh* was not built at that time, as life in S. Domingo during the war was very difficult, and indeed, in 1945, my grandfather and the family immigrated to Caracas, Venezuela.

Years later, after the Previous Rebbe passed away, my father, Efraim Steinmetz, developed a close relationship with the Rebbe and merited to meet him several times. In one of their meetings, the Rebbe expressed to my father his wish to see a kosher *mikveh* built in S. Domingo. My father took his request very seriously and worked diligently for years to complete this undertaking.

He began by sending emissaries to S. Domingo, who even brought with them blueprints received from the Rebbe's office for the construction of a small *mikveh*. Unfortunately, many obstacles came up while trying to carry out the project. However, my father was not deterred.

At one point, he and my mother visited S. Domingo and met with members of its Jewish community. They were warmly welcomed by all present and had the opportunity to speak with them about the importance of having a kosher *mikveh* in the city. Still nothing happened.

Sometime after the S. Domingo visit, my father suffered a stroke which affected his speech. Nevertheless, he expressed the desire that I continue to pursue this project.

Consequently, a *mikveh* expert, Rabbi Gershon Grossbaum of Minnesota, was sent over there in order to assess the terrain and give advice for a successful construction. My father was enthusiastic about the plan, but once again there were unsurmountable obstacles, and the *mikveh* was not built. Apparently, it was still not the right time.

In 2008, Rabbi Shimon and Michal Pelman arrived in S. Domingo, becoming the first ever full-time Chabad emissaries in the Dominican Republic. Rabbi Pelman had heard of my father's relentless efforts to have a *mikveh* built in S. Domingo, and so he contacted him. It seemed that now—at last—it was actually possible to build such a *mikveh*.

My father was very happy to hear the news, and of course was ready to take on the responsibility. A video of my father's JEM interview—in which he discusses the Rebbe's persistence in seeing a *mikveh* built in

S. Domingo — was used to promote this endeavor.

The project took off, and finally, in September of 2017, my sister and I were invited to attend, on behalf of our parents, the inauguration of the beautiful and luxurious kosher *mikveh* sponsored by the Steinmetz and Sragowicz families.

Seventy-seven years after the mission of building a *mikveh* in S. Domingo was entrusted to my grandfather by the Previous Rebbe, and to my father by the Rebbe, it finally became a reality.

Binyomin (C.) between his son Chanania and sister Suzy, at the dedication for the new *mikveh* in S. Domingo.

Courtesy of the Steinmetz family

DR. DONNA HALPER

A New Optimism

Noble confusion cured with one letter

A former radio DJ and music director, Dr. Donna Halper spent twenty-eight years as a consultant for radio stations in the US and Canada. She has authored six books on media-related subjects and has spent the past several decades as a college professor specializing in communication and media studies. She was interviewed in West Hartford, Connecticut, in August of 2018.

Ever since college, I have made my career in radio broadcasting. Being a DJ and music director in cities like Washington, D.C., Cleveland, and New York brought me into contact with many famous people. I've had my name on rock albums, and if you google my name, you'll see my picture with members of the Canadian rock group Rush on the Hollywood Walk of Fame. I mention this only because the fact that I am accustomed to being around famous people has a great deal to do with my story.

In 1976, just after I got a job as a DJ in New York, I developed some serious health problems. I was rushed to the hospital, where they first thought I had appendicitis, but it turned out to be a cyst on one of my fallopian tubes. Back then, the only way known to address this problem was to intervene surgically, which rendered me unable to ever become pregnant.

Before this happened, I had not been sure if I even wanted to have children; but, suddenly, I found myself living in a culture where women are expected to become mothers, but I couldn't. Not ever.

In fairness, I was fine with this, as I realized that the operation had saved my life. If I had not followed the doctors' advice, I would not be telling this story today. So, I accepted it. But I really wondered what should be the role of a woman who cannot be a wife and mother in the traditional sense.

Although I am not Orthodox, I do have a deep respect for Orthodox Judaism. So when someone suggested that Rabbi Kasriel Kastel of the Lubavitch Youth Organization would be the best person for my question, I wrote to him.

"What's the role in Judaism for a woman who can't have children?" I asked. "If a woman's traditional role is to be a mother, what is she to do if she can't? What if she doesn't have a choice, like me?"

After a long correspondence, he encouraged me to bring my questions to the Rebbe. But I was skeptical that the Rebbe would respond to a letter from me, as I was not part of his community. Addressing my hesitancy, Rabbi Kastel suggested that I go see the Rebbe in action at a *farbrengen*. I agreed; I speak a little Yiddish so I thought that I would at least understand the Rebbe's talk.

Watching the Rebbe from the women's section at the *farbrengen*, my first impression was how spiritual this man was. He truly seemed to be a holy person. There were many children in the room, and he spoke with them so kindly, so gently. The kids were sitting there, not moving, mesmerized, taking in every word he said. Later on, I told my friends, "Never in all the years that I've been alive have I seen anything like this."

As I mentioned, I have met and interviewed many important people over the years, so it is hard to impress me. I am the ultimate skeptic. But there was nothing about this man that seemed phony. He was kind, warm and unassuming, and he knew how to speak to children. I was very impressed and, after the *farbrengen* was over, I followed Rabbi Kastel's suggestion and wrote to the Rebbe, though I really didn't expect an answer.

It took a couple of weeks, but he did answer me—in May of 1977. When I read the letter, the first thing that struck me was that his was not a boilerplate letter. This was a correspondence in which the writer invested time and thought. Yes, it was probably typed by a secretary, but there were handwritten notes and words underlined by hand. This answer—a three-page letter no less—truly came from the Rebbe.

FIRST HE ADDRESSED MY QUESTION about the woman's role in Orthodox Judaism, taking issue with my phrasing:

> With regard to your question about the woman's role from the viewpoint of our religion, or, as you refer to it, "Orthodox" Judaism, I must first point out that the division of Judaism

Donna Halper
in the studios
of WNEU Radio
of Northeastern
University in Boston.
1968.

*Courtesy of Donna
Halper*

into "Orthodox, Conservative, Reform," etc. is a purely arti-
ficial one, for all Jews have one and the same Torah, given
by the One and Same G-d, though there are more observant
Jews and less observant Jews. To tag on a "label" does not, of
course, change the reality.

Then he turned to the heart of my question, expressing Judaism's view
on the place of the woman in Jewish life:

> Those who think that the Torah places the woman in an infe-
> rior role to that of the man labor under a misconception, for
> this has no basis in truth. Man and woman are like the head
> and the heart in the physical body: both are equally vital,
> though each has entirely different functions, and only the
> normal functioning of both together ensure a healthy body.
> The same is true of the role of the man and woman in Jewish
> life, and, indeed, in any healthy human society.
> It follows that the heart need not feel inferior to the brain,

although in certain aspects it depends on the brain, just as the brain need not feel inferior to the heart because in certain respects it depends on the latter. Similarly in Jewish life there are duties and functions which G-d has allotted to the woman and those allotted to the man.

In the most beautiful terms, he turned to my specific situation, assuring me that G-d did not expect of me that which was impossible. Although the Jewish approach is generally to consider action even more important than knowledge, in my case, on the issue of having children, G-d would suffice with knowing what was in my heart.

> Where a person, for some reason, is unable to perform a certain *mitzvah* ... there is a ruling in the Torah, *Torat Emet* (so called because all its teachings are true), "the Merciful One excuses a person who is incapable of performing his, or her, duty." Indeed, G-d who knows what is in the heart of everyone, and knowing that were the person able, he or she would have performed it, considers the thought in place of the deed.
>
> Incidentally, it is noteworthy that of the various Divine names, it is the name *Rachamana* ("Merciful One") that is used in the above ruling. This pointedly emphasizes that all G-d's precepts derive from His attribute of mercy and loving-kindness, which, like all Divine attributes, is infinite. It follows that a person who is precluded from performing a *mitzvah* by circumstances *beyond* his or her control is completely excused and exonerated.

The Rebbe was basically telling me that I need not feel bad that I couldn't fulfill this *mitzvah* for reasons beyond my control, because it's the intention that counts. That really resonated with me.

If I wished I could have done the *mitzvah* but it wasn't my fault that I couldn't, I wouldn't be judged harshly for it. I wouldn't be judged at all. G-d would know and understand.

Now, a lot of people might think that all this is obvious. But it wasn't to me. I was raised in an educational system ruled by rabbis who were very rigid. They didn't talk about understanding or forgiveness. But the Rebbe was so different—he was such a compassionate person. He was a

Donna Halper, 5203 8ᵗʰ RD S #523A
Music Director Arlington Va. 22204   (703) 522-1111

16 june 78

Friends:

Several weeks ago, I called and asked
about a bumper sticker--"We Never Lost It"
to replace the badly peeling one on my
car. You so kindly sent me the aforementioned bumper stick
several others, and I
enough. Since I do no
normally charge for th
donation of $10.00--I
give you, but I hope t
for now.

Several stupid que
hate to ask Lubavitche
as I am perhaps betray
knowledge about my fait
defence, I must say I
study as I was growing
didn't feel females ne
more than a superficia
and what I do know I l
later on...) or provin
ignorant. Rabbi Kaste
and be well) kindly ar
questions when I lived
in one afternoon about
he is around while you
please send him my bes
miss having Jews arour

WAVA 10

mouth shut--for me, that would not be the
solution, I'm afraid, and thus, as I continue
to need contact with Jews and there are so
many things I still want to know about, I find
few places that will address themselves to me.
I am what I was the last time I wrote--not a
wife (although I wish I were) and not a
mother (and have no desire to be one, although
I do love kids), a feminist like my namesake
D'vorah, and a woman in a ᵭᵭᵭ tradition made
by and for men, which excludes me from much
of the contact I think I need. I am not
trying to change anyone--I am trying to feel
wanted and included in the community of Israel
and at times I feel totally alienated. Perhaps you don't understand--you don't even know
me, and the few times I did come to Crown
Heights, the men seemed very unwilling to talk
to a strange woman (yes I did dress modestly).
And as for talking with the women, I tried to,
but home-making and childraising are not my
main source of knowledge, I'm afraid...I love
and respect the ideal of the Jewish housewife,
but what about those of us who aren't? Where
do we go? Who wants us until we marry someone and become okay to be talked to?

Enough of this or you'll think I'm not worth
conversing with. My home address is on the
check, should you at least have the time to
answer the questions. I am sorry if I took
too much of your time--believe it or not, I
hate to bother people...especially scholars...
I wish I could be a Torah scholar--I wonder if
it's too late...

Donna

One of Donna's early
letters to Rabbi Kastel.

Courtesy of Rabbi Kastel

world apart from the many rabbis, priests and gurus that I've met. Their
attitude was: "We've got the truth, and that's all there is to it."

I'm sure he would have liked for everyone to become more religious,
but that's not where he started. He met each person on his or her level
and made each person feel—made *me* feel—that I mattered to him.
Even though I was not a member of his community, he genuinely cared
about me as a fellow Jew.

THERE WAS ANOTHER PART OF HIS LETTER that struck me as a very beautiful teaching. He wrote that I need not apologize for asking questions because that is the way to get answers—indeed, that is the Jewish way, and that is why the Jews are described in the Torah as wise and understanding people. We are not expected to rely on faith alone, with one prerequisite that goes all the way back to the time when we received the Torah at Mount Sinai. At that moment, the Jewish people told G-d, "*na'aseh v'nishma*—we will do and we will hear." That is, the doing must come before the understanding. Our fulfillment of G-d's commandments cannot be *conditioned* on knowing their full spiritual significance.

He followed this point with a profound metaphor:

> There is a sound pragmatic, or "business" consideration involved, as, by way of a simple illustration, when one is offered an opportunity to invest a dollar with a view to earning a thousand dollars, though there may be a remote possibility of losing the $1. A normal individual would certainly not hesitate to make this decision.
>
> Similarly, when a Jew decides to act as a Jew by investing a relatively small effort—whether that means restricting himself by keeping kosher, observing Shabbat, etc., the most the person will have lost would be having denied himself certain foods or some convenience on Shabbat. However, if we were to wait with the performance of *mitzvot* until we understand their significance we deprive ourselves of the eternal good which was within easy reach.

Many people have this backwards. They wait around until they understand something before they do it. But the Rebbe was saying that there are some things you might never understand, or you might understand them only when it's too late. So just go out and do the *mitzvah* now. Out of the doing will come wisdom.

The Rebbe was also saying that fulfillment of a *mitzvah* shouldn't be treated like an inconvenience—it should be treated as an opportunity. And that's something that made a lot of sense to me. He wasn't presenting it as a case of "You'd better do this, or else…" He was saying,

"Here is something really meaningful for you, so why wouldn't you want to give it a try?"

This motivated me to keep kosher even though I am not Orthodox. It's a way for me to show respect for my parents, G-d rest their souls. And it's a way to remind myself every day that, in my home, I should have a little bit of holiness — that I should try to remember, even when I eat, that there's an opportunity to be closer to G-d.

I'm not Orthodox, and I could eat bacon, but why would I? By refraining, I am keeping a *mitzvah*, and the more *mitzvot* I keep, the more spiritual benefit I derive.

The Rebbe greets an individual during a meeting of the Machne Israel Special Development Fund. 5 Tishrei, 5748-1987.

Velvel Schildkraut, The Living Archive

RABBI MENACHEM M. SCHNEERSON
Lubavitch
770 Eastern Parkway
Brooklyn. N. Y. 11213
493-9250

מנחם מענדל שניאורסאהן
ליובאוויטש

770 איסטערן פּאַרקוויי
ברוקלין, נ. י.

By the Grace of G-d
13th of Iyar, 5737
Brooklyn, N.Y.

D. L. Halper
c/o WRVR
85 Claremont Avenue
New York, N.Y. 10027

- 2 -

able, he or she would have performed it, considers the thought in place of the deed.

Incidentally, it is noteworthy that of the various Divine names, it is the name רחמנא ('Merciful One') that is used in the above ruling. This pointedly emphasizes that all G-d's precepts derive from His attribute of mercy and lovingkindness, which, like all Divine attributes, is infinite. It follows that where a person is precluded from performing a Mitzva by circumstances beyond his or her control is completely excused and exonerated.

Needless to say, one need not apologise for asking questions. On the contrary, since Jews are described in the Torah as a 'wise and under-standing people,' it is desirable that questions which come within the realm of human understanding should be also be understood and not left to faith alone, wherever this possible. There is only one prerequisite, which goes back to the time when the Torah and Miztvos were given at Sinai, namely that the Torah must be accepted on the basis of Naaseh ('we will do') first, and then v'nishma ('we will understand') - meaning, that the performance of Mitzvos must not be made conditional on the understanding of their deeper significance, etc., nor must the vitality and enthusiasm of the performance be any the less.

This basic principle and attitude is also a matter of common sense. If the Torah is accepted as Divine - otherwise there is no point at all in any questions and discussions, since if it man-made one would be free to do as one pleases - that is, given by a Supreme Being, Whose Essence is beyong human grasp, it would be a contradiction in terms to demand to know the meaning and significance of each Divine Mitzva before performing it, for it would reduce the Supreme Being to the level of the limited human intelligence, which, moreover, is subject to de-velopment, since human understanding increases from day to day with newly acquired knowledge and experince; yet he insists on understanding it today, on his present level.

One might even add
consideration involved,
offered an opportunity
dollars, though there
normal individual woul
larly, when a Jew, on
in a relatively s
Kashrus and Shabbos ob
him by saying, even if
grasp the significance
have lost would be havi
on Shabbos. On the oth
of Mitzvos until he will
will act like any gentile
was his within easy rea
cover the truth, he will

me delay.

n with my birth-
'One who blesses
e of all blessings."
you in all needs.

cole from the view-
udaism,

'orthodox, con-
ll Jews have one
ough there are
n a 'label' does

so been frequently
e woman in an in-
on, for it has no
e heart in the phy-
ely different
her ensure a healthy
an in Jewish life, and,

rain, although in
in need not feel in -
s on the latter.

G-d has allotted to

rm a certain Mitzva
Torah, Toras Emes
iful One excuses a
y." Indeed, G-d
that were the person

- 3 -

Divine Torah, with all the consequences therefrom,

Much more could be said on the subject matter, but I trust the above will suffice. May G-d, whose benevolent Providence extends to each and everyone individually, lead you in the path of Truth.

With blessing M. Schneerson

P.S. Since you refer to women's lib, which has become so popular in recent years, it baffles me that the thrust of the movement is centered on the woman's becoming *similar* to man -- and this is what is termed 'independence' and 'feminist' pride, etc.!

The Rebbe's letter to Donna.
Courtesy of Donna Halper

OVER THE YEARS, I hung onto the Rebbe's letter because it meant so much to me. His emphasis was not on what you can't do, but on what you *can* do. And, for me, that made all the difference.

As he advised, I focused on the *mitzvot* that were possible for me to do. And this is what I would like to communicate to any woman who finds herself in my position. If you can't have children, remember that there are plenty of other *mitzvot* that you can do. If you like children, there are plenty waiting to be adopted. If you don't want to adopt, there are plenty of kids who need mentors. There are kids with disabilities who need someone to invest in them and help them out.

I, myself, became an advocate for a young man with autism. He never spoke until he was twenty-seven years old, and I was told I was wasting my time trying to teach him. And yet every week I came and I taught him and, one day, he looked at me and said, "Hi Donna."

We've been friends ever since. I've been helping him out for thirty-four years now.

If someone had told me years ago that I would be teaching an adult with autism, I would have said, "What? I'm a rock-and-roll DJ!"

But you never know. You never know who G-d is going to put you in touch with, and you never know what *mitzvot* and what opportunities are out there waiting for you.

That's what the Rebbe taught me.

MR. CHARLES S. RAMAT

The Wild Teenager

The man who does what he feels meets the
man who says what he means

Mr. Charles S. Ramat, the former chairman of Neurotrop BioScience, presently serves as president of Ramat Equities Inc., a company that invests in emerging technologies. He and his wife Orah live in New York where he was interviewed in April of 2016.

I am a son of Holocaust survivors. While my parents — Emil and Hana — did not suffer in the concentration camps, they lost their entire families during the war — my father alone lost close to two hundred relatives. My mother, who was a teenager at the time, also lost her family. But she survived by joining a band of partisans and eventually making her way to Budapest.

My parents met after the war and made their home in Vienna, where I was born in 1951. At this time, my father went into exporting hardwoods, a business in which he was very successful. But then, one day, while traveling by trolley, he overheard a very well-dressed Viennese woman talking to the conductor about a Chasidic man seated there, saying, "Too bad Hitler missed that one." My father came home and told my mother, "I've had enough; this is no place for us to be."

My parents moved to Trieste, Italy, where their Catholic neighbors treated them nicely. They thought everything was fine until my older sister came home one day and started crossing herself and reciting Christian prayers.

So they decided to leave Italy, but even though they were very Zionistic, they thought that life in Israel would be too hard, so they immigrated to the United States and settled in Monsey, New York. And it's just interesting to me what my fate could have been — I could've been Hungarian, I could have been Austrian or Italian; I could have been Israeli but I turned out to be American. I guess that is part of the Jewish existence: the lot of the wandering Jew.

IN 1967, WHEN I WAS SIXTEEN and my mother was only forty-two, she found out she had breast cancer. I was a wild teenager at the time—I like to joke that I was almost a juvenile delinquent—so she asked me to go to Israel for a year and learn in *yeshivah*. She said it would help me mature and settle down, and it would give her the peace of mind to focus on fighting her illness.

I would have done anything for my mother, so I went, enrolling in the *yeshivah* that my parents had picked out—Kerem B'Yavneh, where the dean, Rabbi Chaim Goldvicht, took me under his wing.

While there, I very much enjoyed studying Jewish ethics (Mussar), and living in Israel. It was a special time, right after the Six-Day War, when Israel had seized the Golan Heights, and I was part of the first group of Jews to visit it. Later, we even got to ski there, with donkeys carrying our ski equipment up the mountain from the Druze village below, and I recall seeing disabled Syrian tanks sitting by the roadside.

Charles (C.) and his friends, skiing in Israel in the winter of 1967.

Courtesy of Charles Ramat

My mother had been right—Israel did mature me, and when I returned to the United States, I enrolled in Yeshiva University, where I was a straight A student. During this time, Rabbi Goldvicht kept in touch with me, and whenever he came to New York, he would look me up.

One day in 1969, he called to say he was in town and asked if I could drive him to a meeting with the Lubavitcher Rebbe. "Of course," I said. "It would be my pleasure. What time should I pick you up?" It turned out the meeting was at 2:00 AM—something I hadn't bargained for—but since I had committed myself, I drove him. When we got to Chabad Headquarters, he went in to see the Rebbe while I waited in the hallway just outside the Rebbe's office.

By this time, my mother was gravely ill—the cancer was terminal. One of her doctors was advising radical surgery, while another was advising a harsh course of radiation, but neither one offered much hope. The whole family was devastated by this situation, and my parents seemed unable to decide which treatment my mother should pursue. Having lost their entire families in the Holocaust, they had no one to lean on. I felt so much depended on me, and so, taking the opportunity that Rabbi Goldvicht's meeting presented, I decided to ask the Rebbe if I could discuss this issue with him.

I approached the Rebbe as he was saying goodbye to Rabbi Goldvicht, half expecting that he would put me off. It was 3:30 AM, and I was sure he'd say, "I'm tired now. Ask my secretary for an appointment." But instead, he invited me in.

He could not have been more gracious; he could not have been more welcoming. Just looking at his face made me feel calmer; just being in his presence relieved me of some of the anxiety that I had been feeling.

Now, my father had previously spoken about this matter with another Chasidic rebbe, who had recommended that my mother change her name and that we recite a long list of psalms. I expected the Rebbe's advice to be similar, but he surprised me by first asking: "What is your name? ... Where do you live?" Only after he got to know me a bit, did he say, "Now tell me about your mother."

I described her situation in detail. It turned out he knew the doctors who were treating her—which was another thing that surprised me. When he heard their grim prognosis, he was very sympathetic and

Charles's mother,
Hana, visiting him in
Israel. 1967.

*Courtesy of
Charles Ramat*

helped me prepare for the worst.

I am now trying to recollect events that took place half a century ago, and I am paraphrasing the Rebbe's words. I recall him saying, "Everything is in the hands of G-d, but we cannot expect miracles. The fact that she is being treated by reputable doctors is a very, very good thing. But from everything you're telling me, the prognosis is not good. So I would advise you to hope for the best, but prepare for the worst."

Because he was so honest, because he didn't sugarcoat anything, I heard him, where I would not have been willing to hear a rebbe who told me to recite psalms day and night. At that point in my mother's illness I just didn't believe that it could make a difference, and somehow the Rebbe understood my mindset and knew how to speak to me, how to reach me.

Now, I am not saying that the Rebbe would have given the same answer to another person in the same situation. I can only relate what he told *me*. But I sensed that a part of his genius was knowing how to reach each person.

Because he never said that a miracle would happen, because he didn't raise any false hopes, he captured my heart. At that moment, I thought that he was the wisest man on the planet.

When the audience came to an end, he said, "Please keep me informed about your mother's situation." And being the eighteen-year-old wise guy that I was, I shot back with, "Are you just saying that, or do you really want to hear from me?"

He answered, "I would never say something I didn't mean."

After I left—even though the Rebbe had told me to prepare for the worst—I did not feel depressed. On the contrary, I felt that a burden had been lifted from me. My anxiety had stemmed from the fact that my parents seemed incapable of making a decision, and I felt that the burden was on me—my mother's life was in my eighteen-year-old hands. But the gist of what the Rebbe said to me was, "Whatever happens, it will be okay." As a result, I was able to help my mother choose the treatment that would help her preserve some kind of quality of life, instead of torturing her when there was no real chance of recovery.

When her condition deteriorated to the point of no return, we transferred her to a hospice, where we could stay with her until the end. On the ambulance ride over, I was able to say to her, "I'm here with you, I love you; if you can hear what I'm saying, squeeze my hand," and she squeezed my hand. But by the time we got there she was in a complete coma, and three weeks later she died.

Following her passing, I came to see the Rebbe several times, always in the middle of the night for a few minutes, to discuss various life issues. I felt comfortable doing that because I was able to confide in him. And, on each occasion, the Rebbe's response was absolutely deep and incredible ... and tailor made for me.

Charles lighting the *menorah* in his room at Yeshivat Kerem B'Yavneh. 1967.
Courtesy of Charles Ramat

The Rebbe during a meeting of the Machne Israel Special Development Fund.
8 Tishrei, 5749-1988.

*Levi Freidin,
The Living Archive*

AFTER I HAD MARRIED AND STARTED MY OWN FAMILY, I came to see the Rebbe again, and I told him, "Rebbe, I'm having a crisis of faith. I really do not believe. I love Judaism; I love a lot of the rituals, but they are not really part of my life."

He asked me, "Do you keep kosher?"

"No," I replied. And I must tell you, it took a lot of guts to sit in front of the Rebbe and say that. It was actually a terrifying moment, but my relationship with him was based on total honesty, so how could I lie?

"Do you put on *tefillin* every day?" he asked.

Again, I answered, "No."

"Would you be willing to put on *tefillin* every day?"

"No."

He then said to me, "If I ask you to do *one thing* without any precondition, will you promise me you'll do it?"

Because I trusted him completely, I answered, "Yes, anything you ask of me. I promise I will do it."

"Will you and your wife agree to light Shabbat candles every Friday night?"

"Done," I said. And from that point on, we have never missed lighting Shabbat candles. Indeed, Friday night became sacrosanct for our entire family. When our kids were teenagers, they did not go to parties that night. Even though I had all kinds of business dealings going on, I always made a point of being home on Friday night when my wife lit candles.

Lighting Shabbat candles might be a simple *mitzvah* in the scheme of things, but for our family it was life changing. As a result, Shabbat dinner became special. Eating *challah* became special. Opening our home to guests on Shabbat became special.

To me, this was the genius of the Rebbe. Had he insisted that I become fully observant, I might have tried, but it would not have lasted. And yet, this one *mitzvah* has kept my family on a Jewish path throughout our lives, and my daughters have all followed suit.

IN ANOTHER MEETING, I asked the Rebbe what I could do for him in gratitude for all he had done for me. "You can't do anything for me personally," he replied, "but you can do things to help me help others. Look into your heart and see which Chabad project you would like to support. Choose what speaks to you—that way, you will truly invest yourself in our work."

The Rebbe had an unshakable belief that Jews have to take care of other Jews. This struck a chord in me, and of course, I did what he suggested.

One of the Chabad rabbis gave me an overview of the entire Chabad movement, which impressed me to no end. I saw that, in addition to being probably the greatest spiritual leader of our time, the Rebbe was also the greatest CEO, the greatest tactician, and he developed a worldwide organization that does incredible good. And, ever since, I have been proud to support its work.

I got involved with the Lubavitch Youth Organization because working with children appealed to me. I helped build a *matzah* factory where kids could come to learn how to bake *matzah*. I also helped create the first cartoon book on a religious theme with Judah the Maccabee as the superhero. It was very gratifying work, which I would never would have done if not for the Rebbe.

IN CONCLUSION, there is one more thing that I would like to say.

The Rebbe was being sought after by VIPs from all over the world—heads of industry, heads of state. So many politicians running for office made a point of stopping by 770 Eastern Parkway, whether it was to hear the Rebbe's wisdom or to try to get votes from the Lubavitch community. Israeli prime ministers and generals came to discuss issues monumental to the Jewish state and even to discuss battle plans.

And yet, despite all the demands that were made of him, he made time at 3:30 AM for one anxiety-ridden teenage boy. He could only have done so for one reason—because he cared about every Jew.

To me, this was a man who walked his talk, who lived his philosophy. And there are very few religious leaders like him—if any!—on Planet Earth.

Glossary

Ahavat Yisrael, Love of a fellow Jew.

Aleichem shalom, Lit. Peace upon you; the traditional Jewish response after being offered the greeting, "*Shalom aleichem.*"

Aliyah, Immigration to the Land of Israel.

Alter Rebbe, Rabbi Schneur Zalman of Liadi (1745—1812), founder and first Rebbe of Chabad, author of the *Tanya.*

Ashkenazi, Jews of European origin; pertaining to such Jews.

Baal Shem Tov, The name given to Rabbi Yisrael ben Eliezer (1698—1760), the founder of Chasidism.

Baal teshuvah (pl. *baalei teshuvah*), Lit. master of return; a person who turns to G-d in repentance, after willful or unknowing transgression of the Torah's commandments; a Jew of secular or not fully observant background who has decided to undertake full Torah observance.

Baal, An ancient idol (mentioned in the Book of Numbers), popular with the Moabites.

Baruch Hashem, Thank G-d.

Beit cholim, Lit. house of sick, a hospital.

Beit refuah, Lit. house of healing, the Rebbe's term for a hospital.

Bikur cholim, Visiting the sick.

Brit, Circumcision.

Bubby, grandmother.

Chabad, The Chasidic movement founded by Rabbi Schneur Zalman of Liadi. The word Chabad is an acronym for the Hebrew words *chachma, bina, daat,* "wisdom, understanding, and knowledge," — representing the philosophy of the movement. Also known as "Lubavitch."

Chai, Life. Numerical value of eighteen.

Challah, A braided loaf of bread baked in honor of Shabbat.

Chametz, Leavened products derived from wheat, barley, oat, spelt or rye. *Chametz* is forbidden throughout the holiday of Passover.

Chasid/Chasidic/Chasidism, Originally derived from the Hebrew word for "pious." The word *chasid* refers to a follower of Chasidism, the movement founded by Rabbi Yisrael Baal Shem Tov. Chasidism refers to the movement's philosophy. A *chasid* (pl. *chasidim*) approaches the commandments of Judaism with intense joy.

Chet, The eighth letter of the Hebrew alphabet, known as the *Aleph-Bet,* pronounced with a guttural "Ch."

Chitas, The daily study schedule introduced by the Previous Rebbe, Rabbi Yosef Yitzchak. It includes a selection from the *Chumash* (the Five Books of Moses), *Tehillim* (Psalms) and *Tanya* (the seminal work by the Alter Rebbe, founder of the Chabad movement).

Chumash, The Five Books of Moses.

Chupah, The canopy underneath which a Jewish wedding takes place.

Eretz Yisrael, The Land of Israel.

Erev Pesach, The day preceding Passover.

Erev Yom Kippur, The day preceding Yom Kippur.

Etrog (pl. *etrogim*), A yellow citrus fruit; it is one of the Four Species used during the Holiday of Sukkot.

Farbrengen, Public addresses and Torah discourses by the Rebbe, bookended by Chasidic melodies and toasts of *l'chaim.*

Hashem, G-d.

Hei, The fifth letter of the Hebrew alphabet, known as the *Aleph-Bet,* corresponding to "H" in English.

Hoshana Rabbah, The seventh day of Sukkot.

Kaddish, A hymn of praises to G-d recited during the prayer service, in some instances, by mourners in memory of a relative.

Kera, A split.

Ketubot, Marriage contracts.

Kiddush Hashem, The sanctification of G-d's Name.

Kiddush, The blessing traditionally recited over wine on Shabbat and Jewish holidays.

Kitzur Shulchan Aruch, An abbreviated Code of Jewish Law. Compiled by R. Shlomo Ganzfried (Hungary, 1804—1886), as a layperson's version of the original *Shulchan Aruch.*

Knesset, Israel's parliament.

Kos shel brachah, Lit. cup of blessing; receiving line during which the Rebbe distributed wine to individuals after major Jewish holidays.

L'chaim, Lit. to life; toast or blessing often exchanged over wine or other strong drink.

Lag B'omer, The 33rd day of the Omer, a minor festival falling between Passover and Shavuot, commemorating the end of a plague that killed thousands of Rabbi Akiva's students; also the *yahrzeit* of Rabbi Shimon bar Yochai, author of the Zohar.

Lamed, The twelfth letter of the Hebrew alphabet, known as the *Aleph-Bet,* corresponding to "L" in English.

Lekach, Honey cake customarily distributed on the day before Yom Kippur. The Rebbe would continue the *lekach* distribution during Hoshana Rabbah as well.

Litvak, Lithuanian Jew; non-Chasidic, Ashkenazic Jew.

Logotherapy, A form of psychotherapy developed by Dr. Viktor Frankl, which emphasizes the importance of meaning, especially as gained through spiritual values.

Lubavitch, A small town in White Russia that served as the center of the Chabad movement from 1813—1915, and whose name has become synonymous with the movement.

Lulav, A closed frond of a date palm tree; it is one of the Four Species used during the Holiday of Sukkot.

Machne Israel Special Development Fund, Established in 1984 to serve as a major financial resource for the Chabad institutional network. The Rebbe would meet with its supporters in person twice a year.

Rebbe Maharash, Rabbi Shmuel (1834—1882), fourth leader of Chabad-Lubavitch.

Mashiach, **Messiah,** One of the Thirteen Principles of the Jewish faith is that G-d will send this individual to return the Jews to the Land of Israel, rebuild the Holy Temple, and usher in a new era of peace.

Matzah (pl. *matzot),* Unleavened bread eaten on the festival of Passover.

Mesibat Shabbat, A Shabbat party for children.

Mezuzah, A scroll of parchment that is affixed to the doorposts of Jewish homes, containing verses from Deuteronomy that affirm G-d's unity in the world.

Mikveh, A bathing pool in which a person immerses oneself as part of the transition to ritual purity.

Minyan, A quorum of ten men age thirteen or older, required for traditional Jewish public worship.

Mishnah, The first major written work of the Oral Torah.

Mishneh Torah, Maimonides's *magnum opus*, the first complete compendium of Jewish law.

Mitzvah (Pl. *mitzvot*), Lit. commandment; one of the 613 commandments presented by G-d in the Torah.

Motzaei, The evening following Shabbat and Jewish holidays.

Mussar, Category of Jewish philosophic works dealing with personal conduct and character, and methods for self-improvement in these areas. Its approach to self-refinement generally differs from those of Chasidism.

N'shei Chabad, The Lubavitch women's organization.

Pesach, Passover.

Pintele Yid, The core essence of a Jewish soul.

Pre-1A, The equivalent of kindergarten in American Jewish day schools.

Rambam, Rabbi Moses ben Maimon, Maimonides (1135—1204); codifier, philosopher, communal leader, and physician, best known for his writings on Jewish law.

Reb, A title prefacing the name of any adult male, approx. equivalent to the English "Mister."

Rebbetzin, A rabbi's wife.

Sandek, The one who holds a boy who is being circumcised—the highest honor at a *brit*.

Seder, The special service observed on the first two nights of Passover, which includes eating *matzah* and bitter herbs, drinking four cups of wine, and commemorating the exodus from Egypt.

Sephardi, Jews of South European or North African origin; pertaining to such Jews.

Shabbat, The Sabbath, the divinely-ordained day of rest on the seventh day of the week.

Shavuot, The holiday commemorating the giving of the Torah.

Sheitel, A wig.

Shema, The fundamental utterance of Jewish faith: "Hear O Israel, the L-rd is our G-d, the L-rd is one." This is recited daily in the morning and evening prayers and before retiring for the night.

Sheva brachot, The week of festivities following a wedding, during which seven special blessings are recited.

Shochet, One who slaughters and inspects cattle and fowl in the ritually-prescribed manner for kosher consumption.

Shofar, Ram's horn, blown during the prayers on Rosh Hashanah.

Shtiebel, A small, informal house of prayer.

Simchah, Joy.

Simchat Torah, Festival immediately following Sukkot, when the cycle of publicly reading the Torah is annually concluded and recommenced. It is observed with great joy, singing, and the *Hakafot* (circling) procession with the Torah scrolls.

Sukkah, A temporary structure in which Jews dwell during the festival of Sukkot.

Sukkot, Festival of Tabernacles.

Sunday Dollars, The receiving line held every Sunday beginning in 1986 in 770, during which the Rebbe would hand each person a dollar to be given to the charity of their choice. Participants would use the brief meeting to ask for the Rebbe's advice or blessing.

Taharat Hamishpachah, Lit. family purity; the system of laws that govern Jewish marital life.

Talmud, The key text of rabbinic Judaism.

Tanya, The *magnum opus* of the founder of the Alter Rebbe, the founder of the Chabad movement.

Tefillin, A pair of black leather boxes containing inscribed Hebrew parchment scrolls. *Tefillin* are donned by Jewish men once a day, usually during morning prayers.

Tehillim, Psalms.

Tmimut, Carnestness, simplicity.

Torat Emet, The Torah of Truth.

Tzaddik (Pl. *tzaddikim*), A righteous man.

Tzedakah, Charity.

Tzitzit, A four-cornered garment that, according to Torah law, must have special fringes on the corners.

Yahrzeit, Anniversary of someone's passing.

Yarmulke, Skullcap. The head covering worn by Jewish men symbolizing recognition of G-d above.

Yeshivah, Torah academy.

Yetzer Hara, The evil inclination.

Yiddishkeit, Torah Judaism.

Yirei shamayim, G-d-fearing.

Yud, The tenth letter of the Hebrew alphabet, known as the *Aleph-Bet,* corresponding to "Y" in English.

770, Shorthand for 770 Eastern Parkway, the address of the Rebbe's study and synagogue, and the world headquarters of Chabad-Lubavitch, located in Brooklyn, New York.

Acknowledgments

This collection of first-person stories about the Rebbe required the involvement of many people.

First of all, we'd like to express our deepest gratitude to the interviewees for sharing their stories, many of which are very personal. Now, thanks to their generosity of spirit, readers can forever learn from, and be inspired by, their encounters with the Rebbe.

These stories were selected from testimonies recorded by the *My Encounter with the Rebbe* oral history project, and each is a world of its own. Persuading people to share their experiences can be difficult and is but one small facet of the complex undertaking involving investigative research, planning, and travel; conducting the actual interviews; and then transcribing and archiving the recordings.

Rabbi Yechiel Cagen, the director of the *My Encounter* project, has guided and trained many of the project's interviewers through the years. Rabbi Cagen oversaw the production of this book, as he does the weekly publication of *Here's My Story*, where some of these stories were first published in abbreviated form. The interviews in this volume were conducted by Rabbis Mendy Alevsky, Avrohom Moshe Dyce, Mendy Mochkin and Moshe Raichman; as well as by Rabbi Zusha Wolf, who served as our lead interviewer in Israel for many years. Zusha also procured many of the pictures that are displayed in these pages.

The *Here's My Story* weekly publication is made possible by the steadfast financial support of the Crain-Maling Foundation, in addition to ongoing contributions by Nachman and Avrohom Lokshin, as well as weekly sponsors.

Uriela Sagiv, who has served as the book's and the weekly publication's line editor, took the raw interview transcripts and made them readable, all while keeping the narrators' stories accurate in every detail and true to original form. Rabbi Yecheskel Posner, the production manager for this book as well as the weekly publication, coordinated all the moving parts, including content and research. They have both done the yeoman's share of the work, and neither of these publications would have been possible without them.

In order to accurately preserve and present these stories, it is critical to verify every detail to the best of our ability. Thank you to those who carefully reviewed these accounts: Rabbis Menachem Aizenman, Shloimie Chein, Shmuel Posner, Yosef Posner and Mrs. Rivkah Slonim. Thank you also to Mrs. Sheina Herz, Mrs. Ya'akovah Weber and Shalom Goodman for proofreading the manuscript.

Rabbi Yosef Chaim Brook significantly encouraged the publishing of this book, as well as *My Story 1,* and his professional advice was invaluable.

Rabbi Eli Friedman deserves our gratitude for the creative titles and subtitles, engaging the reader. And we would also like to thank Freidi Posner, who translated many long transcripts to English for this book.

A picture is truly worth a thousand words. The many photos in this book bring an added dimension to the stories within. Most of the photographs of the Rebbe presented here were taken by Levi Yitzchok Freidin, Rabbi Chaim B. Halberstam, Yossi Melamed, Velvel Schildkraut, Rabbi Gershon Schusterman and Sam Shlagbaum. We are forever grateful that they seized the moment and captured such unforgettable images. We'd also like to thank Zalman Ceitlin, Motti Hazan and Dovid Leib Lepkivker, who helped navigate our vast photo archive. And a special thanks to all those who contributed the personal photos and documents that adorn this book, as well as to Shaya Gourarie and Zalman Groner, former interviewers for the *My Encounter* project, who collected them.

There are many books containing stories about the Rebbe. We aimed for ascetics that are as unique and beautiful as the contents. Shimon Gorkin's elegant, clean design strikes the perfect balance — highlighting the seriousness of these events while inviting the reader to dive in. The layout of the book was done by Levi Weingarten, who patiently worked on each page until it was just right.

Thank you to the entire JEM staff for their assistance: Chalom Atlan, Mendel Barber, Schneur Bistritsky, Zalman Butman, Betzalel Chaikin, Shalom Ber Eber, Danny Freundlich, Levik Gourarie, Mendel Gourarie, Mendel Greenberg, Levi Greisman, Zushi Greisman, Efroyim Grossberger Noson Grunblatt, Binyomin Gurary, Yoram Henquin, Shmuly

Hurwitz, Schneur Itzinger, Yisroel Kievman, Elchonon Korenblit, Shalom Ber Kratz, Chayim Lieberman, Chaim Loschak, Choli Mishulovin, Bentzion Pearson, Levi Plotkin, Hillel Rosenberg, Yaakov Rosenblatt, Sholom Rosenbluh, Eli Sapochkinsky, Levi Shemtov, Yisroel Slonim, Mendel Spiero, Yaakov Strasberg, Mendel Tenenbaum, Menashe Treitel, Yitzchok Tsap, Levi Vogel and Ezra Weimer.

A special thanks to Yanky Ascher and Yoel Hurwitz for color-correcting the photos, and in some cases restoring them.

The entire JEM organization, as well as the *My Encounter* project, would not be possible without the efforts of Rabbi Elkanah Shmotkin, JEM's executive director. His editorial and creative vision led this publication from concept to completion.

About the Photos of the Rebbe

The majority of the photos of the Rebbe that appear in this book are copyrighted by Jewish Educational Media, Inc., and can be accessed at *TheLivingArchive.org*. If you'd like to learn more about individual photos or to order a print, please scan this code on your mobile device for links to featured photos.

The Living Archive

The Living Archive is a project to restore, preserve and provide access to the video, audio and photographic recordings of the Rebbe's life.

Index

About
My Encounter

Over the course of the Rebbe's lifetime, many tens of thousands of individuals visited with him privately, seeking his counsel and blessing. Many times that number communicated with him in writing. It is largely through these exchanges—personal guidance in times of travail, recommending far-ranging community projects, directing underground activities (in the case of Russian Jewry), counseling Israel's leaders—that the Rebbe influenced the Jewish world, as well as the world at large.

For many decades most of those stories remained undocumented. In 1998, when the *My Encounter with the Rebbe* oral history project was launched by Jewish Educational Media (JEM), this changed. As of this writing, the *My Encounter* staff has recorded more than 1,600 testimonies of individuals from all walks of life—ordinary folks and household names, struggling single mothers and Nobel Prize winners, simple soldiers and IDF officers, artists and politicians, rabbis and laypeople, Jews and non-Jews. The team has traveled to more than fifty cities on six continents in this effort.

Each interview is a world of its own. Ranging between one and seven hours in length, each tells a different personal story. Together, they document the Rebbe's far-reaching influence and impassioned leadership. Perhaps more importantly, they present a roadmap for future generations to follow.

Each interview was meticulously researched in advance of the

Irving Wolinsky being interviewed by the *My Encounter* team in January of 2014.

recording. Once it was completed, it was digitized, archived and transcribed. A number of full-length films have already been produced from these testimonies, and regularly featured in *Living Torah*, the popular video magazine. Residing at JEM.tv, they are watched by hundreds of thousands every week.

The transcripts of these interviews—comprising more than 22,500 pages—have served as the basis for books, articles and other publications by a variety of publishers and authors. JEM's weekly *Here's My Story*, distributed online and in printed form, deserves special mention.

(A separate Hebrew version, *HaSipur Sheli*, is also published weekly.) In the hundreds of weeks since it first began publication, *Here's My Story* has developed an avid readership, becoming a staple in thousands of synagogues, Chabad Houses, schools and private homes.

However, the *My Encounter* staff knows full-well that, as successful as their efforts have been to date, much more remains to be done. There are thousands of individuals still waiting to be interviewed. If you or anyone you know has had a meaningful encounter with the Rebbe, please take a moment to write to: interviews@jemedia.org.

Other books based on
My Encounter with the Rebbe testimonies

My Story 1

Forty-one in-depth interviews featuring fascinating stories of the Rebbe alongside family photos, documents and a stunning selection of portraits of the Rebbe in full color. Available in English, Hebrew and Russian.

Seeds of Wisdom, Vols. 1 & 2

A heartwarming collection of short stories with profound life lessons in relationships, parenting, leadership and personal well-being. A little book with the power to enrich your life and help effect personal growth and meaningful living. Available in English and Hebrew.

One by One

◀ With sixty-six vivid and diverse stories of guidance, perspective and encouragement, read and share the essence of the Rebbe's soul-to-soul leadership—an affordable gift for your friends and family!

To order, visit jemstore.com. For bulk orders, email jem@jemedia.org or call 718-774-6000.

This publication and the entire
My Encounter with the Rebbe *project*
are made possible through the
generous support of the members of

THE

JEM FOUNDATION

ואתה תצוה...להעלות נר תמיד

מוקדש לחיזוק ההתקשרות
לכ"ק אדמו"ר נשיא דורנו

נדפס ע"י ולזכות
הרה"ח"ת ר' לייביש משה וזוגתו מרת רינה
ילדיהם קיילא באשא, בנציון דוד, אליהו,
איסר, רבקה שיינדל אלטא שיחיו
גולדהירש

לזכר נשמות הוריו
ר' מרדכי ב"ר אליהו
נלב"ע כ"ב אייר, תשנ"ה

העניא חאשא בת ר' זוסמאן
נלב"ע ז' אייר, תשע"א

ולזכר נשמות הורי'
ר' יעקב ב"ר מנשה
נלב"ע ח' מנ"א, תש"נ

חוה בת ר' יעקב ישראל
נלב"ע כ"ו טבת, תשס"ח

ת. נ. צ. ב. ה.

In honor of the Bat Mitzvah
of our dear daughter

Chana
חנה שתחי'

May she merit a life of
Torah, marriage and good deeds!

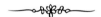

By her parents,
Sholom *and* **Pessy Jacobs**

In honor of **the Rebbe**
and his young shluchim *around the world*

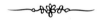

לזכות השלוחים
התּ' לוי, התּ' שניאור זלמן, מינא עטל, התּ' מאיר,
גבריאל נח, מנחם מענדל, חיה מושקא שיחיו

נדפס ע"י ולזכות הוריהם
הרה"ת ר' דוד וזוגתו מרת פערל גאלדא
טייכטל

שמפיין, אילינוי

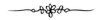

 **Crain-Maling Foundation**

Dedicated in loving memory of my sister
Evan Beatrice-Maling

חוה בת אברהם ע"ה

With her genuine Jewish heart,
she embodied the spirit of giving for
which our people are known

By Dr. Michael Maling